what others are sayir

Through a Season

D0091332

Through a Season of Grief will help many hurting people find the strength to hope again. Here is a book that is practical, biblical, filled with wise counsel, and written with deep compassion for those walking through the "valley of the shadow." Buy two copies—one to read and one to give to a friend.

DR. RAY PRITCHARD, Senior Pastor
Calvary Memorial Church, Oak Park, IL

The truths found in *Through a Season of Grief* will serve as a healing balm for any troubled heart. Bill Dunn and Kathy Leonard have done a masterful job of wrapping practical truths with sincere compassion. This is a book you can confidently give to anyone who has experienced loss without appearing to be "preachy." As a pastor, I look forward to sharing this invaluable resource with many.

DR. ROBERT JEFFRESS, Senior Pastor
First Baptist Church, Wichita Falls, TX

In *Through a Season of Grief* the living God extends His righteous right hand to meet hurting people at their points of deepest need, upholding, embracing, redeeming, and making them whole. I praise Him for such a healing resource!

BRUCE MARCHIANO, Actor and speaker

My husband has recently been diagnosed with advanced cancer. I have found that it is often those outside the storm who give advice to those in the storm. Though they mean well, I think, "They have no idea." In *Through a Season of Grief* you will hear from people who truly understand, for they have been in the storm. They are equipped to bring comfort and wisdom for the hard work of grief.

DEE BRESTIN, Author and speaker

At last, a daily guide through the dying part of living. *Through a Season of Grief* is honest and comprehensive, broad and applicable. A must for every hurting heart.

JANET PASCHAL, Singer and songwriter

Through a Season of Grief is filled with the Holy Spirit's comfort, enabling those experiencing grief to receive God's peace, which is beyond anything you can imagine.

DR. ROBERT ABARNO, Author and counselor

Wake Forest, NC

bill dunn and kathy leonard

through a season of grief

devotions for your journey from mourning to joy

THOMAS NELSON
Since 1798

NASHVILLE   DALLAS   MEXICO CITY   RIO DE JANEIRO

Published in Nashville, Tennessee, by Thomas Nelson. Thomas Nelson is a registered trademark of Thomas Nelson, Inc.

Thomas Nelson, Inc., titles may be purchased in bulk for educational, business, fund-raising, or sales promotional use. For information, please e-mail SpecialMarkets@ThomasNelson.com.

Unless otherwise indicated, Scripture quotations used in this book are from the *Holy Bible: New International Version*®. © 1973, 1978, 1984 by International Bible Society. Used by permission of Zondervan. All rights reserved.

Other Scripture references are from the following sources:

The Amplified Bible: Old Testament. © 1962, 1964 by Zondervan Publishing House (used by permission); and from *The Amplified New Testament.* © 1958 by the Lockman Foundation (used by permission).

The *King James Version.*

The Message. © 1993, 1994, 1995, 1996, 2000, 2001, 2002. Used by permission of NavPress Publishing Group. All rights reserved.

The New American Standard Bible ®, The Lockman Foundation © 1960, 1962, 1963, 1968, 1971, 1972, 1973, 1975, 1977, 1995. Used by permission.

The *New King James Version*®. © 1982 by Thomas Nelson, Inc. Used by permission. All rights reserved.

The Holy Bible, New Living Translation, © 1996. Used by permission of Tyndale House Publishers, Inc., Wheaton, Illinois 60189. All rights reserved.

The *Revised Standard Version* of the Bible. © 1946, 1952, 1971, 1973 by the Division of Christian Education of the National Council of the Churches of Christ in the U.S.A. Used by permission.

Library of Congress Cataloging-in-Publication Data

Dunn, Bill.
    Through a season of grief : devotions for your journey from mourning to joy /
Bill Dunn and Kathy Leonard.
      p. cm.
    Includes bibliographical references.
    ISBN 978-0-7852-6014-1 (pbk.)
    1. Consolation. 2. Grief—Religious aspects—Christianity. 3. Devotional calendars.
I. Leonard, Kathy. II. Title.
    BV4905.3.D86 2004
    242'.4—dc22

2004014211

Printed in the United States of America

17 18 19 20 LSCC 45 44 43 42 41 40

Contents

Welcome

Grief is likely the most difficult journey you will ever take. We pray that these devotions will provide you with instruction, wisdom, hope, and healing as you face grief moment by moment and day by day. May you come to know God in a more intimate and real way as you read the daily Scriptures and the personal testimonies of Christian experts and individuals who, like you, are grieving the death of a loved one.

These devotions are based on the grief recovery support group program called *GriefShare*®. *GriefShare*® groups meet in over four thousand churches around the world. We encourage you to join a *GriefShare*® group where you can express your emotions and receive comfort, instruction, and help from others who have experienced grief.

GriefShare® is a program with direction and purpose. With *GriefShare*® you will learn how to walk the journey of grief and be supported on the way. It is a place where hurting people find healing and hope.

To find the group meeting nearest you, visit www.griefshare.org or call the Church Initiative offices at 1-800-395-5755.

Meet the Experts

The following are the experts who contributed to this book. These Christian teachers, authors, and speakers are respected authorities on grief topics. They will guide you along your personal journey through grief. When referring to an expert in this book, his or her full name is used.

DR. ROBERT ABARNO is a Christian author, counselor, and clinical psychologist. He is the founder of Christ Centered Development, a teaching and equipping ministry in Wake Forest, North Carolina.

KAY ARTHUR of Precept Ministries in Chattanooga, Tennessee (www.precept.org), is a Bible teacher, the author of more than a hundred books, a radio and television hostess, and the principal spokesperson for the *International Inductive Study Bible*.

DR. RICHARD BEWES, a son of English missionaries in East Africa, was the rector of All Souls Church (www.allsouls.org) in London, England, from 1983–2004. He is a well-known speaker on many continents and has written numerous books.

DEE BRESTIN is a conference speaker and the author of many Bible study guides for women (www.deebrestin.com). Her desire is to make Christ's Word relevant to women today.

The late DR. BILL BRIGHT was the founder and president of Campus Crusade for Christ (www.ccci.org). For over fifty years he dedicated his life to helping people find new life and hope through a relationship with Christ.

PASTOR BUCK BUCHANAN served as a senior pastor in the Evangelical Free Church of America for thirty-seven years. He served as the associate pastor of Care and Concerns Ministries at the First Evangelical Free Church of Fullerton, California, for fourteen years.

Rev. Noel Castellanos is the president and founder of the Latino Leadership Foundation, an organization that helps provide leadership development and training for Latino pastors and leaders. He also founded and pastored La Villita Community Church in Chicago, Illinois.

Dr. Tim Clinton is an author and the president of the Executive Board for the American Association of Christian Counselors (www.aacc.net). This organization exists to encourage excellence in Christian counseling.

Dr. Jim Conway is an author and the president of Midlife Dimensions (www.midlife.com). He served as a pastor for almost thirty years.

Rev. John Coulombe serves as pastor to older adults at the First Evangelical Free Church of Fullerton, California (www.fefcful.org), where he has ministered for over thirteen years. He has served in pastorates for the past thirty-seven years. He also works alongside the Christian Association of Senior Adults (CASA).

Dr. Larry Crabb is a well-known conference speaker, Bible teacher, and author. He is the founder of New Way Ministries (www.newwayministries.org), created to help ignite a revolution in how Christians live, think, and relate.

Joni Eareckson Tada is an author, artist, broadcaster, and the founder and president of JAF (Joni and Friends) Ministries (www.joniandfriends.org). Her books and worldwide ministry reflect her experience of God's love and grace since becoming a quadriplegic as a result of a diving accident over thirty years ago.

Elisabeth Elliot was born of missionary parents in Brussels, Belgium, and served as a missionary in Ecuador where her husband, Jim Elliot, was killed by the Auca Indians in 1956. Since her return to the United States in 1963, she has been writing and speaking. For almost thirteen years she ministered to people through her daily radio broadcast, *Gateway to Joy*.

REV. CLAY EVANS was ordained as a minister in 1950. He founded the Fellowship Missionary Baptist Church in Chicago, Illinois, and served as pastor for fifty years. Evans has been a featured soloist on numerous albums of the 250-voice Choir of the Church.

ANNE GRAHAM LOTZ is an author, speaker, and the president of AnGeL Ministries (www.angelministries.org). The daughter of Billy and Ruth Graham, Anne Lotz has hosted a series of *Just Give Me Jesus* revivals and Bible studies across the United States.

JIM GRASSI is an international fishing instructor, pastor, and author. He served as a public administrator for twenty years. Through his ministry, Let's Go Fishing (www.letsgofishing.org), he reaches people with the gospel in unique ways.

DR. JACK HAYFORD is the founding pastor of The Church On The Way in Van Nuys, California (www.jackhayford.com). He has authored more than two dozen books and has written over five hundred songs. Dr. Hayford is also the founder and chancellor of The King's Seminary in Van Nuys.

The late DR. E. V. HILL was recognized as one of the greatest preachers in the world. He was the pastor at Mt. Zion Missionary Baptist Church in Los Angeles for over forty years and preached for more than fifty years.

DR. THOMAS ICE is the executive director of the Pre-Trib Research Center in Arlington, Texas. He has coauthored over twenty books, written several articles, and is a frequent conference speaker.

DR. ROBERT JEFFRESS serves as pastor of the eight-thousand-member First Baptist Church of Wichita Falls, Texas (www.fbcwf.org). He has written several books and hosts the weekly television program *Pathway to Victory*.

BARBARA JOHNSON has lost two sons and is involved in grief ministry. A humorous writer and speaker, she also heads Spatula Ministries in La

Habra, California, supporting parents who have lost children through death or estrangement.

DR. ERWIN W. LUTZER is the senior pastor of the Moody Church in Chicago, Illinois (www.moodychurch.org). He has written over thirty-five books and is the featured speaker on three radio programs heard on Christian stations nationwide: *The Moody Church Hour, Songs in the Night,* and *Running to Win.*

BRUCE MARCHIANO is a professional actor who, having given his life to the Lord in 1989, had the privilege of portraying Jesus in the Visual Bible film production *The Gospel of Matthew.* Known for his joyous and passionate portrayal of the Savior, Bruce now travels the world sharing the Savior and his experiences as an actor portraying Him. His Web address is www.brucemarchiano.com.

CINDY MORGAN, a talented vocalist, earned six Dove Award nominations in 1993, including New Artist of the Year, Female Vocalist of the Year, Contemporary Album of the Year, Contemporary Recorded Song of the Year, and Recorded Music Packaging of the Year.

JAN NORTHINGTON lives in Los Osos, California. She is a CLASS (Christian Leaders, Authors & Speakers Services) graduate and Certified Personality Trainer. Her passion is teaching and speaking. She has authored a book and has written numerous articles for the Christian marketplace.

DR. DAVID OLFORD is the president of Olford Ministries International (www.olford.org) and the director of studies at The Stephen Olford Center for Biblical Preaching. He lectures and teaches regularly at institute events and preaching workshops.

DR. LUIS PALAU is an international evangelist who has spoken via radio and television broadcasts to people in 104 nations and face-to-face to thirteen million people in sixty-eight nations. He is the author of several books on spirituality and the Christian life. He can be reached at www.palau.org.

JANET PASCHAL, a talented singer and songwriter, has appeared with Billy Graham and President George Bush and has toured with Bill and Gloria Gaither. Since 1992, Janet has become the official spokesperson of the Mission of Mercy, an international Christian relief organization. She has received Grammy nominations and is a popular conference speaker and frequent guest on Christian radio and television talk shows.

DR. NORMAN PEART is the founder and pastor of Grace Bible Fellowship, a nondenominational, multiracial church in Cary, North Carolina. He is also a professor at the University of North Carolina.

DR. RAY PRITCHARD is the senior pastor at Calvary Memorial Church in Oak Park, Illinois. He is also an author, conference speaker, and frequent guest on Christian radio and television programs. Dr. Pritchard has ministered extensively overseas, preaching in India, Nepal, Paraguay, Columbia, Haiti, Nigeria, Russia, and Belize.

DR. JOSEPH M. STOWELL was the president of the Moody Bible Institute of Chicago for eighteen years and was featured daily on Moody's *Proclaim!* radio program. He now serves as the executive pastor for Harvest Bible Chapel in Illinois. Dr. Stowell is an internationally recognized speaker and a best-selling author.

DR. JOHN TRENT is a nationally recognized author, speaker, counselor, and business coach. He is the president of Encouraging Words (www.encouragingwords.com), a ministry dedicated to strengthening marriage and family relationships worldwide.

DR. H. NORMAN WRIGHT is a trauma therapist and the author of seventy books. He is on the faculty of Talbot Graduate School of Theology. You can visit his Web site at www.hnormanwright.com.

The following people contributed to this book by sharing their personal stories of grief and grief recovery. We appreciate their openness and willingness to help others.

Annie	Kay
Beth	Linda
Betty	Luevenia
Bruce	Lynn
Chandra	Margi
Cindy G.	Marilyn
Cindy K.	Melba
Cindy M.	Melissa
Darlynn	Nancy
Dora	Nell
Dot	Patricia
Emy	Phyllis
Gretchen	Randy
Heidi	Ruth
Iris	Shelly
Jeffrey	Sue
JoAnn	Sylvia
Jodie	Virgil
John	Wendy

when your dreams fall apart

Understanding Your Grief

Grief is not an enemy or a sign of weakness. It is a sign of being human. Grief is the cost of loving someone.

Since grief comes to everyone, why do some people seem to work through it better than others?

"Some people think that going through the losses or crises of life are the exceptional times," says Dr. H. Norman Wright.

"I see it differently. I see the times of calm as the exceptions. Life really is going through one loss after another, one crisis after another.

"Instead of avoiding talking about these times, let's do our homework. When you know what to expect, you're not thrown by them as much, and you're going to be better able to recover."

Join us each day for the next year as we walk with you on your journey through grief, strengthened and enabled through the Lord Jesus Christ.

"But those who hope in the LORD will renew their strength. They will soar on wings like eagles; they will run and not grow weary, they will walk and not be faint" (Isaiah 40:31).

*Lord God, teach me to embrace my grief and not fight it, so that
I may experience the true healing that comes from You. Amen.*

Grief Is a Unique Experience

You may feel it is useless to talk about your grief because no one truly understands what you are going through.

"You sometimes feel after an experience like this that you're talking a foreign language," says Dora, whose daughter died. "You feel like there's no way anybody can know what you're feeling. There is absolutely no way anyone can know the depth of your pain. So you feel like it's futile to talk about it because words can't express the pain."

Although countless people have experienced grief before you, each person's response to grief is different. Your path of grief will be uniquely your own.

Be encouraged that regardless of how your grief appears to you or others, it has a precious uniqueness to the One who created you. God, who knows intimately your personality, your relationships, and the experiences of your life, knows your grief and isn't shocked or surprised by your responses.

"O LORD, You have examined my heart and know everything about me. . . . Thank you for making me so wonderfully complex. . . . You saw me before I was born. Every day of my life was recorded in your book. Every moment was laid out before a single day had passed" (Psalm 139:1, 14, 16 NLT).

Father, thank You that my way of grieving is distinctly my own, reflective of all You have sovereignly created me to be and experience. Amen.

Grief Runs Deep: Where Is the Hope?

Dr. Joseph Stowell says, "Even though your heart is breaking and tears are clouding your eyes and staining your cheeks, God does give us something worth trusting in tough times. And that's Him, and Him alone."

When your heart is breaking, you can place your hope and trust in the Lord.

"Be strong and take heart, all you who hope in the LORD" (Psalm 31:24).

Anne Graham Lotz defines hope: "Biblical hope is absolute confidence in something you haven't seen or received yet, but you're absolutely confident that whatever God has said is going to come to pass."

She also declares that "Jesus is your hope for the future. One day Jesus Christ will come back, and He will set all of the wrong right. Good will triumph over the bad. Love will triumph over hate. Righteousness will triumph over evil. He's going to make it all right, and you can have absolute confidence that that's going to take place. That's your hope."

Sovereign God, I choose hope. I choose faith. I choose life. Give me an unshakable faith in You. Amen.

Grief Lasts Longer Than Expected

Grief's unexpected turns will throw you again and again. You may feel that for every step forward, you take at least one step back. The grieving process generally takes longer than you ever imagined.

Please don't rush this process. Remember, what you are feeling is not only normal, it is necessary.

"It's been seven years, and I'm still going through it," says Dr. Larry Crabb, whose brother died in a plane crash. "I don't know if it's a very holy thing to admit, but when someone says, 'Well, it's been a week, a month, a year—Larry, for you it's been seven years. Get a grip. Where's your faith in Christ, for goodness' sake?' I get really angry.

"Knowing the Lord and His comfort does not take away the ache; instead, it supports you in the middle of the ache. Until I get home to heaven, there's going to be an ache that won't quit. The grieving process for me is not so much a matter of getting rid of the pain, but not being controlled by the pain."

We read in the Psalms that David grew weary with the process of grief and cried out to the Lord. Then he left the timing in God's hands.

"Be merciful to me, LORD, for I am faint; O LORD, heal me, for my bones are in agony. My soul is in anguish. How long, O LORD, how long? Turn, O LORD, and deliver me; save me because of your unfailing love" (Psalm 6:2–4).

"I am weary with my sighing; Every night I make my bed swim, I dissolve my couch with my tears. My eye has wasted away with grief" (Psalm 6:6–7 NASB).

Heavenly God, I cannot even begin to put my grief in a time frame. Thank you that I don't have to. Comfort me and support me as I lean on You. Amen.

He Will Carry You

The Lord will carry you if you ask Him. When you are feeling so weak you cannot take another step, ask Him to lift you high into His loving arms. Then rest in Him with an open and listening heart. This does not mean your problems will disappear, but it does mean you will have Someone to share them with.

"If you are someone who does not know Jesus Christ as your Savior and you have just been widowed or bereaved, you have a tremendous burden," says Elisabeth Elliot. "You are tired, and it is too big a burden to carry. The Lord says, 'Come to me, you who are tired and over-burdened, and I will give you rest.'"

To receive peace and rest in Christ, the instructions are clear. Jesus says, "Come to me." You must first approach Him and then talk to Him and quietly listen.

"Hear my cry, O God; listen to my prayer. From the ends of the earth I call to you, I call as my heart grows faint; lead me to the rock that is higher than I. For you have been my refuge, a strong tower against the foe" (Psalm 61:1–3).

Lord, I come to You. My heart is worn out, and I need You. Take my heavy burden today. Amen.

Unpredictable Emotions

The unpredictable timing and odd combinations of emotions that hit you during grief can leave you confused and despairing.

"My life was totally flipped upside down emotionally, in every way you could think of," says Sue, whose husband died.

Your emotions not only hit hard, but they can also occur at unexpected moments, which makes the impact seem even worse. Being aware of the unpredictable nature of your emotions will help you stand firm during each new barrage. God's promises in the Bible will also help you to persevere.

In Matthew 5:4 Jesus promises comfort and a blessing for those who go through the process of grief and mourning: "Blessed are those who mourn, for they will be comforted."

Lord, when my emotions come and go with no semblance of order, remind me that this is to be expected during grief, and help me to stand firm. Amen.

Random Emotions

"My emotions occurred spontaneously, and sometimes two or three at the same time," says Cindy, whose daughter passed away.

Although there are stages that are common to the process of grief, they do not occur in a predictable order. Your emotions will be random, sometimes overwhelming, and completely unique.

"Whatever your emotions lead you to feel, it's okay to feel how you're feeling," says Randy, whose sister died. "I think there are several emotions people are going to go through that are beyond their control."

Although you may feel overwhelmed and out of control, you can still have the deep inner peace that comes from God alone. Some people clearly sense the peace of God during times of adversity, but others wonder why they cannot feel it. Be assured that His peace is always available to you. Peace comes through a sincere belief in God's presence and in His promises; it is not dependent on our feelings or sensations. Believe in His promises and rest in His peace today.

"Now may the Lord of peace himself give you peace at all times and in every way. The Lord be with all of you" (2 Thessalonians 3:16).

Lord of peace, when my emotions surprise and confuse me, may I rest in the peace of Your constant presence. Amen.

Grief Is Harder Than You Think

The hardest time to learn about the process of grief is while you are in the midst of it. You may feel that you are taking a crash course in grief and that the learning curve is formidable. But those who seek to understand grief and loss will be better able to recover, so we commend you for your determination and effort to see this process through.

Dr. H. Norman Wright says, "Many of the right things to do in life are the most difficult things to do."

Dear friend, even though you may be in the depths of despair and feel that God is far away, now is the time to cling to whatever knowledge of Him you have. Today is the day to open your mind and heart for deeper understanding.

"If you hang on with whatever it is you know in your heart to be true about Him, then He will come through," says Janet Paschal. "That's a promise."

"I lift up my eyes to the hills—where does my help come from? My help comes from the LORD, the Maker of heaven and earth. He will not let your foot slip—he who watches over you will not slumber" (Psalm 121:1–3).

Lord God, this is so hard. Please keep me from falling. Amen.

Grief Is Disruptive

Grief affects everything you do. It can disrupt every aspect of your life in ways you might not expect.

"I don't think I had time to think because psychologically I wasn't with it," says Nancy, whose husband passed away. "I would do stupid things. I would be coming home thinking I was on X Street, and then I'd realize, *Well, I'm on the wrong street.* It was dumb things like that."

When life seems chaotic and your world has lost its predictable order, remember that God does not change. Like Nancy, you may find yourself driving down the wrong road, but God is with you, and He is able to get you to your destination.

"What a God! His road stretches straight and smooth. Every GOD-direction is road-tested. Everyone who runs toward him makes it" (Psalm 18:30 MSG).

Creator God, You are a steadfast presence in my forever-changed world. Amen.

Identify Your Losses

One reason grief disrupts so many aspects of your life is because your loss is not one isolated loss. You will miss so many qualities and facets of the person you lost that each will become an opportunity to experience grief.

The range of things you need to grieve for may surprise you. Identify your losses and be prepared to grieve for each one.

Use the list below as a starting point.

- your companion
- your encourager
- your source of delight
- your breadwinner
- your housekeeper
- your cook
- your mechanic
- your friend
- your lover

- your "entertainer"
- the one who shares your private jokes
- the one who knows you so well
- the shoulder on which you cry
- the arms that embrace and comfort you
- the one who always cheers you
- your pride and joy

Your list will go on and on. Say your losses out loud to God; speak until you run out of words to say. He knows your deepest needs, and He alone can provide. Do not skip this step.

"And my God will meet all your needs according to his glorious riches in Christ Jesus" (Philippians 4:19).

O God, I have lost so much. Who will fill these gaping holes within me? You, Lord—yes, You. Amen.

Losing a Part of Yourself

The loss of a close family member creates extra depth and complexity to your grief. You shared a special and intimate connection with your loved one, and this relationship helped you define who you were. Losing this person has literally ripped you apart on the inside, leaving you unsure of your own identity.

Dr. Jim Conway, speaking of the death of his wife, says, "When Sally died, it was as if someone took a giant samurai sword and just cut me right down the middle. I kept asking myself and God, 'How am I supposed to go on with one leg, with one arm, with half a brain? How am I supposed to do all of this?'"

There is hope for you. Your identity can be found again when you abide in the Lord Jesus Christ and place your faith in Him. This will not happen overnight, and the process may be very painful. But Jesus will certainly help you as you depend on Him.

"If anyone acknowledges that Jesus is the Son of God, God lives in him and he in God. And so we know and rely on the love God has for us. God is love. Whoever lives in love lives in God, and God in him" (1 John 4:15–16).

Lord Jesus, piece me back together again with Your unfailing love. Amen.

Doubting Your Faith

"I was mad. I felt like the Lord was not there. I had prayed to hear from Him, and I didn't. It seemed as if He wasn't answering my prayers," says Phyllis, who lost her sister. "Emotionally and spiritually I expected something different. I knew that He was there, but I wasn't feeling emotionally like I wanted to feel."

You are not alone, and you are not wrong to have doubts.

David said in the Psalms, "My God, my God, why have you forsaken me? Why are you so far from saving me, so far from the words of my groaning?" (22:1).

Job had similar feelings: "Remember, O God, that my life is but a breath; my eyes will never see happiness again" (7:7). Job thought he would "never see happiness again," but when we read the end of the book of Job, we find that God had something very good in store for him.

God is faithful to do what He says He will do regardless of how you feel or what you believe.

Lord, I'm going to walk this journey by faith because what I feel and see sure isn't helping. Amen.

Spiritual Breakthrough

Your weaknesses and inadequacies make themselves known to you again and again. You can't always count on other people, and you can't count on yourself. No human being can meet all your needs, especially your deepest needs.

"We are living in a broken world," states Barbara Johnson. "We see broken marriages, broken people, broken lives. There's never going to come a time when we've got it all together."

She continues, "As you go through grief, as you center your focus on what is ahead of you as a Christian, that helps you to know that what you're going through isn't going to last. You have to take a day at a time. Tomorrow may be different. Yesterday is a canceled check, tomorrow is a promissory note, but today is cash. You've got today to serve the Lord."

You are at a point where you need to decide whom you will lean on, trust, and put your hope in. Now is the time to search God's Word and hold on to this lifeline. God will meet you where you are, at your point of pain. Seek Him, talk to Him, and learn about Him. He is the only way out of despair.

Listen to God's promise to you and claim it:

"'For I know the plans I have for you,' declares the LORD, 'plans to prosper you and not to harm you, plans to give you hope and a future. Then you will call upon me and come and pray to me, and I will listen to you. You will seek me and find me when you seek me with all your heart'" (Jeremiah 29:11–13).

Lord God, I realize that I need to search the Bible and seek Your way with all the strength I've got left. Amen.

Joy Can Return

It does get better; you will experience joy again.

In her book *A Passage Through Grief,* Barbara Baumgardner writes, "They told me one day I would go twenty-four hours without thinking of my loss. I told them they were crazy.

"They weren't crazy; they were right. At first, I felt guilt, then elation."[1]

God is the source of your hope and joy. Believe these words of Jesus in John 16: "I tell you the truth, you will weep and mourn while the world rejoices. You will grieve, but your grief will turn to joy" (v. 20).

Jesus continued: "A woman giving birth to a child has pain because her time has come; but when her baby is born she forgets the anguish because of her joy that a child is born into the world.

"So with you: Now is your time of grief, but I will see you again and you will rejoice, and no one will take away your joy" (vv. 21–22).

Lord, I cannot even remember what joy feels like, but I believe that someday You will turn my grief to joy, and no one will take that joy away from me. Amen.

Be Equipped for Recovery

If you want to be healed, make a commitment right now to begin the process of grieving. Take steps forward, even when you have to force yourself. These daily devotions introduce you to the tools you need for working through the process of grieving. We want you to be equipped for recovery.

You may feel you are not sure if you can even begin this journey. But be encouraged. Cindy Morgan says, "God takes you as you are. He accepts you, and then His love changes you. You are never beyond hope. Never."

First Peter 1:13 says, "Therefore, prepare your minds for action; be self-controlled; set your hope fully on the grace to be given you when Jesus Christ is revealed."

> *Jesus, it is only by Your grace that I can be healed. I commit my grieving process to You right now, and I promise to see this process through. Amen.*

the seasons of grief

Shock

Shock is a sudden, violent disturbance to the body. The same term is used to describe the effect of an electric current passing through the body. You have likely encountered this paralyzing reaction in grief.

Dr. Norman Peart describes his feelings after the death of his grandmother: "The immediate feeling was that of shock and an awareness that I was not as in control of the world as I once thought. Then it was a numbness, a realization that there's something missing from life now. There was also a great fear as to who could be taken next from my life."

Virgil, who lost his wife, says, "When you go to a funeral, you hear people say, 'Oh, he's holding up so well.' I don't think that's true. I think the person in grief doesn't know what's going on. That's the state I was in." Maybe you can relate to how Virgil felt.

When you are in shock and at that moment you feel powerless to cope and unable to think straight, understand that you don't have to. Yet because of this, it is wise not to make any major changes in your life or decide on any important issues until your shock has subsided.

God will gently lead to safety those who consciously turn to Him and are dependent on His guidance.

"The LORD will give strength to His people; the LORD will bless His people with peace" (Psalm 29:11 NASB).

O Lord, my feet have been swept out from under me, but in Your loving arms I am steady and secure. Amen.

Denial

Are you living in a bad dream? Is every step and every move you make automatic and devoid of emotion? Do you feel suspended in time and unable or unwilling to start up again?

Don't worry. You are experiencing a typical first reaction to grief—denial. Denial is a natural reaction to one of life's most painful events. Your body uses denial as a protective device, be it consciously or subconsciously, to avoid facing reality.

"The clock will mean nothing anymore," says Rev. John Coulombe. "Barely will the calendar. People won't know what day it is, yet their senses are more keenly aware than ever before. It's like a dream that is happening, and they can't get out of it. Everything is in slow motion. But this is normal; this is a response to death."

You must not feel guilty or anxious if you are experiencing denial; God offers you reassurance for this portion of the journey. You can say with confidence, "Even though I walk through the valley of the shadow of death, I will fear no evil, for you [God] are with me; your rod and your staff, they comfort me" (Psalm 23:4).

Oh, Lord God, I am numb in the valley of the shadow of death, but I know You are holding me steady, and You won't ever let me go. Amen.

A Time to Move Forward

Although living in denial may be necessary for a time, at some point you must make a decision to move beyond the denial. This does not mean you will stop grieving altogether, for your healing/grieving process has only just begun. But remember, if you spend too long denying your loss, you will be unable to move forward with life.

Dr. H. Norman Wright says, "You have to come to the place where you admit or recognize 'Yes, I've lost this person. [He or she] is no longer a part of my life.' When you hang on to that person, it's almost like a sense of denial. You remain stuck, and you can't move on with your life."

God will enable you to take the next step. He gently reminds you: "There is a time for everything, and a season for every activity under heaven; a time to be born and a time to die, a time to plant and a time to uproot" (Ecclesiastes 3:1–2).

Holy God, is it time for me to move on from denial? Lead me, Lord. Amen.

Embrace the Grieving Process

It is biblical to grieve. It is necessary to grieve. You must not suppress your heartache and sorrow.

"Weep freely; share your anguish, your deep concern, but always with the joyful assurance that Jesus is with you. The Prince of Peace is with you," said Dr. Bill Bright.

"There is nothing wrong with tears. You miss loved ones who have gone away. But you are not to weep as one who has no hope. Christians can still have joy even in the midst of sorrow. Everyone experiences tragedy, believers and nonbelievers alike. The difference is the believer has Christ with him."

At the graveside of His friend Lazarus, the Bible says that "Jesus wept" (John 11:35). He understands your tears.

Lord Jesus, You are my only hope. Teach me how to grieve. Amen.

Grief Is a Journey

If you want to heal from grief, you must go *through* it; you cannot go *around* it. The grieving process is a healing process. Do not look at healing as a goal you can only attain at the end of the process. Each step you take is part of your healing.

"Grief is a process that is better thought of as a journey," observes Dr. Tim Clinton. "It's just one foot in front of the other. It may seem that others have grieved very quickly, but those who have come through the process too fast have undone business in their lives."

Take a moment to try and identify where you are on your grief journey. If you have admitted you are grieving, then your journey has begun.

Rest assured that the God of all time, the First and the Last, the omniscient and omnipotent God, will be with you every step of the way, and He has already placed your healing in His plan.

"Your word is a lamp to my feet and a light for my path" (Psalm 119:105).

God, all I can do is put one foot in front of the other, but I know for sure that my journey has begun. Amen.

Grief Cannot Be Rushed

Your journey through grief cannot be compared to another person's journey. You will grieve in your way and in your time. Grief does not have a set time limit. The only certainty is that it will take longer than you want it to.

"It's a process that cannot be rushed," says Dr. Robert Jeffress. "As a pastor who has dealt with hundreds and hundreds of people who have gone through a loss, I can tell you that it is a process, and it is a longer process than any of us want to believe.

"Going through grief is like going through a tunnel. The bad news is the tunnel is dark. The good news is that once you enter into that tunnel, you are already on your way out."

Your journey is your own, but you are not alone. Do not be afraid to cry out to God, "How long must I wrestle with my thoughts and every day have sorrow in my heart? How long will my enemy triumph over me?" (Psalm 13:2).

How long, Lord, how long? This tunnel is so dark. Show me Your light. Amen.

Don't Rush Me

Sometimes other people try to help you get out of your grief by offering advice or "constructive criticism." They may admonish you to "get over it" or to "get back into life." These comments can hurt.

Remember, you have an insight into the grieving process that these people do not have. You know that the length of the grieving process is different for each person. You know you have to let the grieving process take place, because if you try to rush it, you will only prolong the healing.

"So many people will say: 'Well, it's been six months. Don't you think you should be over it by now?' But for each person it's different, and to say those things is very hurtful because maybe that person isn't ready," says Emy, a widow.

You cannot rely on other people to say the right words and provide the right comfort, but you can rely on God.

Job's "friends" condemned him and did not understand his grief. "Then Job replied: 'I have heard many things like these; miserable comforters are you all!'" (Job 16:1–2).

Father God, I know that my friends and family mean well, but they just don't understand that I am not there yet. Help me to know when I am. Holy Spirit, You are my Comforter. In You alone will I find refuge. Amen.

Rock Bottom

Your visitors have left and gone home. The house is quiet. The adrenaline that you've been living on has stopped.

According to Dr. E. V. Hill, "Initially, you can expect great strength to do what you have to do. But then you can expect great sorrow. It will start coming in when the phones are no longer ringing and the people are no longer visiting.

"Then you can expect the visit of the devil. He is a booger. He knows when to come and what to say to make you feel even worse."

When your emotions have hit rock bottom, there is only one path to travel, and that is the path to God.

"Even to your old age and gray hairs I am he, I am he who will sustain you, I have made you and I will carry you; I will sustain you and I will rescue you" (Isaiah 46:4).

Lord, in my weakness and the failing of my limbs, lift me into the palm of Your everlasting hand. You alone are my strength and my champion. Amen.

Uncontrollable Emotions

Fear, depression, anger, loneliness, despair—these emotions come and go with dizzying unpredictability. Your life is like a roller-coaster ride that you can't get off.

Stay on the ride. You cannot hurry the grieving process. Each time one of these emotions comes flooding back, it is a sign that you are recovering.

"All the feelings, thoughts, and emotions rush back into my life. It's uncontrollable," says Dr. Norman Peart.

But God is always in control. He is a solid rock, unmoving and unchanging. Build your life's foundation on Him.

"Therefore everyone who hears these words of mine and puts them into practice is like a wise man who built his house on the rock. The rain came down, the streams rose, and the winds blew and beat against that house; yet it did not fall, because it had its foundation on the rock" (Matthew 7:24–25).

Lord, I am hanging on for the endurance of the ride. You are a constant presence through my ups and downs. Amen.

A Series of Losses

Life is a series of losses, and multiple losses will extend your grief journey. Past losses can include the deaths of loved ones and pets, job displacement, the loss of a home, and friends and family moving away. Less tangible losses include not being chosen for a particular project or committee and missing out on special events. If you have not dealt with these losses, you may have feelings of regret or sadness that will affect how you grieve your current loss.

"The old losses actually contaminate, intensify, and complicate this new loss," says Dr. H. Norman Wright.

Once you understand that you are experiencing multiple losses, you will be better prepared for the depth and the different facets of grief that may have been confusing at first. The Bible shows that understanding can lead to peace. Understanding your grieving process will help keep you moving forward and not backward. Be prepared to grieve all your losses on this journey.

"I [Jesus] have told you these things, so that in me you may have peace. In this world you will have trouble. But take heart! I have overcome the world" (John 16:33).

You, almighty Lord, are my Overcomer. Equip me to face life's struggles while resting securely in Your victory and love. Amen.

Loss History

Dr. H. Norman Wright recommends writing a "loss history" to help you identify and work through past losses. Take time to think of and list any losses you have experienced throughout the course of your life. Include any instances where you felt a sense of loss, no matter how unimportant the circumstances may seem now. Think of missed promotions, friends moving away, the deaths of pets, the ends of friendships, job losses, children leaving home, and lost opportunities.

After you have identified each loss, go down through the list and talk about each one (to God or to another person). Talk about how intense it was and how you felt at that time. Take your time doing this. You may need to plan a time each day or week to work through your list.

"If you find there's an emotional connection to some loss," says Dr. Wright, "then maybe you have not really processed it. Maybe it's still affecting your life in some way."

Dr. Wright suggests that you need to come to the point at which you can say of each loss, "Yes, that happened to me, but now I'm going on with my life," compared to "Boy, that happened to me, and it still hurts."

"Remember the days of old" (Deuteronomy 32:7).

God, I didn't realize how much my past losses were affecting me now. Use this exercise to help me recognize and come to terms with each loss on my list. Amen.

Healing

"Just give it time," people say. That is misleading. Time alone will not heal your grief.

"I knew about the process and steps of grief recovery. But still, it felt like the weight of grief on my shoulders would never be lifted," says Dr. Ray Pritchard. "It's okay to feel that way. But know it won't last forever.

"Your feelings at this point aren't the crucial issue. What is important is that you choose to stay close to the Lord and not turn away from Him. If you walk with God as He walks with you, one day you will wake up and say, 'It's a little bit better.'"

God is the source of all healing. Make the decision to remain close to Him despite your emotional struggles.

"I am the LORD, who heals you" (Exodus 15:26).

Jehovah Rapha, healing God, You are my healer, and I choose to walk with You. Amen.

Grief Can Ambush

No matter how long it has been, you still carry a portion of your grief with you. Emotions you already dealt with come flooding back at the most unexpected times. Grief's timing is not your timing.

Elisabeth Elliot says, "One day after my husband died, I was in the grocery store picking up the things that I needed, throwing them into my basket, and suddenly I found myself absolutely shaking with sobs. Fortunately, there was no one else in that particular aisle. I couldn't explain it. Grief does strange things to you at times."

But God holds the master plan for your life. He is never surprised. Although you cannot know the details of the plan, you can know and walk with the Master Planner.

"I trust in you, O LORD; I say, 'You are my God.' My times are in your hands; deliver me from my enemies and from those who pursue me" (Psalm 31:14–15).

God, I do not understand what is going on with me, but I trust that You do. Amen.

Grief Can Feel Unending

You feel as though you've been in this pit, this dark tunnel, on this roller-coaster ride, far too long. Will this grief never end?

"There is no microwave healing. There's no way you can just zap it, and you're better. God's healing takes time, but morning will come," says Barbara Johnson.

What signs of daybreak do you see in your life? If you are walking blindly in the darkness of despair, look to the God of light to show you the way.

"Weeping may remain for a night, but rejoicing comes in the morning" (Psalm 30:5).

> *Lord Jesus, sometimes I feel like my grief will never end. Show me patches of sunlight in my life today that will spur me on with a healing hope. Amen.*

Special Days Trigger Grief

Special days—anniversaries, holidays, birthdays—can act as emotional land mines. The emotions you feel on those days can be as intense or even more intense than the emotions you felt at first.

Dr. Tim Clinton observes, "Too many people are unaware or underaware of the normal grieving process. For example . . . anniversary dates, birthdays, holidays and things like that can evoke a lot of anger. When this happens, people feel like there's something wrong with them or they're not very strong."

These feelings are normal. Knowing this, prepare yourself ahead of time for those special days. Read the Bible to draw strength and comfort from it. Plan a quiet day with close friends or family members who will surround you with love. Remember, when you are discouraged and at a low point relating to your loss, the only remedy is to look to the Father.

"Why are you downcast, O my soul? Why so disturbed within me? Put your hope in God, for I will yet praise Him, my Savior and my God. My soul is downcast within me; therefore I will remember you" (Psalm 42:5–6).

Lord, I look to You when I am struck down again by grief. I will depend on You, and I will praise You; for though I am struck down, I am not destroyed. Amen.

You Cannot Go Back

Remember the good times; cherish the memories, but live each day moving forward. Focus your thoughts on what is before you and how you are going to get there.

"I often tell people that there are three stages you need to think about: You can't go back. You can't stay here. You must go forward," says Dr. Ray Pritchard. "There may be some good things in the past that you wish you could go back to, but in the end you have to let those go."

God's Word speaks to you clearly: "I have set before you life . . . now choose life" (Deuteronomy 30:19).

Yes, Lord, I do choose life. Amen.

You Can't Stay Here

The journey of grief is one that you must ultimately decide to complete. You cannot remain where you are right now. Time moves forward, and so must you.

"You can't stay here because God's Word is always going forward," says Dr. Ray Pritchard.

In Philippians 3:14 Paul says that he moved forward toward "the upward call of God in Christ Jesus" (NASB). The Christian life is not static. It is a walk with God that moves you forward into a larger life with God.

The Lord's plan for your life is pure and simple during this time of grief: "He has told you, O man, what is good; and what does the LORD require of you but to do justice, to love kindness, and to walk humbly with your God?" (Micah 6:8 NASB).

Lord, may I simply walk with You. Take my hand and guide me through every moment of this day. Amen.

Go Forward with God

When it's hard to look forward and it's painful to look back, you need a new perspective, a new focus. Look to the Father and keep your eyes on Him. Every time your thoughts drift away from Him, repeat these words, "Focused on You, Jesus. Focused on You."

If you keep yourself centered in God, you will be able to move forward again. Cindy offers a suggestion from her own experience. She says, "What is at the center of your life? Just for an hour or two hours, put God at the center of your life and see what happens. Then do it for half a day. Then do it for a day, and see what happens. I think you'll start feeling that you're going to be okay, that you can trust God, and that you can do the things you need to do."

"Therefore we do not lose heart. Though outwardly we are wasting away, yet inwardly we are being renewed day by day. . . . So we fix our eyes not on what is seen, but on what is unseen. For what is seen is temporary, but what is unseen is eternal" (2 Corinthians 4:16, 18).

Thank you, God, that I don't have to strive in my journey, because You have already provided the grace I need to make it. Amen.

Women and Men Grieve Differently

Women tend to approach grief differently than men. Often women have a network of friends and relationships already in place, providing them an opportunity for deep personal sharing. Whether you are a man or a woman, you need to vent your emotions, and God uses other people to help you heal.

"Men don't share with each other like women do. They want to get on and get beyond it a lot faster than women do," says Pastor Buck Buchanan. "My advice for them is to get involved in a grief group where they can be encouraged."

Healing will resume when you stop trying to accomplish it by your own strength. God will move through you with His power that far exceeds your own.

"He has said to me, 'My grace is sufficient for you, for power is perfected in weakness.' Most gladly, therefore, I will rather boast about my weaknesses, that the power of Christ may dwell in me" (2 Corinthians 12:9 NASB).

Lord, I need to be honest. The pain is unbearable. Give me the courage to be real with others and to embrace Your power. Amen.

Men in Grief

As you go through life, you fight stereotypes and popular misconceptions. Several notions exist about how "real men" should act in different situations.

Take a moment to identify your own ideas about how men should "handle" grief. When did you form this opinion? Who modeled this behavior for you? Who might be looking to you as a role model?

Here are some comments from men who have experienced grief:

"In our culture especially," says Rev. Noel Castellanos, "the whole macho thing is very prevalent. I think men are afraid to express their feelings. We haven't had too many people show us how to do that. I remember being very moved when I first became a believer as I saw strong Christian men who had the ability to cry and share their weakness and hurt."

Virgil, whose wife died, observes, "Men, as little kids, are told not to cry and it carries through. To solve this problem, fathers should let their little boys cry. It doesn't hurt a thing. It's an emotion God gives us."

"Christ was a man's man," says Jim Grassi. "Eight of the twelve disciples were fishermen. At times, the disciples wept and they felt grief. They had all the normal emotions that God intended people to have."

David, a warrior and king, poured out his emotions to God throughout the Psalms: "I am bowed down and brought very low; all day long I go about mourning. . . . I am feeble and utterly crushed; I groan in anguish of heart. . . . For I am about to fall, and my pain is ever with me" (Psalm 38:6, 8, 17).

Almighty God, let my prayer be like David's prayers. Teach me what manhood really is. Open my heart and mind to want this change. Amen.

Feeling the Need to Be in Control

When life seems to be spinning out of control, you may grasp whatever reins you can find and hang on. Holding those reins gives you a sense of being in control, not only of your life but, more specifically, of your emotions. Emotions can be frightening because they are the least controllable aspect of your nature. Men in particular feel the need to be in control.

"Most men are high on control," says Jim Grassi. "When tragedy strikes, it's a loss of control. You realize just how small you are in the scheme of things and that God is really the One in control. You must release that control and give it back to God and allow Him the full authority in your life."

As long as you are fighting God for control, you will be the loser. Let it all go. Tell Him today that you are tired of fighting, that you want Him to have full authority in your life.

"The mind of sinful man is death, but the mind controlled by the Spirit is life and peace" (Romans 8:6).

> *Holy Spirit, I long for that life and peace. This fight to be strong has depleted the last of my so-called resources. Take my life and lead me on the journey of healing. Amen.*

Facing Your Emotions

Men who seldom express emotions during normal times often find they do not have the tools needed to express their grief in times of bereavement. Their ideas of how a man should behave can hinder the healthy expression of their emotions.

Dr. Larry Crabb says, "Men are real problems and I am one of them. In a way that is different from women, men demand to be able to manage things. A man will naturally not move into chaotic situations where he hasn't got a plan.

"Emotions are probably the least controllable thing about our existence. So when a man begins to honestly face his emotions, his worst terror begins to be realized. He thinks to himself, *If I face what's really happening in my soul, I won't have the resources to handle it; I won't come up with a formula or a game plan.*"

In the Bible, Jacob found it very difficult to move on and to accept comfort. "Then Jacob tore his clothes, put on sackcloth and mourned for his son many days. All his sons and daughters came to comfort him, but he refused to be comforted. 'No,' he said, 'in mourning will I go down to the grave to my son.' So his father wept for him" (Genesis 37:34–35).

Lord God, I understand that the power and strength to heal come from You and not my own ability. I give my life and my struggles to You. Amen.

Uncomfortable Expressing Emotions?

Men tend to grieve alone and to express very little about what they are feeling. But keeping emotions bottled up inside slows the healing process.

Dr. Norman Peart says, "Men are taught that they should not express their emotions because that is a sign of weakness. In reality, expressing emotions is a sign of health because it means you are working through those emotions. You have to be honest with yourself; you do hurt."

God wants you to pour out your emotions to Him: "Trust in him at all times, O people; pour out your hearts to him, for God is our refuge" (Psalm 62:8).

He also directs you to share your emotions with others: "Rejoice with those who rejoice; mourn with those who mourn" (Romans 12:15).

O God, I know that You want me to release my emotions to You and to others. Give me the opportunity and the courage to do that. Uncork my bottled emotions so my healing can continue. Amen.

Society's Superficial Response to Grief

Society often concerns itself with keeping up appearances, maintaining the status quo, and covering up problems, as if pretense will somehow make things right!

"We want everything to be glossed over," Rev. John Coulombe observes. "We want everything to be gilded with gold. We think it should be tidy and nice."

But life is not "tidy and nice" and pretending it is will hinder your healing process and make it even longer.

Remember that your view is not God's. Realizing this, draw close to Him and listen to His wisdom. His perspective on your grief is the one you need to seek.

"'For my thoughts are not your thoughts, neither are your ways my ways,' declares the LORD. 'As the heavens are higher than the earth, so are my ways higher than your ways and my thoughts than your thoughts'" (Isaiah 55:8–9).

Holy God, teach me to grieve wisely, knowing that You truly understand my hurts and my needs and knowing that Your way for me is far better than society's expectations of me. Amen.

Talk About It

Death is a part of life. Everyone experiences the death of a loved one.

"We are social beings, physical beings, and spiritual beings," says Rev. Clay Evans. "When you lose someone you are attached to, it is normal, it is natural, for you to grieve."

If grief is natural and is part of everyone's life, why is there a feeling of discomfort when someone mentions the death of a loved one? Why the embarrassment when tears come during an ordinary conversation?

People in grief may avoid their friends and even their church to prevent these awkward moments. This is not how it should be. Someone needs to move beyond the discomfort. Be the first one to squelch the prevailing attitude of embarrassment and unease, and start talking about grief.

"Bear one another's burdens, and thus fulfill the law of Christ" (Galatians 6:2 NASB).

> *Lord Jesus, grieving is as natural and as common as loving. I want to help make it as acceptable, too. May my healing journey spark healing in those around me. Amen.*

Sharing Your Grief

Which of these sentences best describes you? Your spouse? Siblings? Children?

A. I like to open up and share deep-felt emotions as often as possible.

B. I can think of a million things I'd rather do than bring up the pain again by talking about it.

Every person has his or her own way of reacting to grief, and men and women often respond differently.

"My husband still has a hard time just talking about it," says Dora, who lost her daughter. "I think his way of dealing with it is to dive into work, to avoid it, to not talk about it. Many times it causes problems between us because I want to talk about it. For me, it's like he's not validating my suffering by allowing me to share it with him. For him, it's as if I'm opening up his wounds by wanting him to share it with me."

You cannot change another person to grieve in a way that pleases you, but you can give your concerns about that person to God and pray that he or she will someday open up and release those crippling emotions.

"Therefore confess your sins to each other and pray for each other so that you may be healed. The prayer of a righteous man is powerful and effective" (James 5:16).

Lord God, it's so important that I share my emotions with others. Only You can soften a heart that is hardened. Once again, I give it to You. Amen.

Share Honestly

You need to be honest about your relationship with the person you lost. Sometimes after a death, you may reinvent the relationship you had and make it either better or worse than it really was. Altering the truth will hinder your recovery process.

Remember the good as well as the bad about your relationship, not to feel guilt or sadness, but as an honest release.

"In my integrity you uphold me and set me in your presence forever" (Psalm 41:12).

> *You respect my honesty, O Lord. Forgive me for changing the truth of this past relationship in my mind. My life cannot be rebuilt on the frailty and danger of lies and half-truths.*
>
> *I honestly come before You now and tell You what You already know—the truth about my relationship with the one I lost. Here it is, Lord, the good and the bad. My honesty is stronger and more secure than any lies I have been fooling myself with.*
>
> *Lord, uphold me in my integrity and be with me forever. Amen.*

The First Principle of the Journey: Be Honest

Do you embrace honesty as a foundational principle in your life?

If yes, then *honestly* evaluate your emotions right now. What emotions and struggles have you experienced from the first moment of your grief until now, including those you have not admitted to others? Be honest with yourself and with other people.

"When you are suffering, you may sometimes tend to withdraw, pull back, and pull away," says Anne Graham Lotz. "I do think there is a time for that, and each day you should spend time alone with the Lord. But don't forsake other people, because other people can give you comfort and encouragement and help you keep your focus. Sometimes you can get so preoccupied with the problem that it consumes you. Other people can help give you a balance."

God wants you to be truthful with yourself and with other people. He wants to free you from the debilitating effects of withdrawing and hiding your emotions. Jesus says in the book of John that "the truth will set you free." Read the book of John to learn more about Jesus' teaching, His truth, and true freedom.

"Jesus said, 'If you hold to my teaching, you are really my disciples. Then you will know the truth, and the truth will set you free. . . . So if the Son sets you free, you will be free indeed" (John 8:31–32, 36).

Lord Jesus, I want to be set free. Amen.

The Second Principle of the Journey: Be Expressive

Express your tears and your pain. In order to move on, you cannot push down and pocket your emotions; they must be fully communicated for you to heal.

"Everyone cries," says Dr. H. Norman Wright. "Everyone sheds tears. Some people do it on the outside, but some are only capable of doing it on the inside. From a health perspective, the shedding of tears is very beneficial to physical well-being.

"The people who are unable or haven't developed the capacity to cry are carrying a heavier load of emotion that can actually contribute to some physical difficulties. I don't think you should ever apologize for your tears because you never apologize for something that is a gift from God."

Pull out your emotions. Face the pain head-on. Mourn loudly. Weep bitterly. Be set free.

When Peter realized he had disowned Jesus three times, he "went outside and wept bitterly" (Luke 22:62). When Stephen, the first Christian martyr, died, devout men "made loud lamentation over him" (Acts 8:2 NASB).

Holy God, I'm so adept at pushing down my emotions that I don't know how to pull them up, but I know that I must. Give me the opportunity and the courage to let my emotions pour out freely. Amen.

The Third Principle of the Journey: Be Involved

"Don't imagine that you're gonna tough this out and make it all by yourself," says Dr. Jim Conway.

Do you have a person with whom you can share your innermost feelings about your loss? Take action to find someone. Often it is helpful to find someone who has experienced a loss similar to your own.

Pray first that God will direct you. Then make a list of family members, friends, neighbors, and coworkers with whom you might share. Pick up the phone and plan a time to meet and talk. You might also call your local church and explain that you just need someone to talk to about your situation. Another idea is to find a grief support group where you can share, ventilate, talk, and find support from others who can truly relate.[1]

"Two are better than one, because they have a good return for their work: If one falls down, his friend can help him up" (Ecclesiastes 4:9–10).

Lord, direct me to the person You want me to have as a friend and confidant during this time of grief. Amen.

What Are You Feeling?

To help you express your emotions and share your story with others, it will be helpful to identify and define what you have lost and how you feel about it. Follow these steps:

1. Identify your loss. What did you lose?

2. Determine your specific feelings about that loss.

3. Tell someone: "I'm feeling _____ because of this loss."

Dr. H. Norman Wright says, "What you need is more public affirmation and recognition of the fact that what you went through is a very legitimate loss, and you need to have grieving opportunities for that."

Identifying your losses and your feelings is an important step to take at the personal level, but it is also important to share these feelings with another person and receive his or her affirmation.

"Accept one another, then, just as Christ accepted you, in order to bring praise to God" (Romans 15:7).

Righteous God, what am I feeling, and with whom can I share my feelings? Make this clear to me, and give me the courage to follow through. Amen.

Sudden Loss

Dr. H. Norman Wright says, "Sudden death is a shock to the system. It can often plunge a person into a crisis state. It's the suddenness of it that's just overwhelming. You don't have the resources. It stops you from your walk through life."

The sovereign Lord will remain by your side and will keep you from being destroyed by your emotions and circumstances. Claim His words in the Bible, and stand on the truth of His promises, regardless of what you feel and see. Cling to God with all you have. He will preserve your life.

In the following verse Paul said he felt great pressure and confusion, but God set a limit as to how far this would go: "We are hard pressed on every side, but not crushed; perplexed, but not in despair; persecuted, but not abandoned; struck down, but not destroyed" (2 Corinthians 4:8–9).

> *Savior of my life, I will say it again: The pressure seems unbearable, but it has not crushed me. I am utterly confused and overwhelmed, but I have not given up. My distress is constant, but so are You. I have been forcefully struck down, but I am not destroyed. Amen.*

Grieving Before the Loss

When a person you love is sick or suffering, you begin to grieve before the actual loss. In some cases you may think that most of your grieving is already done. But despite your preparations, the grief that occurs *after* a person's death goes beyond all your expectations.

Dr. Jim Conway lost his wife after a long battle with cancer. He says, "Sally got sick in 1990, and we talked frankly. She went through repeated surgeries, radiation, and chemo over the next seven years. I thought that because we had talked so much that there would be no grief. I really thought that I had resolved all that.

"But it is not like that at all. It was like looking at a video about jumping out of an airplane, free-falling, and finally your parachute opens. All of the previous stuff was just preparatory information, but it was not actually going out of the plane; it was not experiencing grief.

"When Sally died, it was as if somebody pushed me out of the plane, and now I am free-falling—this is what grief is like. You are in free fall. You wonder if the parachute is ever going to open. You wonder if you're going to hit the ground at 120 miles per hour."

Only You, Almighty God, can keep me from falling. I turn to You, believing Your promise: "To him who is able to keep [me] from falling and to present [me] before his glorious presence without fault and with great joy—to the only God our Savior be glory, majesty, power and authority, through Jesus Christ our Lord, before all ages, now and forevermore! Amen" (Jude 24–25).

God's Grace

When you need God's grace the most, God will bless you with a special, dynamic grace to get you through.

Elisabeth Elliot experienced the deaths of her first two husbands. She says, "I think that the reason I did not cry at Jim's or Ad's funeral was because God gives grace to help in time of need. Everybody else at those funeral services was just dissolved in tears. I can honestly say that I really did not feel like crying; I was just so swept away with the glory of the fact that my husbands were with the Lord. I think God gives special grace at times like these to people who need it the most."

As a Christian, God's grace protects you and sustains you in so many ways, even when you are not aware of it. Humans are limited in perception and understanding, but God's grace is infinite. Believe that God's grace is being poured out for you today, and if you need specific grace, ask Him for it. Through Jesus, you can find something to rejoice about in suffering.

"Therefore, since we have been justified through faith, we have peace with God through our Lord Jesus Christ, through whom we have gained access by faith into this grace in which we now stand. And we rejoice in the hope of the glory of God. Not only so, but we also rejoice in our sufferings, because we know that suffering produces perseverance" (Romans 5:1–3).

Heavenly Father, I believe that You are giving me a special grace to help me through the hardest times. I will stand on Your promises even when I cannot see You or feel You. Amen.

Grief Intervention

There are times when the darkness of your grief may so overwhelm you that professional intervention is necessary. If any of the following is true for you, consider seeking professional intervention:

- You are dependent on alcohol or drugs
- You have recurring thoughts about suicide
- You completely withdraw from your family, friends, and colleagues
- You are still depressed after several months

Psalm 73:21–26 states:

I realized how bitter I had become, how pained I had been by all I had seen. I was so foolish and ignorant—I must have seemed like a senseless animal to you. Yet I still belong to you; you are holding my right hand. You will keep on guiding me with your counsel, leading me to a glorious destiny. Whom have I in heaven but you? I desire you more than anything on earth. My health may fail, and my spirit may grow weak, but God remains the strength of my heart; he is mine forever. (NLT)

Please do not hesitate to seek help for problems and needs that require professional treatment. You can ask your pastor or Christian friends for recommendations, search the Internet, or check your local phone book to find the names of Christian counselors and treatment programs.

"Think of it—the LORD has healed me!" (Isaiah 38:20 NLT).

Beloved Lord, grant me the ability to recognize when I need intervention and the courage to seek it out. Amen.

Healthy Grieving: Step One

Grief is a natural, inevitable reaction to loss. You are not given a choice about having grief, but you can choose how you grieve.

Knowing the general process of healthy grieving will assist you on your grief journey. A basic understanding with practical application will enable you to work through the loss in a positive way.

The first step of healthy grieving is to acknowledge and understand your own grief. "The people who recover are the people who admit their loss and are able to talk about it," says Dr. H. Norman Wright.

Understand this step and apply it. Look into your heart and explore your responses to grief so far.

"The LORD does not look at the things man looks at. Man looks at the outward appearance, but the LORD looks at the heart" (1 Samuel 16:7).

Lord, I'm grieving. Help me grieve in my way and my time, but with Your wisdom. Amen.

Healthy Grieving: Step Two

You have already acknowledged that you are grieving, and you have attempted to understand your grief. The next step in healthy grieving is to allow your needs to be recognized by others. To apply this step, you must first recognize these needs for yourself.

Identify your needs right now—physical, emotional, and spiritual. Jot them down on a piece of paper.

Next comes the more difficult part. Let others know your needs, and allow people to help you in a concrete way.

"Grief is not just something you work through on your own," says Dr. Jim Conway. "Most people need outside help because the thing that accomplishes the resolution is talking to somebody. You can accomplish some things on your own, but a support group will be beneficial."

God promises to supply the help that you need, and He will be sure to send the right people. But first you must turn to Jesus and ask for His help.

"Let us then approach the throne of grace with confidence, so that we may receive mercy and find grace to help us in our time of need" (Hebrews 4:16).

Lord God, I have so many needs, and I am tired of trying to be in control. Help me relinquish my needs to You and to others. Amen.

Healthy Grieving: Step Three

The third step in the healthy grieving process is so simple, yet so important; it is to feel free to grieve in your own way. Other people may criticize or make comments about your grieving or the amount of time it is taking you. Realize that your grief is unique. If you are honest with yourself, then you don't need to worry about what others are saying.

Heidi, who lost her husband, says, "One thing that really upset me was when some people said, 'You need to get on with your life. You need to get over the grieving process.' I felt they were wrong because they had never been through this. How could they say that?"

You have to go through the grieving process. Turn to God when you are anxious, uncertain, or frustrated about your grief and about what other people are saying.

"Do not be anxious about anything, but in everything, by prayer and petition, with thanksgiving, present your requests to God. And the peace of God, which transcends all understanding, will guard your hearts and your minds in Christ Jesus" (Philippians 4:6–7).

Father, in my hurt and confusion I come to You. Hold me close and fill me with that indescribable peace. Amen.

Healthy Grieving: Step Four

The fourth step in healthy grieving is to tell your story to others. Give someone an honest account of your loss.

"Grieving means talking about what you're going through in the presence of some other people and letting them react to you," says Dr. Jim Conway.

So how do you find the right people to share with? First consider your family members. Then consider sharing with members of a grief recovery group. If these options are not good for you, as mentioned previously, try to find someone in your church or neighborhood who has experienced a loss similar to yours. If you tell him or her that you need someone to talk to, that person will likely be glad to meet with you.

It may seem easier and more desirable to keep your words, thoughts, and emotions inside and to busy yourself with work and activities to help you forget. But that forgetfulness is short-lived and ultimately ineffective. True healing will only occur when you slow down and let grief run its course.

"Yet it was good of you to share in my troubles" (Philippians 4:14).

Lord Jesus, You know what is best for me much more than I ever will. Open my heart and my mouth and enable me to share my story with others. Amen.

Healthy Grieving: Step Five

Commit to the journey, long or short, that leads back into living life.

"People who handle grief in a most healthy way are those who are willing to admit, 'This hurts. I don't particularly like it, but I really want to go on,'" says Pastor Buck Buchanan.

God will reward your sincere willingness to commit to the journey and to press on.

> Not that I have already obtained it, or have already become perfect, but I press on in order that I may lay hold of that for which also I was laid hold of by Christ Jesus. Brethren, I do not regard myself as having laid hold of it yet; but one thing I do: forgetting what lies behind and reaching forward to what lies ahead, I press on toward the goal for the prize of the upward call of God in Christ Jesus. (Philippians 3:12–14 NASB)

> *Holy Spirit, I commit myself to Your care as I move forward toward life, Your abundant life. Amen.*

Healthy Grieving: Step Six

"Sometimes the best remedy for grief is finding some way to touch somebody else's life," says Dr. Larry Crabb.

Maybe it's time to change the focus of your thoughts from yourself to other people. Open your eyes to the needs around you. Through your experience you have developed new character traits and knowledge, and you have received encouragement and consolation with which you, in turn, can comfort others. Quiet yourself before God and listen for His still, small voice within you. He will direct you to where you are needed.

Holy Lord, in the words of David I pray to You: "Show me your ways, O Lord, teach me your paths; guide me in your truth and teach me, for you are God my Savior, and my hope is in you all day long" (Psalm 25:4–5). Amen.

Healthy Grieving: Step Seven

Trust God and cling to Him. Bring all your questions and feelings honestly to Him. Appeal to Him; cry to Him; yell at Him; confess to Him, and then sit back in His arms and trust.

"Why not trust Him? What do you have to lose?" says Heidi, whose husband died. "If you are already in a situation that seems hopeless and you trust in Him and He doesn't come through for you, then you haven't lost anything. But if you truly trust in God, He is going to come through for you because He loves you so much. At least give Him the opportunity to prove Himself in your life."

The Lord Jesus Christ will prove Himself true and faithful if you will just let Him.

"Trust in the LORD with all your heart and lean not on your own understanding; in all your ways acknowledge him, and he will make your paths straight" (Proverbs 3:5–6).

Lord, You are the only one who will never let me down. You have promised never to pull away from me or forsake me. I put my trust in You, holy God. Amen.

emotions of grief

Your Emotions

Your emotions can be intense, draining, and hard to hold back; they run deep and are tangled up inside you.

Everyone goes through some unexpected emotions, and it helps for you to identify and sort out the emotions that apply to you. This is part of the healing process.

Which emotions have you experienced during the grieving process?

• denial	• rage	• loneliness
• rejection	• confusion	• helplessness
• guilt	• anxiety	• disappointment
• anger	• sadness	• resentment
• jealousy	• inadequacy	• vindictiveness
• fear	• envy	• depression
• pain	• dread	• bitterness
• loss	• anguish	• dismay
• sorrow	• betrayal	• abandonment
• apathy	• distrust	• lack of control

Jesus can identify with your sorrows.

"He was despised and rejected by men, a man of sorrows, and familiar with suffering. Like one from whom men hide their faces he was despised, and we esteemed him not" (Isaiah 53:3).

Lord Jesus, You alone know my suffering and pain. Please sort through these emotions with me. Amen.

Sudden and Unpredictable

Emotions during grief do not occur in an orderly fashion. You cannot follow a checklist and mark off the emotions you are finished with and then move on to the next. They come suddenly and unpredictably.

"People ask me, 'How are you doing?' And I say, 'Wonderful.' One moment I'm sobbing uncontrollably—I carry Kleenex around in my pocket—and the next moment I'm so exhilarated with joy with all that God is doing in my life," says Dr. Jim Conway.

Circumstances will change. People will change. Surroundings will change. But the Bible leads you to the one sure thing: "I the LORD do not change" (Malachi 3:6).

Almighty, unchanging God, I grasp on to Your hand as my emotions confuse and overwhelm me. You alone cannot be moved, and I am confident that as long as I remain in You, I, too, will not be moved. Amen.

Out of Control

Not only are your emotions unpredictable, but they may also seem uncontrollable. This changing nature combined with the intensity of the emotions can cause you to feel disoriented, forgetful, and over-powered.

"There was this overwhelming feeling of being out of control . . . overwhelmed and watching life pass by," says Cindy following her daughter's death.

Your response to these uncontrollable emotions can be confusing to you as well as to others; for instance, sometimes you may want people with you, and sometimes you do not. You may also act in ways you later regret.

Job expressed this sentiment: "If only my anguish could be weighed and all my misery be placed on the scales! It would surely outweigh the sand of the seas—no wonder my words have been impetuous" (Job 6:2–3).

Precious Lord, You know the desires of my heart. In my confusion give me peace to know that You are in control of all life and You do not make mistakes. Amen.

This Can't Be Happening

Although your mind knows the facts, your heart is often reluctant to accept the death of someone you know and love.

"You may have a tendency to deny," says Dr. H. Norman Wright. "Denial covers over the sharpness of the pain."

Denial is a process that occurs during grieving to minimize the struggle. This is a natural and transitional part of your healing journey.

Randy shares how he experienced denial after his sister died, but over time, he found that denial was impossible: "After the funeral I was basically in denial. I tried to dive into my work and forget about it. It's taken a long time. Little things will remind me: things that she did, places she went to. Things like that will all of a sudden bring this very empty, hollow feeling inside me, where I can't breathe. I feel like the air is just sucked out of me. It's been five years, but trying to deny it or to ignore it is not possible."

You may be tempted to "dive into" your work and fill your mind with anything but the truth of the situation. But the book of Proverbs tells us to be open to the truth and to pursue it: "Buy the truth and do not sell it; get wisdom, discipline and understanding" (23:23).

Jesus, give me the courage to face the truth. With Your help I know I can do it. Amen.

Isolation

Sometimes you just want everyone to leave you alone. So you build a protective wall around yourself, not only to keep other people out, but also to guard against unwanted emotions. You may think you are playing it safe, but instead you are blocking out the healing.

"There are people who love you and want to pray for you and want to talk with you," says Dr. Tim Clinton. "If you allow that to happen, God puts great salve on deep wounds."

Doesn't that sound wonderful—a great salve on deep wounds? Jeremiah cried out to God for just such a thing and found Him to be faithful and true.

"Is there no balm in Gilead? Is there no physician there? Why then is there no healing for the wound of my people?" (Jeremiah 8:22).

"'But I will restore you to health and heal your wounds,' declares the LORD, 'because you are called an outcast, Zion for whom no one cares'" (Jeremiah 30:17).

Faithful God, bring me out of my self-imposed isolation that I may be healed by the Balm of Gilead—Jesus Christ. Amen.

Suppression Can Lead to Explosion

Are you quelling your emotions within you and consciously keeping them at bay? Think about the amount of force and energy this involves. Your emotions may be packed in so tightly that the pressure could build up to the point of possible explosion.

"You can delay the grieving process by denying it or just not allowing yourself to cry or to face it," says Dr. H. Norman Wright. "It's like you put a lid on your life and on your emotions. It is a form of repression, and whenever you repress any of your feelings, you bury them alive. Someday there will be a resurrection, but you will not be in charge of it. It could come through depression. It could come out through explosiveness."

In the midst of overwhelming emotional suffering and pressure, Jesus looked to God with determination.

"And being in anguish he prayed more earnestly, and his sweat was like drops of blood falling to the ground" (Luke 22:44).

Holy God, may my resolve to release my emotional pressure and to seek You be as earnest as Jesus' prayer. Amen.

An Excessive Need to Tell Your Story

You may be a person who feels the need to express your story to anyone and everyone who will listen. You have felt the healing salve that comes from sharing with others, and you may think that telling your story repeatedly will result in greater healing.

Sharing your experience with others is a crucial step on your healing journey, but use wisdom in discerning if your timing is appropriate.

Luevenia experienced the death of her husband. She says, "When I talked about my husband's death to people who weren't close to me, it was boring for them. They got tired of it. But it's ever present with me."

God's Word offers advice on timing for all situations in life. "There is a time for everything, and a season for every activity under heaven. . . . a time to tear and a time to mend, a time to be silent and a time to speak" (Ecclesiastes 3:1, 7).

Lord, I praise You that sharing comes easily to me, and I praise You for the taste of healing that it brings. Give me the wisdom to hold my tongue when I should be listening instead of speaking. Amen.

Rage!

Rage. Have you felt it? Screaming, wailing, intense, and coming up out of nowhere. It is defined in *Webster's Dictionary* as "violent and uncontrolled anger; a fit of violent wrath."

If you can relate to the above descriptions, you are experiencing an emotion common to the grieving process.

"I think the rage I had inside caused my high blood pressure, and I didn't know how to express my anger," says Annie after her father died.

Your anger does need to be expressed, but it must be done slowly and not impulsively. Impulsive anger deals with "personal rights" and "my plan," the kind of anger that shows you are still trying to remain in control. As God is "slow to anger," so are you encouraged to have this attribute.

"He who is slow to anger is better than the mighty. And he who rules his spirit, than he who captures a city" (Proverbs 16:32 NASB).

Impulsive anger can hurt others and cause new problems for you. But the dynamic of being "slow to anger" allows you to express your anger, to see the cause of it, and to deal with it.

Lord, give my rage a slow fuse and keep it from becoming a hungry, devouring flame. Amen.

Anger: Your Strongest Emotion

The Bible instructs you to be angry! "Be angry, and yet do not sin; do not let the sun go down on your anger" (Ephesians 4:26 NASB). Anger by itself is not a sin, and it is one of the most common emotions associated with grief.

"I went through that shock and denial period for about three months," says Dora after the death of her daughter. "Then suddenly, as the shock wore off and the reality set in—anger. Intense anger. Just wanting to wail, to scream from the depths. There's no way I could express as much anger as I was feeling."

You need to release your anger in a way that is productive for healing and not harmful to others around you. To release your anger does not mean to lash out, to throw a fit, or to lose control of it; releasing your anger involves the open and honest expression of your emotions in a way that is physically, mentally, and emotionally freeing. You can do this by expressing your anger to God in prayer (don't hold back!). You can release your anger in the presence of a person who will listen quietly and neither judge nor offer advice. Another healthy way to release anger is to write down every angry thought that comes to mind until you cannot think of another angry sentence to write. Some people find that expressing their anger out loud—and loudly—in a private place is helpful.

The fact that you should "not let the sun go down on your anger" means you should deal with it when it is present. Don't go to sleep and forget it, only to have it come back in greater strength later.

Holy Spirit, grant me the freedom and opportunity to release my anger in a way that helps, not hurts. Amen.

Anger: Where Does It Come From?

You are probably doing your best to get back in control of your life. But life cannot be controlled, and anger and frustration often come as a result.

Dr. Larry Crabb states: "If I say, 'I know what I need to live, and it's not God,' I have a very wrong definition of life. Jesus, of course, had it right. He said, 'This is life: There can be no God but Jesus Christ.'

"But when I hear that, something in me says, *Oh, no. No, no, that's not life. Life is having the doctor say I'm healthy. Life is having my wife say 'I love you' as opposed to 'I'm leaving you.'* When I misdefine life and make it something else, then God becomes my enemy. He's not cooperative. And I get furious."

And when God is not "cooperating," you may attempt to handle the grieving process on your own, and fail.

"There is a way which seems right to a man, but its end is the way of death" (Proverbs 16:25 NASB).

Lord, I get so angry when I feel out of control. I just want to get a grip on things again. Teach me that by giving You control of my life, I will be empowered. Amen.

Anger: Directed at People or
Situations Surrounding Your Loss

Anger does not necessarily follow a logical path. Different people will focus their anger in different directions. For instance, you might be angry with people or at circumstances surrounding your loss.

"I remember being angry at first toward my sister-in-law because she was the one who told me [about the car crash]," says Jodie, whose husband was killed. "That made me mad. I had to really ask the Lord to heal that anger. He's faithful."

Heidi shares, "In the situation surrounding my husband's death, there were a lot of people involved in making the decision for him to leave that night. There are times when I want to get angry about the way things were done."

Do you need healing from misdirected anger?

"O LORD my God, I called to you for help and you healed me" (Psalm 30:2).

"If we confess our sins, he is faithful and just and will forgive us our sins and purify us from all unrighteousness" (1 John 1:9).

Father God, I am angry, and that's okay, but turn my anger away from false, destructive paths. Amen.

Anger: Directed at the Person You Lost

"People who lose someone can be really angry. They may be thinking, *How dare you die and leave me! How dare you reject me! How dare you leave me in these circumstances!*" observes Dr. Robert Abarno.

You may be directing your anger at the person you lost. Why? Because he or she left you, because of what you wish your relationship had been, because of all the unfinished, unorganized business that you ended up with. This anger is a natural reaction that you should not feel guilty about.

Your anger may stem from feelings of abandonment. But remember, you are not alone. God promises in His Word that He will never abandon you. His presence is eternal; His faithfulness to you is sure.

"The LORD himself goes before you and will be with you; he will never leave you nor forsake you. Do not be afraid; do not be discouraged" (Deuteronomy 31:8).

Lord Jesus, I trust that You will never leave me and never give up on me. Amen.

Anger: Directed Toward God

Some people have trouble admitting they are angry with God; others express it quite freely.

"I shook my fist at Him in anger. I blamed God," says Lynn, whose twin brother died.

If you are angry with God, He knows it whether you express it or not. You might as well be honest with Him about your anger. But in your anger, know that He is still faithful, and He will not turn away from you. Nothing you do will keep Him from loving you.

"I am convinced that neither death nor life, neither angels nor demons, neither the present nor the future, nor any powers, neither height nor depth, nor anything else in all creation, will be able to separate us from the love of God that is in Christ Jesus our Lord" (Romans 8:38–39).

God, I'm so angry at You, but at the same time grateful for Your faithfulness to me. Amen.

Anger: Be Honest About Your Feelings

No matter where your anger is directed, you must be honest about what you are feeling. Honesty with yourself and others is an important step on your grief journey.

"You might as well tell the truth to God, because He knows anyhow," says Dee Brestin.

Suppressed and silent anger will intensify and hurt only you.

"But when I was silent and still, not even saying anything good, my anguish increased. My heart grew hot within me, and as I meditated, the fire burned" (Psalm 39:2–3).

Lord God, You know me inside and out. I don't want to hurt anyone, but I do want to be true. Show me how. Amen.

Anger: Know Its Limits

You have a choice to make about your anger. You can either let anger take control of you and allow it to be your master, or you can deal with your anger and grow in strength and healing.

To effectively deal with your anger, first, be aware of its source. What triggers those feelings? You also need to know how far you can let your anger go before it has gone too far. By understanding the limits of your anger, you will be able to release it in a way that is healthy for you and for those around you.

"Anger is legitimate. There's nothing wrong with anger in and of itself. But you can't turn your anger loose and just let it fall where it may," says Pastor Buck Buchanan.

The book of Proverbs offers sound advice: "A fool gives full vent to his anger, but a wise man keeps himself under control" (29:11).

Lord God, give me the wisdom to know when to hold my anger in check. Amen.

Anger Can Lead to Bitterness

Your perspective on people and life can become poisoned by bitterness. Bitterness never makes things right, never satisfies your heart, and will always block your journey through grief. See bitterness as your enemy and flee from it.

Dr. Tim Clinton says, "Resentment is anger with a history. And bitterness? A lot of people become bitter over life's issues. It's often said that when you're dealing with hardship and hurt in your life, and great pain, you can either become bitter or you can become better. Challenge yourself always to let God do a work through you so you can become stronger and more effective."

The history that bitterness dwells on is like a stack of IOUs of what you think people should have done and how situations should have worked out. The only way to be free is to tear up the IOUs and let the bitterness go.

Bitterness prevents you from being able to receive God's free gift of grace.

"See to it that no one comes short of the grace of God; that no root of bitterness springing up causes trouble, and by it many be defiled" (Hebrews 12:15 NASB).

Lord Jesus, remove the poison of bitterness from my life, and let me see Your good work in this situation. Amen.

Is Anger Good or Bad?

God sometimes exhibits anger, and you are made in His image. God is described in Exodus 34:6 as "compassionate and gracious" and "slow to anger."

Jesus Christ was the perfect model of human behavior for you to follow, and at times Jesus was angry. In Mark 3:5 he was angered by the stubborn hearts of the Pharisees who refused to see the truth: "He looked around at them in anger . . . deeply distressed at their stubborn hearts."

Dr. Tim Clinton says, "Anger is a God-given emotion. In Scripture God was often angry at unrighteousness and injustice. It's okay to be angry, especially at injustice. It's okay to be angry at loss.

"To deny your anger is simply to let it turn inward. Angry people can't see life around them. Angry people can't see joy around them. Angry people can't see people around them. And hence, they can't enjoy life."

Lord Jesus, I'm intelligent enough to know that anger should not control me. I also understand that it needs to be properly released for my benefit and for others around me. Help me follow through on what I know is right for me to do. Amen.

Right Anger Versus Wrong Anger

In the following two verses, the Bible specifically talks about "right" anger, "wrong" anger, and the effects of each.

"A hot-tempered man stirs up strife, but he who is slow to anger appeases contention" (Proverbs 15:18 AMP).

Your slowly released anger "appeases contention"; it brings about peace and calm to your strife. Think about that.

James 1:19–20 says, "This you know, my beloved brethren. But let everyone be quick to hear, slow to speak and slow to anger; for the anger of man does not achieve the righteousness of God" (NASB).

What kind of anger is not righteous? Human anger. Human impulse is to either let it rip or to hold it in so tight that the pressure becomes dangerous. God's anger is wise and effective in bringing healing and not harm.

Righteous Lord, I see now that anger is not necessarily a bad thing. Teach me more. Amen.

Dealing with Anger: Redirect Toward Mourning

Dealing with your anger in a positive way may sound good, but how exactly is it done? One suggestion is to let your anger surface and then redirect it toward mourning. Consider your anger solely in the context of your loss. You may be putting all your energy into your anger to avoid a torrent of tears; this, in turn, has kept you from grieving.

"I'd like to remind you that Jesus Christ wept," says Dr. Erwin Lutzer. "I'd like to remind you that it says in the New Testament that when Stephen died, they took him to his burial and great lamentation was made over him.

"It's okay to grieve. There are those who do not grieve, and later on it begins to catch up with them. So you go through that process as long as you understand that it is a process of transition and healing."

Expressing tears is part of the grieving process; it is part of the healing. Use your anger to help you move forward toward healing, and keep in mind that your anger and tears won't last forever.

Let your mourning lead you toward hope. No matter where you are in grief, you can always have hope.

"Brothers, we do not want you to be ignorant about those who fall asleep, or to grieve like the rest of men, who have no hope" (1 Thessalonians 4:13).

Lord, let my anger turn to grieving and let my grieving lead to hope. Amen.

Dealing with Anger: Write About Angry Feelings

As you attempt to deal with your anger, you may find it helpful to write about your angry feelings. Writing about your feelings will help to unload some of that pressure because it gives you a way to express your emotions.

Barbara Johnson says, "The anger comes and just seems to flood you. But there are a lot of ways to dilute the anger. If you have lost a loved one, write a letter. That will help you unload some of those feelings you have."

Address your letter to the person causing you the most anger and distress. It could be your lost loved one, a family member, or someone involved in the circumstances surrounding the death. You might be angry mostly with yourself. If your anger is directed at God, write a letter to Him. He alone can deliver you from your anger.

"May my cry come before you, O LORD; give me understanding according to your word. May my supplication come before you; deliver me according to your promise" (Psalm 119:169–170).

Precious Savior, deliver me from this anger. Amen.

Dealing with Anger: Bible Verses

Another practical suggestion for dealing with anger is to draw help from Bible verses. Dr. John Trent recommends that you start by writing down an appropriate Bible verse on a three-by-five card. Every time you begin to feel angry, take out the card and read the verse. Then write the date on the back of the card and place a check mark next to it.

This practice will first of all link God's Word with your active anger. It will also provide a written record of how angry you are and whether or not you are showing improvement. As you continue this practice, you will begin to realize that anger is a choice.

"But if serving the LORD seems undesirable to you, then choose for yourselves this day whom you will serve. . . . But as for me and my household, we will serve the LORD" (Joshua 24:15).

Almighty God, grant me the perseverance to follow through on these anger management ideas and to follow through in a relationship with You. Amen.

Dealing with Anger: Choose to Move Past It

Perhaps you are at the point at which you must now choose to move past your anger and bitterness. You have allowed yourself the time and opportunity to slowly vent your anger, and you have honestly expressed those feelings with others. When you are ready to move beyond your anger, be prepared to stick with that decision.

The night Heidi's husband died in a plane crash, she prayed, "God, I know that You have a plan for my life. And I don't want bitterness and anger to well up in my heart, because I have two young children, and we have to go on with our lives."

Heidi says, "I made a decision that night not to become bitter and angry about the situation and not to blame God. Sure, I asked why and I didn't understand, but I wasn't going to blame God, and I wasn't going to blame other people."

You, too, can choose to move past anger with the Lord's help.

"I thank Christ Jesus our Lord, who has given me strength, that he considered me faithful" (1 Timothy 1:12).

Jesus, strengthen me to move beyond my anger and bitterness and to stay there. Amen.

Dealing with Anger: Ask God for Help

You may feel helpless in the face of your anger. You cannot deal with it on your own. The most important step you can take is to ask God for help.

"God will give you the opportunity to be angry," says Rev. Noel Castellanos. "He's not going to take that freedom away from you, but when you're done, behind all of that stuff you don't understand, there's a loving God who can redeem any situation. You can allow that deep anger in an authentic, honest way to be converted into a plea for help."

Give your burden of anger to God, and He will give you rest.

"Come to me, all you who are weary and burdened, and I will give you rest. Take my yoke upon you and learn from me, for I am gentle and humble in heart and you will find rest for your souls. For my yoke is easy and my burden is light" (Matthew 11:28–30).

Lord Jesus, I give my anger and my struggles to You. I come to You to learn and to rest. Amen.

Blame

Humans seem to have a natural tendency to want to place blame, as if that would help resolve the feelings of distress and pain. But blame is a black hole that will suck you down further and further.

"As a pastor, I've seen people respond to grief in every way," says Dr. Jack Hayford. "I think of the beauty of recent events in my own congregation. There was a young couple who were instantly separated by the intervention of death while they were at a national park. He fell into a rushing river and was trapped beneath a log where he could not get out. There was no way to attempt rescue because of the force of the stream. His wife was standing right there, not ten feet away, watching him drown, seeing it happen.

"To watch that family move into an openness to the comfort of the Spirit of God, to not blame God, to recognize an accident for what it is, to believe that God didn't design it, but He did foresee it and that His comfort and presence would be with them is a tremendously thrilling thing to witness."

Jesus urges you not to be troubled by blame, but to move forward in the peace and comfort of the Holy Spirit of God.

"But the Counselor, the Holy Spirit, whom the Father will send in my name, will teach you all things and will remind you of everything I have said to you. Peace I leave with you; my peace I give you. I do not give to you as the world gives. Do not let your hearts be troubled and do not be afraid" (John 14:26–27).

Holy God, this blame isn't accomplishing anything but added pain for me. Send me Your comforting Spirit to guide my thoughts into a clear perspective. Amen.

Bitterness Leads to Resentment

Other families around you are still together—happy and oblivious to your brokenness and pain. *Why me and not you?* you might be wondering. Your wondering can turn into bitterness and resentment.

Dr. Robert Jeffress says, "There can almost be a resentment on the part of Christians against other Christians who may not be going through grief. 'Why aren't they experiencing what I'm experiencing? Why is God picking on me?'"

Many problems can arise from the improper handling of your emotions during grief. You can't avoid having the emotions, but how you respond to them will determine whether you proceed in a healthy manner or are doomed to unnecessary detours on your grief journey. Ultimately, unless you deal with the issues behind your emotions, your life may be moved toward bitterness and resentment.

"I loathe my own life; I will give full vent to my complaint; I will speak in the bitterness of my soul," Job complained at first.

But then he changed his focus and persevered in faith and trust: "I know that Thou canst do all things, and that no purpose of Thine can be thwarted. . . . Therefore I retract, and I repent in dust and ashes" (Job 10:1; 42:2, 6 NASB).

Turn to God, who knows the bitterness in your heart and wants to replace it with His loving comfort.

> *Lord of all, forgive my bitterness and resentment and fill me instead with the love, peace, and trust that only You can provide. Amen.*

Bitterness Leads to Depression

"Bitterness is a terrible temptation to harbor your own troubles and problems and chew on them and indulge in self-pity," says Elisabeth Elliot.

What troublesome thoughts are you harboring and chewing on again and again?

"Bitterness very often leads to depression," continues Elliot. "I am convinced that a great deal of depression is the fruit of bitterness, which is unresolved sin or anger or pain."

Bitterness hurts only you. You are allowing those thoughts to take you off the path of healing. But you can control your thoughts. Whenever bitterness tries to seep in, renounce it in the name of Christ and see it as your enemy.

The Bible discusses handling this spiritual battle within the mind:

"For though we live in the world, we do not wage war as the world does. The weapons we fight with are not the weapons of the world. On the contrary, they have divine power to demolish strongholds. We demolish arguments and every pretension that sets itself up against the knowledge of God, and we take captive every thought to make it obedient to Christ" (2 Corinthians 10:3–5).

Lord, I'm fighting a losing battle on my own, but with You I have the power to win. Amen.

Freedom from Bitterness

There is hope. You can be free from bitter thoughts.

"I'd shut my eyes and see gravestones and all sorts of things. I was walking in places in my mind that I wasn't supposed to be walking in," says Cindy, whose daughter died.

"Even now, when I look at the past and get really sad, I think, *You know what? Today's a good day. It's raining, but my baby is in bed asleep, and my five-year-old is at school, and today is a good day.*

"Then when I look at the future and start thinking about things that could possibly go wrong, I think, *You know what? I'm not gonna go there, 'cause God isn't walking with me there.*"

Tackle one bitter thought at a time. When bitter thoughts come into your mind, repeat Cindy's words, "I'm not gonna go there, 'cause God isn't walking with me there."

"Therefore do not worry about tomorrow, for tomorrow will worry about itself" (Matthew 6:34).

Lord Jesus, with You I can live one moment at a time and work my way toward freedom from my bitter thoughts. Amen.

Regret

Regret is a strong emotion you will likely encounter during grief. Perhaps you have regrets over things you wish you had said or done while your loved one was still alive. A frequent thought might be, *If only I had . . .*

You are not alone, my friend.

Annie, who lost her father, says, "I lay awake at night thinking, *O Lord, I wish I had taken him to Duke Hospital. Why didn't I think about it?* I just kept punishing myself. But one of my friends said, 'You did all you knew to do.' Which is true."

Do not condemn yourself. Look to Christ Jesus for help in facing these regrets.

"There is therefore now no condemnation for those who are in Christ Jesus. For the law of the Spirit of life in Christ Jesus has set you free from the law of sin and of death" (Romans 8:1–2 NASB).

Lord Jesus, set me free from my regrets. Thank you for not condemning me. Amen.

If Only I Had . . .

"In God's economy you can't go back and say, 'I should have done this,' 'I should have done that,' or 'I didn't do this right,'" says Barbara Johnson, "because you did the best you could at the time that you did it. God knows your heart, and you can't live in a state of regret or wishing you had done something differently."

Many times you may beat yourself up thinking about the things you did wrong in regard to your loved one, or you are plagued with thoughts about what you could have done differently.

John's son committed suicide. He says, "Afterwards, I remembered every time that I had mistreated him or punished him unjustly. I recalled every time I had yelled at him out of frustration and anger—everything I had done wrong as a parent to him."

John realized that his thoughts of blame, regret, and self-condemnation were harmful and they needed to stop. He knew that good, uplifting, and strengthening thoughts were from God and he needed to focus on them. He says, "God in His grace also reminded me of when I would come home and eat lunch with my son and we would have little talks. The little things we did were good. We did have some really good times."

Remember the good times, and counter your "if onlys" with Scripture. God's Word is powerful and will help you conquer the negative thoughts that play in your head. Replace harmful thoughts with God's healing words.

"You were taught, with regard to your former way of life, to put off your old self, which is being corrupted by its deceitful desires; to be made new in the attitude of your minds; and to put on the new self, created to be like God in true righteousness and holiness" (Ephesians 4:22–24).

Lord God, teach me to put off my old habits of self-condemnation and bitter regret and replace them with a new attitude of prayer and Christlikeness. Amen.

Relief

Relief is also a common emotion associated with grief, especially if your loved one was in pain or suffering.

Janet Paschal's grandfather had Alzheimer's disease. She says, "We had watched him change, and it was a very slow loss, a very slow process. So there was a sense of relief when he died, but at the same time, there was a selfish part of me that wanted him back, that didn't want to surrender him."

You may feel relief because the burden of responsibility has been lifted with the death of your loved one. Don't feel guilty about your relief. This response is natural and expected, particularly after a long struggle or illness.

"We count those blessed who endured. You have heard of the endurance of Job and have seen the outcome of the Lord's dealings, that the Lord is full of compassion and is merciful" (James 5:11 NASB).

Lord God, my feelings confuse and somewhat embarrass me. Thank you for granting me endurance, and please continue to guide me on my journey through grief. Amen.

Loneliness

The loneliness of loss—do you feel it? This can be one of the most painful emotions in grieving.

Luevenia, whose husband passed away, says, "There's no way I'll ever be the same. I just can't be. I'm so lonely. The evenings are the toughest because I can get out during the day and do things."

The Lord Jesus knows what it's like to be lonely. He's been there. He knows it well.

You may be lonely, but you are never alone because God is with you every moment, and He can transform your lonely life in ways you cannot imagine. "God sets the lonely in families, he leads forth the prisoners with singing; but the rebellious live in a sun-scorched land" (Psalm 68:6).

> *Holy God, I am a prisoner of loneliness. I know that things will never be the same as they were, but You promise in Your Word that You will "lead forth the prisoners with singing." Lead on, Lord. Amen.*

Remedy for Loneliness

Become involved with a Christ-centered grief support group. Many churches have small groups that can aid you in your healing from grief.

"You feel like you're losing it, and then you hear these other people who have similar incidents happening in their lives. You realize that God prepared the body in such a way that you've got to go through this process before you can heal," says Nancy following her husband's death.

God does not want you to be alone.

"I will come down and speak with you there, and I will take of the Spirit that is on you and put the Spirit on them. They will help you carry the burden . . . so that you will not have to carry it alone" (Numbers 11:17).

A grief support group should have a focus beyond grief itself. In other words, the group should do more than share stories and release emotions. A group with the objective of introducing biblical help for grieving individuals will provide the tools needed to face life's difficulties and to move toward a new and abundant life. The *GriefShare®* groups are designed for this purpose.

Faithful God, give me the courage and desire to pick up the phone and find a support group to aid me in my healing. Amen.

Remedy for Loneliness: Develop a Hobby or Skill

Starting a new hobby may sound unappealing and uninteresting at this point in your life. But we encourage you to do it anyway. Remember, you are not developing this hobby for the sake of the activity; you are using it as a tool to deal with loneliness.

"My life was so much a part of my husband's," says Patricia. "He was so dependent upon me; he could not function without me on a twenty-four-hour basis. When he died, I said, 'What am I going to do?' All of my time had been spent taking care of him. I was totally lost. I didn't know what to do.

"It was just a few months later that my daughter worked in vacation Bible school, and she said, 'Mom, why don't you come and help me?' So I did. That really began my ministry here. I began working in the nursery on Sunday evenings, one night a month. Then I saw an opportunity to help in the children's department during the week on a volunteer basis.

"The Lord has just opened up a whole new opportunity, a whole new life for me. I knew from the beginning that I was not going to stay home and get the rocking-chair rot."

God has appointed you with certain gifts to use in helping others or in bringing joy to others' lives. Try out a new hobby or volunteer to do something you've never done before. Again, you may not be doing this because you desire to, but because you need to.

"There are different spiritual gifts, but the same Spirit gives them. . . . The evidence of the Spirit's presence is given to each person for the common good of everyone" (1 Corinthians 12:4, 7 NLT).

Lord God, place in my path a new opportunity to serve You and to take great steps forward in healing. Amen.

Remedy for Loneliness: Reach Out

One of the most effective ways to come out of loneliness is to reach out to others who are hurting or in need. Even if you don't feel like reaching out, discipline yourself to do it anyway.

Dr. Ray Pritchard says, "There comes a time when you have to wipe the tears away. There comes a time when you have to stop thinking about what you have lost and start thinking about the needs of the people around you.

"I don't say that's easy. I don't think you can always do that overnight. For some people it will be after a period of weeks, for some after a period of months. For me it was a year after my father died.

"It might be as simple as baking cookies for the neighbors, going to visit the hospital, going to the nursing home. It might be as simple as writing letters to others who have also lost loved ones and sharing with others what God has given you. There is an amazing therapeutic value in not only telling your own story, but in pointing people back to God."

To escape loneliness and despair, you must take action and reach out to others, and you will experience the light of hope rising up in your life.

"If you give yourself to the hungry, and satisfy the desire of the afflicted, then your light will rise in darkness, and your gloom will become like midday" (Isaiah 58:10 NASB).

O Lord, loneliness and despair have weighed me down for too long. I want to reach out to others and experience Your hope and Your light. Amen.

Loneliness Trap: Clutter

To have a new hobby or to embark on a new endeavor to serve others is good, but overcrowding your life with activities can distract you from the process of grieving. You need time to be quiet, to relax, to meditate, and to pray.

Dr. Jim Conway says, "I remember a woman coming to one of the groups who said, 'My husband has been gone for about a year, and I'm just not getting any better.' She listed off half a dozen activities that she'd started since her husband died, as if being more active would help her through the process.

"I said to her, 'You know, you've been running from grief, but you have not yet started to grieve.'"

Use wisdom in the choices you make during grief, choices about your time, commitments, activities, and behaviors. Grief must be faced and then journeyed through, and the wisdom and strength to persevere is found in the Lord.

> Consider it pure joy, my brothers, whenever you face trials of many kinds, because you know that the testing of your faith develops perseverance. Perseverance must finish its work so that you may be mature and complete, not lacking anything. If any of you lacks wisdom, he should ask God, who gives generously to all without finding fault, and it will be given to him. (James 1:2–5)

Father, please give me the wisdom to know when to be active and when to slow down, when to work and when to relax. Amen.

Loneliness Trap: Avoid Premature Romantic Relationships

"You need to realize you can exist without another person," says Dr. H. Norman Wright.

For those who have lost a mate, you may be tempted to jump into a relationship too quickly in order to avoid the pain you are feeling. But if you bring the unresolved pain of grief into a new relationship, then the relationship is already on rocky ground.

"I tried to have a relationship," says Melissa, a widow, "but it just didn't work. I guess maybe it was for all the wrong reasons anyway. But I would tell people who are out looking: Don't look. The Lord knows what you need, and He will bring the right mate for you when it is time."

In seeking to solve one problem, you may create a host of others. Seek only to serve God, and everything else will fall into place.

"So do not worry, saying, 'What shall we eat?' or 'What shall we drink?' or 'What shall we wear?' For the pagans run after all these things, and your heavenly Father knows that you need them. But seek first his kingdom and his righteousness, and all these things will be given to you as well" (Matthew 6:31–33).

Holy God, all I need is You. Help me to believe it and to act on it. Amen.

Growing Through Loneliness

Loneliness is never comfortable, but if you ask Him, the Lord can bring something good out of it.

"The Lord sees to it that you find yourself in a lonely position sometimes," says Elisabeth Elliot, "not necessarily geographically. You can be in a crowded room and still be lonely.

"Oswald Chambers has something very interesting to say about that, 'Friendship with a person who has not been disciplined by loneliness is a very dangerous kind of friendship.'

"You need to recognize God's discipline of loneliness when it is assigned to you and receive it with both hands saying, 'Lord, I would not have chosen this, but I will receive it. Now teach me what I can only learn in loneliness.'"

It is not God's plan to give you everything you want for your life or to ensure that your life is comfortable and problem-free. God has made life so that it is filled with times of receiving and times of letting go. He wants you to learn to be content where you are now because He is with you.

"I know what it is to be in need, and I know what it is to have plenty. I have learned the secret of being content in any and every situation, whether well fed or hungry, whether living in plenty or in want. I can do everything through him who gives me strength" (Philippians 4:12–13).

Lord God, teach me what I can learn in loneliness. Amen.

Fear of the Future

"When you have an anxiety or fear, this is a feeling of concern about the future. Sometimes you may ask the question, what if . . . ? And you answer it yourself. Then you ask the question again, and the second time you answer it, you embellish the answer.

"You can actually create a genuine fear of the future by what goes on in your mind," says Dr. H. Norman Wright.

The Bible says that God is love. It also says that love cannot co-exist with fear. So if Jesus lives in you, you do not need to fear. If you have accepted Christ as your Lord and Savior, then He dwells in you and in your mind.

"There is no fear in love. But perfect love drives out fear, because fear has to do with punishment. The one who fears is not made perfect in love" (1 John 4:18).

Lord Jesus, I believe in You, and I want You to live in me. Forgive me for all my sins. Amen.

Depression

Are you experiencing a complete lack of energy? Difficulty sleeping? Trouble concentrating? Constant fatigue? No sense of enjoyment? Apathy?

If your answer is "yes," then depression has come to you.

"Loss is one of the main causes of depression," states Dr. H. Norman Wright.

It is okay to be depressed; even Jesus was depressed when facing death: "He began to show grief and distress of mind and was deeply depressed" (Matthew 26:37 AMP).

You might be wondering about the difference between depression and sadness.

Dr. Wright explains, "Sadness doesn't last as long; it's not as intense, and it doesn't immobilize you. Depression lasts longer, and it does immobilize you. With sadness, you can still go about your work. Maybe with depression, you can do it at 70 percent of your capacity.

"The depression is there sometimes to numb you against the pain. Now, if the depression lasts and lingers for months, then maybe it has taken hold of you. But it's going to come."

Take comfort from the fact that your depression is normal and expected with the loss of a loved one. Going from one emotion to the next is part of your movement through grief, so continue to take one step at a time and lean on the steady, secure arms of God.

Jesus, I am senseless and paralyzed in the face of my depression. You, too, have felt this emotion. Help me to realize that depression does come to those in grief, and it's okay to feel this way. Comfort me, Lord. Amen.

Depression: When to Seek Help

If your depression persists for months and becomes a way of life, it is no longer normal grieving. You do not have to live with this.

If it goes on and on, get help. Talk to a Christian counselor or your pastor or a doctor. This type of depression is what doctors would call *clinical depression,* and there is help for that.

Dr. Ray Pritchard says, "Don't give up. Pick up the phone. Call a friend. If that friend can't help you, call another friend. If the people at one church cannot help you, call another Christian church."

Take action to find help for your depression. And if that fails, try again.

"Blessed is the man who perseveres under trial, because when he has stood the test, he will receive the crown of life that God has promised to those who love him" (James 1:12).

> *Father, it is only by Your grace that I can stand through this trial. Open the doors of help for me and strengthen me to walk through them. Amen.*

Unresolved Grief

Unresolved grief multiplies your problems. So express your emotions, share your story, get angry if you need to, and tell God how you really feel. The person you lost would not want you to become trapped in a continual cycle of grief. It is not a betrayal of that person for you to get better. Getting better means you move away from the disabling aspects of grief. You don't stop missing the person or feeling the hole left in your heart.

Cindy recalls her husband's words to her at some point after their daughter died: "Why don't you take where you've been and what you've done and go forward with it and be proud that you survived it? Reach out to others who might be in need, and just be thankful that we had her."

Your steps through the grieving process may be halting, baby steps. As difficult as this may be, God wants you to walk forward through your grief. Remember the words of David in Psalm 23:4: "Even though I walk through the valley of the shadow of death, I will fear no evil, for you are with me."

"By his light I walked through darkness!" (Job 29:3).

God, shine Your light in every corner of my being and show me the areas of my grief that I need to face and resolve. Amen.

Express Your Emotions Freely

The grieving customs in ancient Israel involved a great deal of free expression, especially compared to today's culture.

After King Saul, his son, and Israel's army were defeated, "David and all the men with him took hold of their clothes and tore them. They mourned and wept and fasted till evening for Saul and his son Jonathan, and for the army of the LORD and the house of Israel, because they had fallen by the sword" (2 Samuel 1:11–12).

First of all, David and all the men mourned their loss together as a group. "Group grieving" is an effective tool for the journey, but in today's culture it is something that you must seek out, usually in the form of a support group.

The second action of David and his men was to take hold of their clothes and tear them. They released their energy in a way that was physical, yet not harmful.

Lastly, and still as a group, they "mourned and wept and fasted till evening." In their culture they were free to openly express and share their grieving emotions, and they were expected to do so.

Think of the forms of mourning that you have engaged in. How does it compare to the mourning of David and his men? You can learn from the past and be a part of an improved future.

Glorious Lord, I want to express my emotions freely, actively, and without embarrassment. Amen.

Doubting God's Goodness

Is God truly good? What does it mean to you personally that God is good?

Dr. Larry Crabb says, "When you see a child suffer, when the doctor says certain things to you, you really wonder if God is good.

"'God, where are You? If You're good, then it seems to me that things should work out like this—' and I impose my definition of good on God. And I say, 'This is what the word *good* means: It means that I won't get cancer again. It means my wife won't die prematurely. It means my kids will be healthy and I will make enough money to pay the bills.'

"When I look at God and say, 'You're not cooperating with my definition of good,' the natural consequence is not trust, not worship. It's idolatry. I'm going to find some other god that agrees with my definition of good. Satan comes along and basically says, 'I'll arrange for what you want.' And you'll have certain pleasures for a season, and then it'll be awful."

It is not God's intention to give us everything we want. Getting what we want is not the key to happiness, peace, or contentment. Since we cannot see the full picture and do not have all the facts, our judgment is skewed. God would not be God if He could not see all things and judge all situations for the ultimate good.

God's Word is absolute truth; don't let your doubts get in the way of His perfect plan.

"You are talking like a foolish woman. Shall we accept good from God, and not trouble?" (Job 2:10).

Most Holy God, my limited view is getting in the way of truth. Even when I don't feel it, help me to know without a doubt Your goodness and faithfulness to me. Amen.

False Guilt: Satan's Lies

"Yes, Satan knows when to come. He lays it on you," explained Dr. E. V. Hill. "I just want you to know it's not of God; it's the devil. God isn't punishing you at all. The devil's doing that."

The guilt and blame you hear echoing in your head is Satan lying to you. Understand and believe this.

Dr. Hill said, "So watch the fact that it's not the voice of the Holy Spirit. It's the visitation of the devil. Rebuke it as such. Stick with your faith in God no matter how it hurts. And God has a great reward for you."

When guilt rears its head, stay focused on the truth and do not be deceived by lies.

"He [the devil] was a murderer from the beginning, not holding to the truth, for there is no truth in him. When he lies, he speaks his native language, for he is a liar and the father of lies" (John 8:44).

Holy Spirit of God, teach me to recognize Your voice and to follow it with assurance. Amen.

Physical Symptoms

Has grief impacted your body as well as your mind?

"Physical problems can run the gamut," says Dr. H. Norman Wright. "There can be stomachaches, headaches, anxiety, rapid pulse, heaviness of heart. It can affect your blood pressure. Sleep disturbances come as insomnia or sleeping ten, twelve, or fourteen hours a day. You lack energy, just plodding through the day, looking at the clock, hoping it's time to go to bed."

How you feel physically can deeply affect how you feel emotionally. So make sure that the basics are covered. Eat healthy food, exercise on a consistent basis, and get plenty of sleep.

Remember, healing is a journey you travel both physically and mentally. Face each difficulty one day at a time, one step at a time, until its completion. Counter each problem with the assurance of Scripture. Remain faithful till the end, and you will be victorious over every problem that sets itself up against you during this time.

"In all these things we are more than conquerors through him who loved us" (Romans 8:37).

In You, victorious Lord, I am more than a conqueror over these physical problems. Show me how to endure and to win! Amen.

Emotional Safety Valve #1: Lift Your Fears to Jesus

Overwhelmed by your emotions? On the verge of emotional shutdown? Feeling as if there is no future but despair? Try lifting your fears to Jesus.

"People who don't know Christ have a different perspective on this because they have no option other than despair," says Dr. Jim Conway. "They only have the option of using their own energy or other people around them to try and make this adjustment. They don't have the person of God living in them, giving them the capacity to adjust and the sense that there is a future."

You do have an option. Choose faith in the Lord Jesus Christ. Make it a habit to mentally and verbally give each emotion to Him the moment that emotion arrives. You may want to picture yourself wrapping up that emotion in a package and handing it into His loving, powerful arms to keep. Repeat this exercise as needed, and trust in God to take those burdens each time.

You can take this action because God cares for you. First Peter 5:7 says, "Cast all your anxiety on him because he cares for you."

Second Chronicles 15:7 says, "As for you, be strong and do not give up, for your work will be rewarded."

Lord, I am constantly tormented by these thoughts and emotions. I need to give each one to You, one at a time. Take them from me, and I will trust in You for strength and healing. Amen.

Emotional Safety Valve #2: Forgive

Forgiveness is getting your heart right with God by making the choice to forgive others and by receiving God's forgiveness. Forgiveness does not mean you are relieving someone of responsibility for his or her actions. Forgiveness does not necessarily mean you trust that person. Forgiveness is the act of letting God's love flow through you.

Think about the above definition for a moment.

Doug Easterday says, "You're not alleviating responsibility from anyone by forgiving them. You are transferring it to where it really belongs and that's with God. They will answer to God someday, but if you're requiring them to answer to you, then you have as big a problem as they do."

Forgiveness is obedience to God.

"Then Peter came to Jesus and asked, 'Lord, how many times shall I forgive my brother when he sins against me? Up to seven times?' Jesus answered, 'I tell you, not seven times, but seventy-seven times'" (Matthew 18:21–22).

> *Lord, it is only by Your power that I can forgive. Keep me from destroying myself with unforgiveness. Amen.*

Choosing to Forgive

Forgiveness is a choice, not a feeling.

"It's not really possible to say, 'I can't forgive.' What you're really saying is, 'I won't forgive,'" says Doug Easterday. "You're the only one who can make this choice. Therefore, you have something to say about your own destiny if you choose to forgive."

In the Sermon on the Mount, Jesus taught His followers how to pray (Matthew 6:9–13). This needs to be your prayer if you are a follower of Jesus Christ. Choose to pray these words now:

> *Our Father which art in heaven, Hallowed be thy name. Thy kingdom come, Thy will be done in earth, as it is in heaven. Give us this day our daily bread.* And forgive us our debts, as we forgive our debtors. *And lead us not into temptation, but deliver us from evil: For thine is the kingdom, and the power, and the glory, for ever. Amen.* (KJV, emphasis added)

Forgiveness Leads to Healing

Death often happens in the context of medical decisions, family choices, and reactions. The situation is often attended with uncertainty and a high level of stress. Because of this it is often easy to feel unforgiveness toward some people who were involved.

"I believe that unless you are willing to forgive," says Kay Arthur, "you will not be healed."

If you truly desire to get your heart right with God and to heal, you must forgive as God has forgiven you.

"If I don't forgive, what I'm saying is that what the person did to me is more important to me than going on with God," states Doug Easterday.

Are you willing to be healed? Then "forgive as the Lord forgave you" (Colossians 3:13).

Lord, I do want healing. Enable me to forgive. Amen.

Forgiveness Leads to Freedom

How do you know if forgiveness has taken place?

"You'll know that you are forgiven if you can let God's love flow through you to that person," says Doug Easterday. "If the person walked in, would you let that love be expressed? If you answered no, then forgiveness has not taken place. 'Well, he or she doesn't deserve it.' Then forgiveness has not fully taken place. 'Well, I don't know if I can.' Then forgiveness needs to go deeper.

Forgiveness is like an onion; there are layers to it. The first layer of an onion is still an onion, but there is more onion underneath. Forgiveness often has layers to it. Forgiveness is not entirely complete until all the layers are gone, and then you can say, 'I can forgive, because I choose to.' When you can let the Lord flow His love through you, then you can say, 'I know that I'm walking right with God in forgiveness.'"

When you have forgiven, you are free and released from self-induced bondage.

"For if you forgive men when they sin against you, your heavenly Father will also forgive you. But if you do not forgive men their sins, your Father will not forgive your sins" (Matthew 6:14–15).

Father, grant me the ability to forgive, and free my heart to love again. Amen.

Forward, Backward

Do not be discouraged if it feels as though you are going backward at times—sometimes forward, sometimes backward. That is the natural process of grief.

If you are bringing your hurts and fears to God, if you desire to move forward toward healing, if you are learning about the grieving process and trying to apply some things you have learned, then you are making progress, even when you do not feel you are.

Dora, whose daughter passed away, says, "Sometimes you will think, *Last week I could cope with this, and this week I can't,* and then you'll think, *I'm not getting any better. I'm not making any progress.* Then you'll take a big leap forward. There's no timeline."

You, too, will take that big leap forward as time goes on. For now, concentrate on the small victories over the pain—fewer tears, a smile, helping another person, reading and understanding a Bible passage, replacing a negative thought with a positive thought, forgiving a wrong.

"We also pray that you will be strengthened with his glorious power so that you will have all the patience and endurance you need" (Colossians 1:11 NLT).

Father God, when I get discouraged because it feels like I'm going backward and not forward, help me to stop trying so hard and allow You to be my support and strength. Amen.

Destructive Choices

In an effort to escape the pain, you may sometimes look for short-term solutions such as alcohol, overwork, drugs, or sex. These destructive choices have two elements in common:

1. They prolong the actual grieving process.

2. They break down the values and priorities that a person had embraced beforehand.

Dr. Robert Abarno says, "It's called displacement. When you don't face the issue and you don't want to accept the answer 'I am the problem,' you may displace it by getting into alcohol or relationships or drugs or whatever. But that is temporary. It just doesn't do the job."

A quick fix lasts only a moment, but God is forever. Seek to please the Spirit, and you will move forward in healing.

"The one who sows to please his sinful nature, from that nature will reap destruction; the one who sows to please the Spirit, from the Spirit will reap eternal life. Let us not become weary in doing good, for at the proper time we will reap a harvest if we do not give up" (Galatians 6:8–9).

Heavenly Father, I need to get off this road of destruction and onto the road of life. Lead me there. Amen.

Compulsive Behaviors

A compulsive behavior is an activity you feel compelled to do excessively in order to distract yourself from the pain. It is something you do to avoid grief.

Many people associate compulsive behaviors with negative actions such as overeating, not eating, drinking too much alcohol, or abusing drugs. But compulsive behaviors can also include activities that are normally thought of as good—working, cleaning, serving at church, or remodeling the house. These behaviors become compulsive when a person continues to overdo an activity to avoid the pain.

A compulsive behavior "always offers more than it provides," says Dr. John Trent. Therefore, you might keep increasing your activity or behavior to find that original satisfaction and comfort, which is now elusive.

"Genuine healing from grief," says Dr. Trent, "comes not in an artificial climate, which all those are—activity or drugs or whatever, it comes through the reality of knowing Jesus Christ."

Honor God with your behavior, and know that true satisfaction is found in Him.

"Do you not know that your body is a temple of the Holy Spirit, who is in you, whom you have received from God? You are not your own; you were bought at a price. Therefore honor God with your body" (1 Corinthians 6:19–20).

Lord Jesus, I want to know You. Dwell within me as I seek to honor You with my actions and behaviors. Amen.

Compulsive Behaviors Hinder Healing

Dr. H. Norman Wright says, "The person who has a tendency toward any kind of compulsive behavior or addiction might see this come to the forefront even more so during grief."

Along with drug and alcohol abuse and excessive diet habits and activity, other compulsive behaviors associated with grief include anger and violence. You may have found that you will submit yourself to anything to escape the pain of grief.

These behaviors may temporarily sedate the pain, but they will hinder and even block your healing. If you are willing to try anything to find true healing, then try a personal relationship with Jesus Christ. Remember, God loves you unconditionally. If you already have a relationship with Christ, then take action to make daily changes in your life based on what you know to be true about God's character and His faithfulness. Allow yourself to be guided and transformed each day by the power of God's spirit.

It is wise to take some time to think and pray about your compulsive behavior and identify whether or not your behavior is grief-induced or if you have been struggling with this problem for much longer. If you have a compulsive behavior that is out of your control, please seek help through your church or a Christian organization. You must learn to cope with and heal from this behavior so that you can heal from your grief.

"I have seen his ways, but I will heal him; I will guide him and restore comfort to him" (Isaiah 57:18).

Lord Jesus, I want a fresh start with You. Show me how. Amen.

Tempted to Give Up?

You may feel you would rather escape than endure. But remember, it is always too soon to give up. God sent His angels to rescue Daniel only *after* he was in the lion's den (Daniel 6:19–21). Paul says God rescued him *after* he had the "sentence of death" within him (2 Corinthians 1:9). God rescued Peter from prison *the night before* he was to be executed (Acts 12:4–11). Even at the last moment, He can rescue you. Never give up.

"Whatever string you can find to hold on to, whatever you know about God in your heart, hang on to it with everything you have. Then stand back and see His glory," says Janet Paschal, whose grandfather died.

When it seems that there is nothing left to live for, God will prove Himself true. Focus on Him and do not let your thoughts stray for a moment.

Job initially wanted God to take his life: "Oh, that I might have my request, that God would grant what I hope for, that God would be willing to crush me, to let loose his hand and cut me off!" (Job 6:8–9). But if God had granted Job's request, he would never have seen God's blessing in the end.

The book of Habakkuk encourages you to trust in God and persevere no matter how bad things seem: "Though the fig tree does not bud and there are no grapes on the vines, though the olive crop fails and the fields produce no food, though there are no sheep in the pen and no cattle in the stalls, yet will I rejoice in the LORD, I will be joyful in God my Savior" (Habakkuk 3:17–19).

> *Savior God, I see nothing but darkness, but in this darkness I grasp at a pinpoint of light, which is my knowledge of You. I will hold on to this, Lord, with all the strength I can muster, for You alone are my hope. Amen.*

When You Want to End the Pain

One of the most destructive choices you could consider as you deal with grief and loss is the possibility of suicide. Although your motivation may be to end the pain, you will actually inflict a greater pain on those you leave behind.

For those of you who have lost a loved one through suicide, you know firsthand the deep heartache and overwhelming emotions that occur as a result.

Shelly's son committed suicide. She shares: "There was pain so deep that I didn't know if I was going to be able to get up sometimes. I was like, 'Lord, I don't think I can go another twenty-five years or however long I may have on this earth. I don't think I can handle this amount of pain.'"

Katie, whose husband committed suicide, says, "Nobody knows what it is like until you have to go through it."

These emotions are normal, but if you actually begin to form a plan to end your life—if you feel it is worthless to continue or that you cannot handle the pain any longer—you need to call your pastor or a doctor immediately. You need professional support for this kind of crisis.

Your friends cannot take the place of professional counselors, but they will be a support for you. Many people love you dearly and would give anything to reach out and help you. Remember, though, that other people cannot know what you are thinking or feeling unless you open up and tell them. Reach out to other people, continue to build relationships, and do not close yourself off. Let people love you even when they don't understand you.

Jesus has promised you hope and healing for the future. You will receive and be reminded of this hope through your relationships with other people as you let God's love flow through them to you. Let God minister His love to you today.

"The Father himself loves you dearly" (John 16:27 NLT).

Holy God, teach me how to love and be loved. Amen.

Cling to God

"The eternal God is your refuge, and underneath are the everlasting arms" (Deuteronomy 33:27).

God is a big God. His strength and power are beyond comprehension. When it seems a major effort to get out of bed and function, when you cannot think straight, when holding on to any kind of hope seems impossible, this is the time to pray and to understand that with God all things are possible.

"How do I cling to God?" asks Kay Arthur, whose husband committed suicide. She answers, "I cling to God by finding out everything I can about God and then not letting go of it. I hold on, if I have to, literally by my fingernails. I know that when I hang on by my fingernails, I'm going to feel underneath me the Everlasting Arms, which are going to hold me and sustain me."

When your faith is only the size of a tiny, tiny mustard seed, you can move a large mountain because you believe in the power of God. You have chosen to trust in Him, and He will be there to give you strength.

"He replied, 'Because you have so little faith. I tell you the truth, if you have faith as small as a mustard seed, you can say to this mountain, "Move from here to there" and it will move. Nothing will be impossible for you'" (Matthew 17:20). Even a little faith, when it is in a big God, is sufficient.

Almighty God, I will cling to You with every ounce of strength I have left. Please give me more faith. Amen.

The Lowest Point

"The bottom is a lot deeper than you would even think," says Dr. John Trent.

If you feel as if these dark days will never pass, we want to assure you that there is hope because of Jesus. He suffered and died and rose again on the third day.

Those early disciples saw Jesus put to death on a cross and were as hopeless as anyone ever was. All their dreams and hopes died with Him. Yet when they saw Jesus alive from the dead, it changed everything.

Even during the heaviest, most hurtful times of your grieving experience, you, too, can share the hope that only Jesus brings.

"We have this hope as an anchor for the soul, firm and secure" (Hebrews 6:19).

Jesus, my hope is in You. Amen.

God's Blanket of Love

"Have mercy on me, O God, have mercy! I look to you for protection. I will hide beneath the shadow of your wings until this violent storm is past. I cry out to God Most High, to God who will fulfill his purpose for me. He will send help from heaven to save me. . . . My God will send forth his unfailing love and faithfulness" (Psalm 57:1–3 NLT).

When you are at your lowest point and it seems as though no one can reach you, God can. He is there for you, if you will just accept His help.

"God has to be a comfort blanket to you," says Barbara Johnson. "Until you accept that comfort blanket of God's love, you are going to be struggling or hurting. God's comfort blanket makes you feel so secure and so loved. His comfort blanket has sustained me."

God's everlasting arms will always be underneath you, upholding you through the pain. His love will always surround you, enveloping you in comfort and security. His wisdom will guide you through each day. Talk to God today. Tell Him that you need His help, His love, His comfort, and His everlasting presence.

"The LORD's unfailing love surrounds the man who trusts in him" (Psalm 32:10).

Saving God, I need Your help. I need to know and experience Your love and comfort in my life today. Thank you for loving me. Amen.

when your spouse dies

One-Flesh Relationship

A part of who you are is gone. Your identity is shaken to the very core. You wonder if you will ever feel normal again or if you will ever enjoy life again.

"When you lose a mate, you lose part of yourself," says Dr. Jim Conway. "It's as if you've had an amputation of an arm or a leg. I think that you don't really recover; you adjust, and the process of adjusting varies with every individual. There's no formula."

The pain that comes from the loss of a spouse is much deeper than most people realize because in a marital relationship two people become one flesh.

"The man said, 'This is now bone of my bones and flesh of my flesh; she shall be called "woman," for she was taken out of man.' For this reason a man will leave his father and mother and be united to his wife, and they will become one flesh" (Genesis 2:23–24).

When part of your flesh is abruptly taken away, there is a ripping and a tearing that leaves a huge, open wound.

"Until you have experienced the death of a spouse, there is no way you can tell someone how deep the hurt is. The Lord says that we are one flesh, and suddenly half of that flesh is torn from us," says Beth.

Lord God, a part of me is gone and will never be recovered. What do I do now? Amen.

Shared Dreams

You had so many dreams and plans together. Your future was anticipated as a twosome.

Emy, whose husband died, says, "We did not do everything we had always hoped. The golden years were not golden. Some of our dreams were really dashed. But you have to realize that life is not given to you as a rose garden, and you don't appreciate the heights until you go through the valleys."

Right now you may feel completely hopeless, and all you can see in your mind is ruined dreams. But as you look toward the future, focus beyond the debris and find the light. There is a light in your darkness, and that light is the Lord Jesus Christ.

"You will do well to pay attention to it, as to a light shining in a dark place, until the day dawns and the morning star rises in your hearts" (2 Peter 1:19).

Lord Jesus, help me to see beyond my broken dreams and to follow the light that will lead me into a new day. Amen.

Shared Knowledge of Each Other

"When you're married so long, you know what the other person is thinking before he even speaks. Your minds are so close that you miss that too," says Nancy after the death of her husband.

What a blessing to have someone who knew you so well and who loved you just the way you are.

Let God fill this need in your life. He knows you inside and out. He knows even the number of hairs on your head (Luke 12:7). Nothing about you is hidden from God. He loves you unconditionally.

"O LORD, you have searched me and you know me. You know when I sit and when I rise; you perceive my thoughts from afar. You discern my going out and my lying down; you are familiar with all my ways. Before a word is on my tongue you know it completely, O LORD" (Psalm 139:1–4).

Lord God, You know me better than I know myself. I want our relationship to grow deep and strong. Amen.

Shared Identity

You shared a one-flesh relationship. Your identities, your very beings, were interwoven with each other. When your spouse died, you lost a large part of your identity, leaving you unsure of who you are.

Marie, whose husband passed away, says, "It was like trying to discover who I was all over again. For so many years I was a wife and a mother, and now all of a sudden, I'm no longer _____'s wife. After being married seventeen years, I had to figure out, what do I do with my life now?"

In order to find yourself, you must first find the Lord Jesus. And if you already know the Lord, then just as He established your identity during your marriage, He will show you who you are now.

"I am the vine; you are the branches. If a man remains in me and I in him, he will bear much fruit; apart from me you can do nothing. If anyone does not remain in me, he is like a branch that is thrown away and withers; such branches are picked up, thrown into the fire and burned" (John 15:5–6).

Lord, my life is an outgrowth of Yours. May I build my new identity on this strong foundation. Amen.

Who Am I?

"Who am I?" asks Heidi. "I had identified with this person; I had become one with this person. Our hopes and dreams were together. And now, who am I?"

When you are confused and uncertain, and you don't even know who you are anymore, remember that these feelings are expected with the loss of a spouse. Spend time working through these bewildering thoughts, and don't rush this process.

Trying to skip steps on your grief journey will not aid your healing; it will only set you back. Your identity is not gone; it just needs to be rediscovered.

"Know that the LORD is God. It is he who made us, and we are his; we are his people, the sheep of his pasture" (Psalm 100:3).

Lord, show me what it means to belong to You. Amen.

Loss of Purpose and Direction

You may feel as though you have no purpose, that there's nothing left for you to do. This feeling can be particularly strong if your spouse underwent a long illness and you had put all your time and energy into caring for him or her.

"Don't get caught up in the fact that you have lost someone," says Patricia, who is a widow, "but that God has something out there for you and that your life is not over. It may be the beginning of something very special that He has planned for you. It may be something that you would not be able to do if He had kept that one person on earth with you."

You are going to have a new, changed identity. God is calling you for a specific purpose, and you can trust Him to accomplish His purpose in your life.

"I cry out to God Most High, to God, who fulfills [his purpose] for me" (Psalm 57:2).

"The LORD will fulfill [his purpose] for me; your love, O LORD, endures forever—do not abandon the works of your hands" (Psalm 138:8).

Lord God, I don't feel purposeful at all right now, but I'm starting to be curious about what it is You want me to do. Amen.

No Longer a Couple

Many things in society today are couple oriented, and you are probably very conscious of and disturbed by the fact that you are no longer part of a couple.

"Socially, you feel like an outcast. You go into a group you used to be part of as a couple, and all of a sudden you feel so alone," says Rev. John Coulombe.

This feeling of loneliness and the consciousness that you are not part of a couple may cause you to avoid going into group situations where most of the other people are couples. God disagrees with the idea that three's a crowd. He reveals in His Word that great strength is available when three people come together.

Ecclesiastes 4:12 says, "Though one may be overpowered, two can defend themselves. A cord of three strands is not quickly broken."

Matthew 18:20 says, "For where two or three come together in my name, there am I with them."

Give your friends a chance, and don't think you are no longer welcome because your spouse is not with you. Let God give you the courage to go into situations in which you may feel awkward or unwanted.

Powerful God, I've been prejudging my friends and assuming they don't really want me around. My relationships with friends are different now, but different does not mean less loving or caring. Clear my vision to see how these relationships can become fuller and deeper because of You. Amen.

Feeling Alone

Along with all your other pain, the sense of being totally alone can press in on you. You are facing life alone now, and you may feel more acutely than ever the loss of the deep and intimate connection you shared with your spouse.

Dr. Ray Pritchard says, "There's a tremendous difference between being alone and being lonely. When you're alone, you simply have no other people around, but you feel no particular loss. You are lonely when other people may be around, but you feel that there is no one around to connect with you at a deep, personal level.

"Be completely honest about your loneliness. It is not a sin to feel lonely. I just think you shouldn't stay that way. Be honest with God, and then pick up the phone and call a friend; call a pastor; call someone in your church. Don't sit by yourself feeling as if you are completely helpless. I know how hard it is to pick up the phone, but how much worse it is to stay that way for days and weeks and months and feel as if no one cares."

Though you may feel friendless and forsaken, the Lord is always with you. He will be your refuge, and He will give you the strength to carry on if you just ask Him.

"God is our refuge and strength, a very present help in trouble" (Psalm 46:1 NASB).

Heavenly Father, You are a constant Presence on this journey. Amen.

When Loneliness Hits

When does loneliness hit you the hardest?

"Getting into bed at night—it was the biggest, loneliest bed. So far I have not been able to pull the covers down on that side," Luevenia says following her husband's death.

JoAnn answers, "When you're used to having a partner and going out together and doing stuff together, it's difficult when all of a sudden you don't have anybody."

Nell, also widowed, says, "At night, especially when I would come to church, there were times I didn't want to go back home. It would just make me nervous to think about going back home and being by myself."

Do not fear or try to avoid those situations where loneliness creeps in and seems unbearable. Face the loneliness with Jesus at your side and know that this is a time of deep loneliness; feel the loneliness and do not try to block it out. Express your emotions and then keep walking with Jesus.

"I guide you in the way of wisdom and lead you along straight paths. When you walk, your steps will not be hampered; when you run, you will not stumble. Hold on to instruction, do not let it go; guard it well, for it is your life" (Proverbs 4:11–13).

Jesus, guide me in wisdom. Walk with me in my path of loneliness and bring me safely through. Amen.

Companionship Is Gone

Picture yourself at the dinner table laughing with your spouse. Picture your spouse in his or her favorite room or chair. Picture your spouse hugging you while you cry.

"The greatest loss is the company of that person, having him there," says Nancy, who lost her husband. "He had a favorite chair. You look over at that chair, and he is no longer in that chair. He was always there to lift me up if something was wrong."

Now picture yourself at the dinner table dining with Jesus. Picture yourself in your favorite room or chair with Jesus close by your side. Lastly, picture Jesus enfolding you in His arms, covering you completely with the sleeves of His robe and just pouring out His love into your whole being.

Be filled with His great love today.

"This is how God showed his love among us: He sent his one and only Son into the world that we might live through him. . . . And so we know and rely on the love God has for us. God is love. Whoever lives in love lives in God, and God in him" (1 John 4:9, 16).

Lord Jesus, today I will crawl into Your arms of love and just rest. Amen.

Making Decisions

With the death of a spouse, you are suddenly faced with a myriad of decisions you must make on your own, and these decisions bombard you right alongside your tangled, unpredictable, and overwhelming emotions.

"I had never bought a car in my life!" says Gretchen. "He just all of a sudden one day would come in with a new car. We didn't particularly talk about it. He knew and I knew when the time came that he would depreciate them out, and then I would get that car, and he would get a new one."

Decisions can range from what to serve the children for breakfast to how to buy a car. These decisions come daily, and they cannot be ignored. Take heart; God will give you the strength and the wisdom to make the right choices. You can trust that He is helping you even when you are not aware of it.

"The lot is cast into the lap, but its every decision is from the LORD" (Proverbs 16:33).

God, I must tackle these decisions one at a time. Hear my prayers for each decision and answer them—one at time. Amen.

Endless Details

The loss of a spouse leaves you with endless details and paperwork at a time when you are not emotionally equipped for such matters.

Marilyn shares: "Some of them are just little legal things you have to go through. All of a sudden you can't do it *this* way anymore; it has to be *that* way. You have to mark the dreaded box 'widow.' You realize suddenly you have become a different identity. But when I've really prayed over these things, the Lord has given me peace that I'll get through this."

The Lord is faithful, and you will meet and accomplish one detail at a time, one day at a time, by His strength.

"For when I am weak, then I am strong" (2 Corinthians 12:10).

Lord Jesus, Your power shines through me when I admit my weakness and my dependence on You. By Your grace I am stronger than I ever was before. Amen.

Determine Your Responsibilities

You have certain responsibilities and commitments you must fulfill each day regardless of how you feel about them and regardless of how you feel on that particular day. These responsibilities may have multiplied since the loss of your loved one.

"Right after the accident the main thing was to keep my children's lives as normal as possible," says Heidi.

Make a list of your daily responsibilities and consider asking other family members and friends to take care of several items on your list. Then commit yourself daily to getting up and fulfilling each of your remaining responsibilities in a way that pleases God.

"The plans of the diligent lead to profit as surely as haste leads to poverty" (Proverbs 21:5).

Lord and Savior, when my responsibilities overwhelm me, help me to face them with a heart attitude that pleases You. Amen.

Competing Emotional Needs

As a parent, especially if you have younger children living at home, you have the extra burden of giving comfort and encouragement to them, even as you need the same comfort and encouragement yourself.

Jodie, whose husband died, says, "I was parenting on my own. I was doing this hectic teaching schedule. I needed to be strong for my sons. At night I would cry and cry unto the Lord.

"The Lord proved Himself so faithful. One of the things that I have learned is that God has all the resources I need. I had a real concern about raising my children by myself. I prayed a lot for guidance and wisdom and strength. God gave me one verse that says, 'He'll gently lead those who are with young.' I took that to heart and knew it was from the Lord."

The Lord is your shepherd. He will care for you, protect you, comfort you, and lead you.

"He tends his flock like a shepherd: He gathers the lambs in his arms and carries them close to his heart; he gently leads those that have young" (Isaiah 40:11).

Shepherd me, Lord. Amen.

Discover Your Inner Resources

You may be surprised at what you can do when you don't have any alternative.

"You will make it through," says Beth, whose husband died. "It's like a deep tunnel, and you're in the middle of the tunnel. There's no light at all, and you don't think you're going to make it. But if you just keep pressing on toward the Lord, you will make it to the end. That is a promise."

Keep pressing on. You *will* make it.

"But the Lord stood at my side and gave me strength . . . and I was delivered from the lion's mouth" (2 Timothy 4:17).

Lord, I will keep taking one step at a time. Deliver me from my weaknesses and doubts. Amen.

Responding to Loss

In Genesis 23, the Bible relates the story of the death and burial of Sarah, Abraham's wife. The chapter begins, "Sarah lived to be a hundred and twenty-seven years old. She died at Kiriath Arba (that is, Hebron) in the land of Canaan, and Abraham went to mourn for Sarah and to weep over her."

Abraham's immediate response was to mourn and weep for his wife. He made a clear choice to mourn. How have you done this?

Rev. Noel Castellanos says that in healthy grieving "there are more than just a few tears. There is a real sense of honesty about the pain. To deal with grief in a healthy way, there has to be a time of just expressing your deep hurt."

Holy God, I choose to mourn and to express my grief freely, knowing that this is the only path to healing. Amen.

Moving On

A journey through grief completely consumes your time, energy, and thoughts. You walk through life oblivious to what is happening around you. This overwhelming consumption will gradually cease as you move forward through grief.

"There was a time after my husband passed away that people would ask me how I was doing," says Marie. "I would say that I'm getting through this second by second. Then, it was minute by minute. Then one day I realized that I was coming along quite well. One day, I went outside and looked up and there was the sky. I hadn't seen the sky in years or heard the birds because I was just so consumed with everything."

Your hope lies in God. Cast your cares on Him; lay your burdens at His feet. In His great compassion and love, He will sustain you.

"Yet this I call to mind and therefore I have hope: Because of the LORD's great love we are not consumed, for his compassions never fail. They are new every morning; great is your faithfulness" (Lamentations 3:21–23).

Holy Lord, I want to hear the birds and see Your sky again. Amen.

Saying Good-Bye

Saying good-bye is not a one-time action. It is a process with many different steps, difficult steps. It's okay if you don't feel ready for this now. Understand that saying good-bye occurs gradually over time.

One step is to visit the places you used to go as a couple, and create new memories there.

Virgil's wife died. He says, "My one son came over and said, 'Dad, you've got to get out. Mom's not coming back.' Grief recovery means being able to move forward in spite of the pain."

The Lord God will go before you and will enable you to say good-bye.

"Righteousness goes before him and prepares the way for his steps" (Psalm 85:13).

Righteous God, strengthen me, one step at a time, to face the old precious memories and to create wonderful new ones. Amen.

Another Step in Saying Good-Bye

Sooner or later you are faced with the necessary step of dealing with your spouse's possessions. This is an important part of saying good-bye. Again, don't rush the grieving process; just follow this step when you are ready.

Margi had some dear friends who spent the last week of her husband's life at her house helping out. These friends were having financial troubles, and after her husband's death, Margi chose to give her husband's nice work clothes to them. She also remembered her husband's ex-students, neighborhood boys who knew him, and, of course, her son.

She says: "My husband probably had a hundred ties. I gave them away to different people because I knew that my husband had touched their lives in some way.

"I knew that it meant something to others, and that's why I was able to give some of his things away. My husband had a little cedar chest from when he was a boy my son's age. I gave that to my son one Christmas and then an arrowhead collection and several things like that."

Your spouse's memory can live on in the lives of loved ones around you. Whom can you touch today with a memory of your spouse?

"I thank my God every time I remember you" (Philippians 1:3).

Lord God, may the precious memories of my spouse bring joy to me and to those around me. Amen.

The Lord Is Your Helper

In your grieving, who or what has been your greatest resource? Whom have you relied on the most to help you through?

Let God be your most important resource; you must let Him help.

"So we say with confidence, 'The Lord is my helper; I will not be afraid. What can man do to me?'" (Hebrews 13:6).

God's strength is available at any given moment, but you must continue to use it.

Melba, whose husband died, says, "I felt the strength of the Lord from the very beginning. Actually, I thought being alone was just going to be terrible. And it hasn't been terrible. I'm coping with it."

Lord Jesus, I know Your strength is available, but sometimes I don't feel it. Help me to understand that Your strength, stability, and security is so much more than just a feeling inside. Amen.

The Lord Will Be Your Husband

"The Scripture that really turned my life around was Isaiah 54," says Melissa. "When I read it the day after my husband died, it was very personal to me. It was written just for me. God said that He would be my husband, and for every single woman out there, He said He will be your husband. He's the best provider you could ever have, and He's the best husband that you ever dreamed of."

Melissa discovered that although she had known Jesus as her Savior, she had never relied on Him as her provider.

"For your Maker is your husband—the LORD Almighty is his name—the Holy One of Israel is your Redeemer; he is called the God of all the earth" (Isaiah 54:5).

Pick up your Bible and talk to Him. Let Him fill your life.

Lord, I need to know You as my husband and provider. Show me how. Amen.

Let the Peace of God Reign

Are you letting God's peace reign in your life? Every time something else threatens to take over your life—unwelcome thoughts or emotions—grasp on to His peace and rely on His eternal promises.

"There's a verse in Colossians that says, 'Let His peace reign in Your heart,'" says Ruth, whose husband died. "Every time I realized I wasn't letting it reign, I would just grab back on to what the Lord had told me and let it reign."

It is truly possible to let peace rule your life.

"Let the peace of Christ rule in your hearts, since as members of one body you were called to peace. And be thankful" (Colossians 3:15).

Lord Jesus, I want to let Your peace take the throne of my life. Amen.

Remarriage?

Your source of wholeness and identity should come from your relationship with the Lord, not from another person. It is only when you are truly living for the Lord and are fully content to accept Him as your sole provider that He would send another mate into your life.

Do not rush into remarriage.

"We're in a hurry-up, throwaway, disposable, microwavable world," says Gretchen, a widow. "And we do not want to wait. God doesn't do everything yesterday. He answers our prayers, but it's 'Yes' and 'No' and 'Wait.' Most of the time it's 'Wait.' It's in His timing and not our timing. We want everything in our timing."

Be satisfied with your singleness, and let God supply your needs according to His perfect plan.

"He who did not spare his own Son, but gave him up for us all—how will he not also, along with him, graciously give us all things?" (Romans 8:32).

Savior God, I want to know You more fully than I do now. Amen.

Don't Rush into Remarriage

Dr. Jim Conway says, "In the early days of losing Sally, there was a desperateness, 'What am I going to do for all of the holes that have been left by her death?' She was not just a wife. We wrote books together; we traveled together; we stood side by side as we did seminars; we managed the office together; we did the counseling together. We were just totally intertwined.

"In the early days of panic there's this urgency to try to replace that, to find somebody else who can help you in all of these areas of life. But it's the worst time to do this because you're just under so much other stress. The choices you make would be panic choices instead of choices that are best for you."

You are only ready for the potential of remarriage when you no longer need that relationship to feel whole. Let God fill your gaping holes, and trust Him to direct the paths of your future relationships. Your relationship with God must be your primary concern.

"May the God of hope fill you with all joy and peace as you trust in him, so that you may overflow with hope by the power of the Holy Spirit" (Romans 15:13).

Holy Spirit, I trust in You to fill me and to guide me. Give me Your hope that overflows. Amen.

Why Remarry?

Do you need this new relationship to feel whole?

If you answered "Yes" to the above question, then you are not ready for the potential of remarriage.

If you answered "No," then spend some time thinking carefully about why you want to remarry.

Gretchen advises, "To those people who hurry into marriage and feel like they cannot get by without having a partner, I would say above everything else, 'Just get on your hands and knees and pray to the Lord.' If He doesn't send the person there, you might as well hang it up. It's not going to work out. If it's not from the Lord, I'd rather stay single."

Don't rush into remarriage to deaden the pain of your grief; you will simply bring that pain into the new relationship. New relationships must be built on one foundation.

"But the one who hears my words and does not put them into practice is like a man who built a house on the ground without a foundation. The moment the torrent struck that house, it collapsed and its destruction was complete" (Luke 6:49).

Strong Father, may the building blocks of this relationship come only from You. Amen.

Your New Relationship

Ask yourself two questions:

1. Is my new relationship God-centered or me-centered?

2. Why do I want this new relationship?

Gretchen says, "Over the years I have seen people so desperate for marriage right after their husbands had died. They were so desperate to get married again that they would just run the men down. I've seen men do the same thing with women. They would think, *I just can't do without a person in the house with me,* and it didn't work out. It wasn't God-centered. It was me-centered."

Take an honest look at your new relationship and decide if this relationship will bring honor and glory to God. If you aren't sure, then wait, pray, and seek God's guidance to distinguish His will from your will. His will is always best for you.

"Do not conform any longer to the pattern of this world, but be transformed by the renewing of your mind. Then you will be able to test and approve what God's will is—his good, pleasing and perfect will" (Romans 12:2).

Thy will be done, Lord, not mine. Amen.

God Will Provide

"I'm finally at a point where I can honestly say if I don't get married again, it's fine, because the Lord is my husband," says Margi, whose husband died.

Trust God in your pain. Commit yourself to Him. Remember, He sees your whole life from beginning to end. He knows what you need better than you or anyone else!

"He placed his right hand on me and said: 'Do not be afraid. I am the First and the Last'" (Revelation 1:17).

Some people feel a need to remarry and others do not. Although we have been talking about remarriage, not everyone wants to remarry or should remarry. God has a future planned just for you.

Jesus, You are all I need. I don't know what my future holds, but I know that all things will work out for the best if You are in control. Amen.

Remarriage: Decide Deliberately

Make the decision not to make any big decisions too quickly. Give God time to heal your heart and to minister to you. He knows what you need and when you need it.

Dr. Ray Pritchard describes three decisions that a person who has lost a spouse must make:

"Decision number one is: 'In my pain and in my grief am I willing to trust God, and am I completely committed to doing His will even when things are tumbling in around me?'

"Decision number two is this: 'What are the basic responsibilities of my life and am I willing to do them?'

"And number three: Make the decision that you're not going to make any big decisions very quickly. Give God time to heal your heart. Give Him time to wrap His arms around you. Give Him time for the body of Christ to minister to you. I think it is often a mistake to jump into another relationship too soon after you have lost a mate."

Commit yourself to God first and to your current responsibilities next.

"So then, those who suffer according to God's will should commit themselves to their faithful Creator and continue to do good" (1 Peter 4:19).

Faithful Creator, I will take my time making these big decisions and just rest and trust in You. Amen.

Men Often Rush Remarriage

Men are more likely than women to jump into a new relationship prematurely. Women often already have a network of relationships to support them in times of grieving, whereas often a man's only close relationship was with his wife.

Jim Grassi, internationally known outdoorsman, recommends that men take time together away from the hustle and bustle of daily life and spend time studying God's Word and sharing with one another in God's great outdoors.

He says, "Jesus was a practical, real guy, and He dealt with real guys. He asked them to put down their musty nets and go out and fish for men instead of fishing for fish. He had those quiet times with the guys, and He took them to places that were different. He took them out of Capernaum and put them into other settings where He could have that time. In His own life when He went out in the wilderness for forty days, He went to a different place than He was used to so that He could listen to God."

Follow Christ's example for your life and put down your own musty nets of thoughts and emotions. Call a friend or a group of friends and make plans to go camping, fishing, or hiking in God's creation. And when you get there, read God's Word together and listen and share.

"The heavens declare the glory of God; the skies proclaim the work of his hands. Day after day they pour forth speech; night after night they display knowledge" (Psalm 19:1–2).

Jesus, show me how I can get away from the busyness of my daily life and find a place to meet with You. Amen.

Contributing to a New Relationship

If parts of you are still broken or needy, another person can feel attracted to the idea of helping to repair or rebuild you. That individual may feel falsely strengthened by the idea that you need him or her to grow and heal, when, in fact, it is God whom you both need.

Before pursuing a new relationship, think about what you will contribute to that relationship, not what you "need" or what you can get from the relationship. The attitudes, qualities, and wisdom you bring to a new relationship should strengthen the relationship, causing both individuals to draw closer to God.

"'Who is he who will devote himself to be close to me?' declares the LORD. 'So you will be my people, and I will be your God'" (Jeremiah 30:21–22).

Lord Jesus, I devote my life to You. I pray that everyone who comes into contact with me will see a glimpse of You and that any new relationship I might be involved in is centered on You. Amen.

Freedom to Remarry

God may at some point bring another person into your life, and you are then free to pursue a relationship. You may have to give yourself permission to do so because of the loyalty you feel to the spouse you have lost. He or she will always be a part of your life; you are not being disloyal by moving forward again.

"I did have to give myself permission to date again," says Jodie, who lost her husband, "but I really was not looking for a second husband. I guess the Lord just opened my eyes when it was time."

God will provide in a way that is right for you. In the meantime, walk in the freedom that God has for you.

"You, my brothers, were called to be free. But do not use your freedom to indulge the sinful nature; rather, serve one another in love" (Galatians 5:13).

Lord God, make sense of my conflicting thoughts and emotions, and give me wisdom in the decisions I make today. Amen.

Feeling Guilty?

After an appropriate time of grieving the death of your spouse and after experiencing personal healing from your loss, you might consider dating. New dating relationships can cause you to feel guilty. You may feel you shouldn't be having fun and that you are being disloyal to your lost spouse. These feelings are certainly natural and will take some time getting over.

"When you first start dating, you feel guilty for enjoying yourself. That was a little awkward getting past," says Marie, who lost her husband.

You are not betraying or abandoning your loved one by dating again. God does not want you to feel guilty about this. You are free to date, and you are free to not date.

"This then is how we know that we belong to the truth, and how we set our hearts at rest in his presence whenever our hearts condemn us. For God is greater than our hearts, and he knows everything" (1 John 3:19–20).

Heavenly Jesus, You are greater than all my worries. I bow down to Your wisdom for my life. Amen.

Others May Not Approve

Even if the Lord brings a new mate into your life, you may encounter people who don't approve of your remarriage.

"There were certain people, of course, who thought that a year was not long enough," says Jodie after the death of her husband.

Can you truly say this person was sent to you from God for the purpose of remarriage? If you have that godly assurance, then make your decisions based on His plan, not on the opinions of others.

Keep in mind that these people may disapprove only because they want what's best for you. Pray for them to know and understand God's will, and do not be embarrassed or ashamed about your remarriage decision.

"Do not be afraid; you will not suffer shame. Do not fear disgrace; you will not be humiliated. You will forget the shame of your youth and remember no more the reproach of your widowhood" (Isaiah 54:4).

Holy God, speak Your words of love through me so that others may come to know You as a result of my life and my new relationship. Amen.

Anticipatory Grief Not Understood

Your spouse may have experienced a long illness before his or her death. As a result, this "anticipatory grief" enabled you to achieve a level of grieving beforehand. This doesn't mean you will be exempt from grief and pain when your loved one dies—actually, you might be amazed at how much grieving you will still need to do. Anticipatory grief doesn't make grieving easier, but it can shorten the process for some people.

As a result of anticipatory grief, you may be ready to build a new relationship earlier than others think is appropriate.

Dr. H. Norman Wright says, "A lot of the grieving will occur during a time of sickness and decline. You will experience it together and maybe with other friends. After that grieving, it can take less time to get through the grieving process. So, at six months or eight months, a remaining spouse may begin looking around and wanting to build a new relationship, and other people may become judgmental.

"When somebody starts dating six months or so later and even marries within a year, it doesn't mean that they did not have a good relationship. There is a lot of anticipatory grief that goes on."

Let God's words encourage you:

"Be joyful in hope, patient in affliction, faithful in prayer" (Romans 12:12).

Oh Lord, when people judge and misunderstand me, it hurts so much. But I don't want to live my life to please them; I want to live my life to please You. May my words, thoughts, and decisions be pleasing to You today. In Jesus' name, Amen.

Godly Support from Others

Praise God when you have received godly support and wise counsel from other people in your decision to remarry. Persevere in prayer if you do not yet have this blessing. Christ-based guidance and encouragement will help to direct your path.

Beth, now remarried, says, "My two daughters were extremely supportive. In many ways they had to be because I married a man who is a number of years younger than I am. My first husband had been a number of years older than I was. Maybe psychologically I thought, *I don't want to be a widow again.* I don't know. But my girls were supportive of that also."

God wants you to seek the advice of others, and He will give you discernment to filter out the directions that are not from Him.

"Plans fail for lack of counsel, but with many advisers they succeed" (Proverbs 15:22).

Wonderful Lord, all wisdom, power, counsel, and understanding belong to You. Lead me to those people who will support me in following Your path for my life. Amen.

The Big Decision

Remarriage?!!

The remarriage decision should be made in the context of

- the power of an active prayer life
- personal study of God's Word
- the wisdom of godly counsel

"Don't put God in a box," says Jodie. "He sees your whole life from beginning to end. He sees what you will need one day when you're old and your children are gone. It is not His intention that a man or woman should be alone. He created Adam and Eve to be together, to be companions."

God will not send everyone a second mate, but He will surely send you a companion, a true friend who will support you in your relationship with God and throughout life's difficulties. No matter what decisions you are faced with, be it remarriage or something else entirely, you must equip yourself to decide wisely. First, decide to live your life through God's power. Second, act on it, making all decisions in light of His Word.

"For the kingdom of God is not a matter of talk but of power" (1 Corinthians 4:20).

Lord God, I commit to active prayer, personal Bible study, and godly counsel before making the decision to remarry. I know that with this life commitment Your power will be unleashed in my life and all glory will belong to You. Amen.

Do God's Will

Where does God want to use you right now? What is His will for your life? You may feel that God is not speaking loud enough and is not answering your prayers fast enough for you to find out.

Keep yourself from "quick fixes" or "obvious answers" to your own prayers if you aren't certain they are in God's perfect plan. Persevere daily in listening to and learning from Him. He has not abandoned you. He is working for your best in all things.

"And we know that in all things God works for the good of those who love him, who have been called according to his purpose" (Romans 8:28).

God, I commit my life to be used by You according to Your perfect plan. Amen.

An Active Prayer Life

How can you know what God is saying to you if you only take time to listen every once in a while? Or if your prayers are mechanical and rushed? Or if the motivations behind your prayers are entirely self-serving?

Pray and listen. Daily, hourly. Pray and listen for His voice every morning when you wake up, throughout the day as you fulfill your daily tasks, and when you turn off the light at night.

First Thessalonians 5:17 instructs you to "pray continually." What does that mean to you? The task may seem frustratingly impossible, but, praise God, it doesn't have to be so.

"In the same way, the Spirit helps us in our weakness. We do not know what we ought to pray for, but the Spirit himself intercedes for us with groans that words cannot express" (Romans 8:26).

God's Spirit lives within those who know Jesus as Lord and Savior. He knows your struggles, and He also knows the sincere desires of your heart. Praying continually in the Spirit is as easy as breathing. When you breathe in, whisper a prayer—a praise, a thank-you, an endearment, a cry, a question, or a fear.

Take a deep, relaxing breath right now and pray:

Holy Spirit, fill me; move through me; intercede with the Father for me; open my ears and quiet my heart to hear You today. Amen. Come, Lord Jesus.

Bible Study

"When Christians are afraid about what lies ahead," says Dr. Richard Bewes, "the great panacea is to read the Scriptures. Read the Scriptures day by day. It's when you lose your anchorage in the Scriptures that you lose your hold upon life itself and upon the future."

With God, there is no need to fear. You can live each day on His sure foundation, certain about your life's direction and your future. This assurance is found in the Bible. Listen to the benefits of reading the Scriptures:

> The law of the LORD is perfect, *reviving the soul.* The statutes of the LORD are trustworthy, *making wise the simple.* The precepts of the LORD are right, *giving joy to the heart.* The commands of the LORD are radiant, *giving light to the eyes.* The fear of the LORD is pure, *enduring forever.* The ordinances of the LORD are sure and altogether righteous. They are more precious than gold, than much pure gold; they are sweeter than honey, than honey from the comb. (Psalm 19:7–10, italics added)

God's promises are for you. Your life can be transformed through Christ Jesus and through His Word. Seek His truth in the Holy Scriptures, and start living a new and abundant life right now. Let His Word be your anchor.

Lord God, forgive me for not faithfully reading the Bible. Help me to make a commitment and to stick with it. Amen.

Keeping Your Mind on Jesus

Controlling your thoughts is one of the most difficult things to do. You probably find it easy to worry, to daydream, to let your imagination run wild, and to let unbidden thoughts creep in and take over. But, oh, the repercussions of this lack of control.

God tells you in Philippians 4:8 where to direct your thoughts: "Finally, brothers, whatever is true, whatever is noble, whatever is right, whatever is pure, whatever is lovely, whatever is admirable—if anything is excellent or praiseworthy—think about such things."

Daily prayer and Bible study will help you keep your mind on Christ Jesus and will help you stay in God's will.

Holy God, today, through Your enabling, I will drive out unhealthy thoughts and replace them with Philippians 4:8 thoughts. Amen.

One Healing Relationship

Remember, there is only one relationship that can heal your broken heart. Jesus Christ is the Great Healer. He has experienced what you have experienced; He alone knows your grief and suffering.

"In all their affliction He was afflicted, and the angel of His presence saved them; in His love and in His mercy He redeemed them; and He lifted them and carried them all the days of old" (Isaiah 63:9 NASB).

Don't search for someone or something to fill the holes in your life. Let Jesus fill you. He is right there waiting for you with outstretched arms.

"After a certain period of time, I did want another person to fill the hole," says Melissa, whose husband died, "but as I grew in the Lord, I knew that it wasn't possible."

Lord, true healing is found in a relationship with You. May I fall into Your embrace today. Amen.

No Friend Like Jesus

"I welcome anyone who may be processing grief, who does not have the resource of the person of Jesus Christ, to come to know Him as your personal Savior," invites Dr. Joseph Stowell. "While you still may weep, and your stomach may still be in a knot, and your mind may be confused for the next six months, there will be a Friend who will walk with you and guide you through the depths of it all. There is no friend like Jesus!"

Don't attempt to get through grief using your own strength and risking a temporal or shallow healing. Choose Christ so that your healing may be full and complete, and you will gain a friend like no other.

"When Jesus saw their faith, he said, 'Friend, your sins are forgiven'" (Luke 5:20).

Lord Jesus, I want You to be master of my life. Please forgive me for my selfish sins, and lead on, Friend. Amen.

your family and grief

Coping with the Loss of a Child

To lose a child of any age—from an infant to an adult child—is one of the greatest shocks a parent can experience. The death of a child is tragic and feels entirely wrong.

"It's so out of sequence and just so unnatural when your child, whom you protected all your life, dies. Is there something you could have done to have spared this?" says Pastor Buck Buchanan.

This grief can be very deep. You will likely relate to the waves of grief and sorrow expressed in Matthew 2:18: "A voice is heard in Ramah, weeping and great mourning, Rachel weeping for her children and refusing to be comforted, because they are no more."

God knows your sorrow, and no matter how dark or painful your situation, Jesus can bring you hope. Sometimes, though, you feel like rejecting that hope and embracing your despair, as if hopefulness is somehow a betrayal to your child. Do not let Satan manipulate your thoughts in that way. Seek God and allow Him to light your path.

Lord and Savior, You are the only one who knows my sorrow. My body is enveloped in pain and wracked by grief, but I know there is hope because of You. Help me to live out that hope. Amen.

The Loss of a Child: Bitterness and Blame

"The bottom line is no matter whom you point a finger at and expect that person in some way to take the blame or pay you back—there is no way this will bring closure or peace to your heart," says Shelly, whose son died. Another person cannot bear your pain for you; only Christ can bear your pain.

She continues, "In the same way, you can't pay God back for your sins. It took the blood of Christ to wash them because you can't pay back for what you've done, and it becomes a futile battle that leads you into a spiral of bitterness that could just choke you.

"So greater and quicker is the healing to rise above it and just say, 'Lord, let me walk in the light of understanding today that You're with me, that You love me, that it's okay.'"

Let it go. Free yourself from the bitterness and blame that will ultimately consume you. Write down Shelly's words and repeat them as a daily prayer: Lord, let me walk in the light of understanding today that You're with me, You love me, and that it's okay.

"Come . . . let us walk in the light of the LORD. . . . The people walking in darkness have seen a great light; on those living in the land of the shadow of death a light has dawned" (Isaiah 2:5; 9:2).

Lord, You're with me, You love me, and it's okay. Amen.

Is Bitterness the Only Option?

For those who do not believe in the world to come, bitterness is indeed the only option.

But for those who believe in an eternal, glorious life, ruled by a God who is higher, wiser, and more powerful than all, these people have hope—the true, godly hope that they will see their loved ones again, reunited in His loving presence. To ensure this hope, you must surrender your life to Him and commit yourself to serving Him and learning more about Him.

Jesus died as the payback for the sins of all people; He took the blame. But Jesus rose from the dead. He defeated death and now lives eternally so that you, too, can experience eternal life with Him. He loves you that much!

Through Christ you can be reconciled to God, no matter what you have done in the past. Repent (turn from) your sins today and turn straight into His loving arms.

The Bible offers a simple plan of salvation to those who come with a sincere heart: "If you confess with your mouth, 'Jesus is Lord,' and believe in your heart that God raised him from the dead, you will be saved. For it is with your heart that you believe and are justified, and it is with your mouth that you confess and are saved" (Romans 10:9–10).

Lord Jesus, I believe that You are the Son of God and that You died on the cross to save me from my sins. I turn away from my sinful ways right now and surrender myself to You. Thank you, Amen.

Treasure Your Memories

Children are a gift from the Lord. You want the best for your children—long, happy lives, spiritual growth, and fulfillment. But every day is a gift from God. Even in your loss, it's good to be thankful for the time you did have together.

Rate yourself: Have you been mostly (a) thankful for all the wonderful times with your child or (b) bitter about the times you won't have with your child?

"I had her for almost five years," says Cindy, who lost her daughter. "I'm the lucky one. I try not to focus on what is so bad, and I try to say, 'Okay, I can't change it, so let's look at what's good or at what's not so bad.'"

The Bible says that Jesus loves children dearly. Be assured that your child is precious to Jesus and so are you. "He took the children in his arms, put his hands on them and blessed them" (Mark 10:16).

After the prayer today, spend time thinking about some joyous and humorous times you had with your child.

Lord of heaven, calm my heart and help me to remember right now the precious memories I can learn from, grow from, and treasure in my heart daily. Amen.

Troubled Thoughts

You do not need to be constantly burdened by sorrowful thoughts.

"Listen to my prayer, O God, do not ignore my plea; hear me and answer me. My thoughts trouble me and I am distraught" (Psalm 55:1–2).

Author, speaker, and humorist Barbara Johnson lost two of her sons. She shares how God gave her a special memory of one of her sons to replace the bad thoughts that were overwhelming her. She says, "The memory is so special that when I talk about my son and I think about it, God windshield-wipes the pain, and I can enjoy the other memories and think on things that are good and happy and fun and pure. And God, in time, does erase the painful memories. It's so important to think of the fun times."

Ask God for a special memory of your child to replace the negative pictures in your mind. Focus your thoughts on that special memory. Share it with others, and treasure it.

Lord God, remind me of the happy memories, the fun times, and the laughter, and may those memories bring a smile to my face and to others around me. Amen.

Children Are with the Lord

Christians believe the only way to enter heaven is through God's Son, Jesus. But what about infants and small children who never reach the age to make a decision to receive Jesus?

Dr. Luis Palau says, "I am convinced that little children who die in innocence, who don't know right from wrong, are covered by the blood of Jesus Christ, and they are in the presence of the living God. The Bible clearly teaches that a brief life is not an incomplete life. We have our ideas of how long we should live, but the Bible says that every one of our days was written in God's book before they even happened.

"All is well with your little child because she's [he's] in the presence of God the Father in absolute perfection. And you can rest on that because that's what the Word of God teaches."

Little ones are not only in heaven, but are also safe in a joyous, precious place close to the heavenly Father. On earth, children are sometimes looked down upon, but in heaven they hold a special place of honor.

The value of children was emphasized by Jesus who said in Matthew 18:10 that children have angels assigned to each of them in heaven. These angels are in intimate contact with the Father, whose nature is revealed throughout the Bible. Being true to His nature, the Father's concern could not stop at the death of a child.

"See that you do not despise one of these little ones, for I say to you, that their angels in heaven continually behold the face of My Father who is in heaven" (Matthew 18:10 NASB).

Holy Father, as I close my eyes right now, please give me an assurance of the peace and joy that my child is experiencing in heaven right now. Amen.

Reunited Because of Christ

David noticed that his servants were whispering among themselves and he realized the child was dead. "Is the child dead?" he asked. "Yes," they replied, "he is dead."

Then David got up from the ground. After he had washed, put on lotions and changed his clothes, he went into the house of the LORD and worshiped. Then he went to his own house, and at his request they served him food, and he ate.

His servants asked him, "Why are you acting this way? While the child was alive, you fasted and wept, but now that the child is dead, you get up and eat!" He answered, "While the child was still alive, I fasted and wept. I thought, 'Who knows? The LORD may be gracious to me and let the child live.' But now that he is dead, why should I fast? Can I bring him back again? I will go to him, but he will not return to me." (2 Samuel 12:19–23)

David said with assurance, "I will go to him." David's young child was gone, but he knew with certainty that he would see that child again. He made the important decision to go on living in the meantime. David knew that his son was already in the presence of the living God.

If David, who lived in Old Testament times, had this certainty, how much more certain can we be about our own children now that Jesus Christ has come and given us a greater hope?

Thank you, Jesus, that you care so much for me and for my child. I want to surrender my sinful life to You, so that I, too, will spend eternity in Your loving presence. Amen.

Treasures in Heaven

The Bible admonishes you to lay up your treasures in heaven (Matthew 6:20). But how difficult that is to do when your treasure is an infant child!

Dot lost three of her infant children. She says, "At the funeral of our first child, the preacher used the Scripture about not laying up your treasures here on earth. That was always a comfort to know that my children were going to be in heaven. I've found great comfort in the fact that they are not gone; they've just been lifted to a higher plane."

God knows your child more intimately than even you do. He created your precious child with the gentlest of hands. God was with your child before he or she was born, and He will tenderly watch over your child forever.

"Your eyes saw my unformed body. All the days ordained for me were written in your book before one of them came to be" (Psalm 139:16).

Heavenly Jesus, bring me words of true comfort today. Thank you that my baby is alive and well with You. Amen.

God Relates to Your Loss

God's Son died; He was buried; and on the third day He rose again. There is hope because of Jesus.

According to Dr. Bill Bright, "God has demonstrated His love for you by personally visiting this planet earth. He left His place of glory, came as a man (the God/man), died on the cross for your sins, and was raised from the dead as a demonstration of His love.

"A woman said, 'Where was God when my son was killed during the war?' And a wise, spiritually mature friend said, 'He was where he was when His own Son died on the cross for our sins.' God knows all about your problems. He wants to help you, but in your anger and resentment, and oftentimes hatred, He cannot help you. It is only when you say, 'Oh God, help me,' in a spirit of humility, that He envelops you with His love, forgiveness, and grace."

God knows your deepest fears, hurts, and needs.

"For God so loved the world that he gave his one and only Son, that whoever believes in him shall not perish but have eternal life" (John 3:16).

Oh God, help me. Amen.

Your Family Needs Your Support

As difficult as it is, your life must go on. No, you'll never feel the same again, and that hurt place in your heart will never be fully healed on this side of heaven. But the others—your family—they need you to be involved in their everyday lives. They need your help as they journey through grief.

"Your family deserves you as a 100 percent person," says Barbara Johnson, whose two sons died. "They don't deserve only half of you. But so many times parents are so wrapped up in that grief. They keep rotating back to that other time instead of saying, 'Hey, I'm still alive. I have children who need me.' This is a new life. The other chapter is done, but the book goes on."

Provide your family with the love, attention, and nurturing they so desperately need from you.

"If anyone does not provide for his relatives, and especially for his immediate family, he has denied the faith and is worse than an unbeliever" (1 Timothy 5:8).

Lord, thank you that as I provide for others, You, in turn, will provide for me. Amen.

Grief Can Lead to Divorce

Tragically, the majority of marriages do not survive the loss of a child. Make your marriage the exception. Choose to persevere and never to give up.

These three people remained with their spouses and worked through the emotional struggles, only to come out better on the other side.

Dora, speaking of her daughter's death, says, "You'll be here at one point in your grief, and your spouse is over here and the two never meet for months and months. Then all of a sudden when you do meet, you find that you're two different people. And you really have to work to get back on that same level of communication. It's real tough, but in many ways I feel like my husband and I are bonded for life because of our suffering."

Jeff, who lost his son, says, "I think it's made our relationship stronger. We communicated so well through the death of our son and after. We've talked more in the last three years than we did in the previous nine or ten."

Teresa's daughter died. She says, "When you do lash out, because none of us are perfect, the other spouse has to be mature and say, 'Well, come on, Sweetie, I know this may be an emotional time right now. I know you didn't mean that. I know we're under a lot of emotional strain right now and a lot of adversity, but let's just pull this thing together,' and just immediately grab hands and start praying."

Take courage from the testimonies of these couples and focus on God. Even when you are both going in opposite directions, you will surely meet if you keep your eyes on God's plan for your life.

"'For this reason a man will leave his father and mother and be united to his wife, and the two will become one flesh.' So they are no longer two, but one. Therefore what God has joined together, let man not separate" (Mark 10:7–9).

Lord, it is Your will that my spouse and I remain together. Give me the strength to persevere. Now is the time to begin. Amen.

Grief Can Rob You of Intimacy

Men and women view intimacy in different ways, and the loss of a child or a loved one will affect the intimacy in your marriage.

Shelly, who lost her son, says, "We tried to pull from one another what we needed to be pulling from the Lord. It's almost like we had to allow ourselves to go our separate ways and deal with the grief and let ourselves be built up from the Source who could really meet that need before we had something to offer each other . . . Many say that most marriages don't make it through something like this, and it's nice to be a testimony that a marriage can make it through."

God alone can meet your needs. When you despair because your spouse is not acting or responding in the way that you think is best, you must be proactive and not reactive. Hold to the "I must change first" principle: "Lord, my spouse is driving me crazy. One of us needs to change. I volunteer. Change me."

When you gain your strength from the true Source, you will be better able to build a new intimacy with your spouse.

> Since, then, you have been raised with Christ, set your hearts on things above, where Christ is seated at the right hand of God . . . Put on the new self, which is being renewed in knowledge in the image of its Creator. . . . Therefore, as God's chosen people, holy and dearly loved, clothe yourselves with compassion, kindness, humility, gentleness and patience. Bear with each other and forgive whatever grievances you may have against one another. Forgive as the Lord forgave you. And over all these virtues put on love, which binds them all together in perfect unity. Let the peace of Christ rule in your hearts, since as members of one body you were called to peace. And be thankful. (Colossians 3:1, 10, 12–15)

> *Lord, teach me Your love. Amen.*

Sexual Intimacy Is Possible Again

It is not unusual for profound grief to impact sexual intimacy in a marriage.

"With me, it was very hard to go back to a sexual relationship after my parents died," says Sylvia. "My husband could not really understand why this bothered me, but he saw me through it, and we've been married forty-eight years."

Your marriage can survive and come out stronger. Persevere in love, and do not let your feelings rule your actions.

The wife's body does not belong to her alone but also to her husband. In the same way, the husband's body does not belong to him alone but also to his wife. Do not deprive each other except by mutual consent and for a time, so that you may devote yourselves to prayer. Then come together again so that Satan will not tempt you because of your lack of self-control. (1 Corinthians 7:14–15)

Holy God, sexual intimacy just doesn't feel right anymore. Help me to rise above my emotions and move toward Your love. When I move toward You, my love for my spouse will be carefully and securely strengthened again. Amen.

Growing Closer to Your Spouse

Sometimes when a couple loses a child, they react by targeting each other. As a result, they begin to grow apart. Quinton and Teresa experienced the death of their daughter. They offer a few suggestions to help you and your spouse grow closer during this time.

1. Apologize daily for anything you may have said or done to hurt the other person in the past twenty-four hours.

2. Be the first person to give in. You do not have to agree with the other person's view, but acknowledge the parts you do agree with and apologize.

3. Pray together daily, whether you feel like it or not.

4. Say something encouraging to your spouse each day.

5. Reflect on the good times together.

6. Be sensitive to the other person's feelings and needs, which may be different from your own.

7. Do not isolate yourself from your spouse.

8. Attend a Bible study together.

"Out of respect for Christ, be courteously reverent to one another. Wives, understand and support your husbands in ways that show your support for Christ. . . . Husbands, go all out in your love for your wives, exactly as Christ did for the church—a love marked by giving, not getting" (Ephesians 5:21–22, 25 MSG).

Dear Lord, sometimes I feel that the gap between my spouse and me is growing larger each day. Please help us to come together again. Amen.

Your Words

"The good man brings good things out of the good stored up in his heart, and the evil man brings evil things out of the evil stored up in his heart. For out of the overflow of his heart his mouth speaks" (Luke 6:45).

Sometimes as a result of grief, you may find yourself directing words of blame, anger, scorn, or irritation at your spouse without giving much consideration to those words. Perhaps it is time to think about some of the things you've said and consider why you said them. Your words are likely revealing emotions you are holding inside you, and these emotions need to be addressed.

"God allows pressures in your life to reveal to you what's inside you," says Iris. "The Bible says what's in your heart comes out of your mouth. For years I was trying to tell my husband what I thought God was trying to show him, but I'm seeing more and more that God's trying to reveal to me what's in me. As He shows me what's in me that is wrong, I can confess it to Him. And the Bible says if you confess it, He takes it away as far as the east is from the west."

After a time of self-examination, if you come to realize that you have said or done something wrong—yes, confess it to God, but also take the time to confess and apologize to the person you have wronged. You can also share with the other person what you have learned about yourself and ask for prayer to handle things better the next time.

Father, forgive me for saying unkind words to my spouse. Help me to be better aware of any emotions I'm holding inside so that I can work through them. Amen.

Grief Can Cause Family Conflicts

Grief puts an awful strain on families, often leading to family conflicts. What conflicts have you and your family experienced as a result of your loss? Emotions are running high, and the last thing you want to deal with is further strife.

Annie, whose father died, says, "It was so hard after he died because of the conflict within my family over settling the estate. We had so many differences of opinion. It was very heartbreaking. I never thought that my loved ones would react like they did. Now I look back, and I realize that they also were grieving. Once we were past settling the property, getting the property sold and everything divided, now gradually we're getting back together. Money can really cause problems in a family."

Understand that each person in your family is grieving in his or her own way, and before you make important family decisions, pray together for God's wisdom and guidance. Do not be afraid of ridicule or rejection from your family members for recommending prayer— prayer is powerful, and you are wise to suggest it.

"It is to a man's honor to avoid strife, but every fool is quick to quarrel" (Proverbs 20:3).

Savior God, I pray that everyone in my family can come to an agreement about what is best to do. Give each of us a peace and a feeling of confirmation that our decision is the right one. Amen.

Family Ties

"God saved my family from destruction. I think that the enemy was trying to come in and destroy us. But God said, 'No,'" says Darlynn, whose grandmother died.

Grief can cause intense strain on your family, regardless of how close you may have been before the loss. But God placed you within a family for you to support one another. He does not want you to quarrel. When you do, you are giving Satan the opportunity to destroy what is good.

It is okay to express your differences, but personal attacks and hurtful accusations are always out of line. Your home must be a safe place where love is the context in which disagreements are worked out.

"You want something but don't get it. . . . You quarrel and fight. You do not have, because you do not ask God" (James 4:2).

Ask God for help right away. Stop the grumbling and dissension before they have a chance to grow.

Righteous God, please strengthen our failing family ties, and bond us together each day in love. Amen.

Unanswered Questions

Suicide always leaves unanswered questions.

"Just this week I spoke with a darling father," says Barbara Johnson. "He was about forty years old and had a seventeen-year-old son. He went to wake him up in the morning for school and found him hanging from a chandelier. There's no preparation for this. A darling Christian boy, active in his church; his father was a wonderful Christian man. So there's no explanation for this.

"That is when you have to claim Deuteronomy 29:29, 'The secret things belong to the LORD.' And this is a secret thing. No one will ever know the reason why this thing happened, this side of heaven. As I counsel many parents who have lost children to suicide, that is the hardest one to deal with. They want to blame themselves. I try to tell them that their child went out to meet a just and a loving God. And only God knows the answers. You can't blame yourself for what your kids do, or grab on to guilt."

No, you cannot blame yourself. There is no responsibility or control when it comes to suicide.

"Now I know in part; then I shall know fully" (1 Corinthians 13:12).

Holy Father, I will never truly know the reason for this suicide until I get to heaven. Every time I start to point the finger of blame, gently cover my hand with Yours and restore me in Your peaceful presence. Amen.

Believers Go to Heaven

If a person is a believer in Jesus Christ, nothing can separate him or her from the love of God. Not even suicide can take a believer out of His hands.

"Suicide is a very difficult topic," says Dr. Erwin Lutzer, "but let me simply say something that I think needs to be said: I have known genuine Christians who have committed suicide, and I expect to see them in heaven."

If you have lost a loved one to suicide, do not weary yourself with the burden of wondering if he or she is in heaven. God alone knows the hearts of people, and He is a just and merciful God.

Take the time now to get your heart right with the Lord. Surrender your life to the healing Christ; and obey what is written in His Word. Know for certain that as a believer you will live in His presence forever in heaven.

"For my Father's will is that everyone who looks to the Son and believes in him shall have eternal life, and I will raise him up at the last day" (John 6:40).

Savior Jesus, I give my life to You and seek to please You all of my days. You are my hope and my life. Amen.

Others Do Not Know What to Say

"We were so deep in our grief that we didn't know how to ask for help," Shelly says of her son's suicide. "We didn't know how to communicate that. There were times I wished someone would have intruded upon our grief and said, 'Do you need someone to talk to? Do you need someone to share with?'"

If you have lost someone to suicide, there are times when even those closest to you don't know what to say. They may even pull back. This isn't because they don't love you. It's because they simply are at a loss for words and don't know how to respond. Explain to them or show them that what you need is a friend.

"[Love] bears all things, believes all things, hopes all things, endures all things. Love never fails" (1 Corinthians 13:7–8 NASB).

Lord, when I don't know what to say and my friends don't know what to say, let us all just rest in Your love. Teach us to love one another. Amen.

Suicide: Cultural Taboo

Suicide is considered taboo in today's society. Often people do not know what to say to you or how to respond to you if you have lost a loved one to suicide. As a result, people often avoid you instead of risking discomfort or awkwardness. This is uncomfortable for you as well, but you must get beyond those feelings and ask others for the help you need.

One way to seek help is through a grief recovery support group. In this setting you can find people who will be concerned friends, who will not worry about the "right" words to say or the "best" way to respond to you. They will accept you, love you, and not have expectations of you.

"A word fitly spoken is like apples of gold in settings of silver" (Proverbs 25:11 NKJV).

O God, help me to reach out and seek help from others who are grieving, too. Amen.

Forgive Everyone Involved

When someone close to you has taken his or her life, a natural tendency is to try and understand the reason for it and to place blame. Be cautious. Focusing on blame will only make you bitter. Bitterness will not resolve any issues, but will block your healing.

Shelly lost her son through suicide. She says, "Yes, there are people we could blame. But the greater challenge to us as Christians was to rise up and say, 'We forgive. We're not going to hold them accountable in any way, shape, or form.'

"We did whatever we had to do to align ourselves in a way that we could imagine the Lord Jesus Christ doing. When we were willing to do that, we released healing, and we released miracles."

Turn your thoughts to the things of God—His words, His attributes, His creation, His promises—and not to blame.

"But there is forgiveness with thee" (Psalm 130:4 KJV).

Lord, forgive me and open my heart to forgive others who are involved in this situation. Amen.

Children in Grief Need Unconditional Love

Children need special attention when they grieve because they are not equipped with the emotional maturity of adults. Their world has fallen apart, and what they need most of all is the assurance of your unconditional love.

"There wasn't anybody to help me when my dad died," says Barbara Johnson. "I had a mother and a sister, but everyone was so busy. I went through my teenage years by myself without a whole lot of help. I did pay a price for that because emotionally I needed some help, and I needed comforting.

"For other parents who have lost a child: Remember, the other siblings are hurting too. Reach out to these kids and unconditionally love them—just love these kids right where they are and let them know that love is the healing factor and that they're not to blame. Sometimes children have a tendency to blame themselves if there's an accident or a tragedy. But I think we have to put the blame aside and just show a lot of love and a lot of understanding."

Do not put this off. Go to your other children right now and tell them how much you love them. Look them in the eyes; hold them in your arms, and just love. God loves you and calls you His child. Now pass that love on to your children.

"How great is the love the Father has lavished on us, that we should be called children of God! And that is what we are!" (1 John 3:1).

Forgive me, Father, for neglecting to comfort the hurt and pain that my other children are feeling. Comfort me as I comfort them. Amen.

Children in Grief May Act Out Their Hurt

Your children may surprise you by the misbehavior they display while grieving. But you need to remember the source of their misbehavior: They feel hurt and do not know what to do with that feeling.

Shelly, whose son passed away, talks about the response of her other son: "He was the passive child between two demanding children. He often didn't express himself and held everything inside. So it was out of character for him to rise up with anger and to put holes in the walls and to be so frustrated in the way that he was.

"After seeking God, what I felt in my heart was that it was his survival he was going through. He was dealing with pain so deep, and he was too young to understand that death is a permanent thing. It's something you can't change; you can't go back; there's no way to rectify what has happened. You just have to accept it. That was so hard for him to deal with. It's almost like he came out fighting.

"And when we were able to accept that this was a part of the process that he had to go through and just cover it in love, we removed some of the stressors in his life, and we allowed him that time."

You still have to be the parent, and your children need you to continue to communicate clear boundaries to them. But choose the issues that you want to address. Over everything else give them oceans of love and grace.

"As a father has compassion on his children, so the LORD has compassion on those who fear him" (Psalm 103:13).

Lord, show me how to be there for my child. Show me how to remove the stressors in his or her life, and open the flow of love and understanding between us. Amen.

Parents Must Model Healthy Grief

Children need their parents to model healthy behaviors. They need to see their parents dealing with grief in a healthy way so that they can learn to do the same.

"I was real open with my grief at first," says Jodie of her husband's death. "I think that is why the boys were comfortable bringing up their dad and saying, 'I really miss Dad.' We could talk about it, and that was good because my oldest is not real expressive about his emotions. That made it easier for me to pull his emotions out too."

Jodie's sons followed her lead in coping with grief. You may desire to model healthy grief, but are not sure how to do so. Take heart; you are better equipped than you think.

These daily devotions are a guide for your journey, not only your journey of grief, but also your journey of knowledge and wisdom. You are learning from others who have traveled before you and are seeking truth and healing in God's Word. Teach your children the source of true healing and make it your priority. Lead them to Jesus.

"Jesus said, 'Let the little children come to me, and do not hinder them, for the kingdom of heaven belongs to such as these'" (Matthew 19:14).

Heavenly Jesus, I want to learn more and more about You so that I can teach my children the certainty and assurance found in a life with You. Amen.

Be Honest with Your Grieving Children

You may wonder how much to say to your children about the loss of their sibling, parent, relative, or friend. Of course, you have to gauge it to their ages and attention spans, but with this in mind, we encourage you to be honest and open with your children.

"As parents you want to protect them; you want to make it right for them, and yet you don't know that what you're doing is actually not hurting them," says Dora. "When we first got back from the hospital after their sister died, we were at a loss for words, and we probably did all the wrong things. They wanted to know how she died, and my husband said, 'Well, she fell asleep; it's just like falling asleep, only she just didn't wake up. It was very comfortable.' Neither one of my girls could sleep after that for months because they were afraid they were going to die. Their comprehension is so limited at that age."

God understands that you do not know what to say. He will enable you. Be truthful, yet compassionate with your children, and pray continually for His guidance. Encourage the children to ask you questions, and keep the lines of communication open at all times. Also, seek help from experienced parents or a counselor for advice on how to explain such things to children.

"Not that we are competent in ourselves to claim anything for ourselves, but our competence comes from God" (2 Corinthians 3:5).

Holy God, open my mouth to honestly talk and share with my children. Help me to be available and approachable to them. Amen.

Your Child May Need Further Help

When children grieve, they do not have the same capacity to understand death that adults have. Be aware of any changes in your child's mood or any odd behaviors that may indicate confusion or a misunderstanding of death. Get your child to talk to you, and explore his or her fears and questions together.

Heidi shares, "About a month after my husband died, my son was very angry. My mother had come to stay with us for a while and had been there for about a month. I think his thinking was that if she'll leave, my daddy will come back. He became very angry toward her and wanted her to leave. It was at that point that I realized there was anger building up, and I didn't know how to deal with it because I was going through my own emotions. I did seek counsel for my son; we put him in counseling, and it was the most wonderful thing for him because he was able to talk out his feelings."

You may need to seek counseling for your child to help him or her open up further. Pray about this possibility, and always take time to talk to your child and teach your child about the true healing that only comes through Jesus Christ.

"God shall wipe away all tears from their eyes" (Revelation 7:17 KJV).

Savior God, healing is found in You alone. Bond my family together in the unity of Your healing love as we travel this journey of grief together. Amen.

Don't Hide Your Emotions

Think back over the past few days and identify times when you held back your true emotions and "put on a happy face" for the sake of your children. Your children are experiencing different degrees of the same feelings you are. If you cover up your emotions, your children will follow your example.

One suggestion to help your family communicate their emotions to each other is with a "Feelings Chart." Write on the chart "Today I feel . . ." (You may want to have a space for each family member.) Then, draw faces or write down emotions on several circles of heavy paper, which will attach to the end of your daily statement (Velcro works great). Remember that younger children may need simpler words and pictures, but older children and adults will need a wide range of words to help them better identify and express their emotions.

Here are some ideas: *sad, lonely, angry, confused, guilty, bitter, rejected, helpless, afraid, worried, disappointed, resentful, jealous, inadequate, vindictive, depressed, lost, abandoned, betrayed, sorrowful, better, so-so, relieved, okay, not bad, hopeful, peaceful, reassured, thankful, secure, insecure, unloved, loved, encouraged, joyful.*

Each day find the emotion that best describes how you feel at any given time and place that word on the chart. Have your other family members do this as well.

God promises to be with you through all of your emotional turmoil. He also promises to comfort, heal, and strengthen you. God's Word is full of promises for you.

"There hath not failed one word of all his good promise" (1 Kings 8:56 KJV).

Thank you, Father, that You will never fail me. Help me to see the big picture beyond my tangled emotions. Amen.

Helping Children Grieve

Children can accept loss if there is something to hope for, something to look forward to. But if they view their lives as one loss after another, recovery is extremely difficult.

Here are some general guidelines in helping your children grieve:

1. Understand that children have feelings even if they do not show them. A child's initial response, like adults, is denial.

2. Tell your children about the feelings you are struggling with.

3. Tell them they are not responsible for the loss.

4. Help them understand what has happened. Share just enough details to satisfy their questions, avoiding anything that would traumatize them.

5. Be there for them. They need more than words. Your presence can help them grieve the loss.

6. Help them remember the good times, and encourage them to share their emotions.

7. Empathize with their hurt without condoning any wrong behavior.

"Can a mother forget the baby at her breast and have no compassion on the child she has borne? Though she may forget, I will not forget you!" (Isaiah 49:15).

Lord, You love my children even more than I do. Give me the wisdom to care for them and nurture them through my grief. Amen.

where is god?

The Why of Death

Right now you might not be feeling very close to God. You might be thinking, *Where is God? Does God really care? How could He let this happen? What does my future hold?*

Dr. Robert Jeffress shares the response of a man who lost three of his seven children through horrible deaths to leukemia: "When somebody asks him, 'How could you keep believing in a God who would allow you and your children to experience such a tragedy?', this is what he says, 'In those kind of experiences you have two choices: You can either give up or you can keep believing in God even when it doesn't make sense. Faith means something when it's exercised in the darkness.'"

Dr. Jeffress adds his own insight: "I believe that faith means something when you don't understand the whys. I don't think God ever condemns you for asking why. But in the ultimate analysis, the question is not why but it is Who? God calls on you to believe in Him who said, 'I am the way, the truth, and the life. No man comes to the Father but by me. I am the resurrection and the life. He who believes in me, though he were dead, yet shall he live again' [John 14:6, 11:25]. Ultimately you must trust in that."

Lord God, I have so many questions and doubts and feelings of guilt and blame. Where do I go from here? Lead me in Your way, truth, and life. Amen.

Questions Are Natural

It is natural to have questions when unwanted and unexpected loss comes into your life. The more traumatic the loss, the greater the questions.

Dr. Tim Clinton says, "Not long ago when I lost my mother, I struggled with the question why. Why so early? Why so quickly? When you ask why, you are in essence validating your own humanness and realizing you are not in control."

Express your questions freely, but realize that you cannot control your life or anyone else's. The sovereign God is higher than all, and His ways are beyond comprehension.

"'For my thoughts are not your thoughts, neither are your ways my ways,' declares the LORD" (Isaiah 55:8).

Sovereign God, I have so many whys. I could go on and on, but nothing will change no matter how many times I ask. I do not understand this. I do not understand You. But I realize I am not meant to. You, O Lord, are high above all, and I must give my questions to You once and for all. Amen.

What to Do with the Whys?

"What do you do with the whys?" asks Kay Arthur, whose husband committed suicide. She answers, "You have to lay them at the feet of Omniscience and, by faith, leave them there and say, 'If You want to show me why, God, fine. If not, I'm going to cling to who You are and what You promise.' When you're asking why, and you're in the dark, and you don't have any reasons, you are to cling to Him in hope. He is the God of all hope. The thing that you have to realize is you are here for a much larger purpose than you realize."

Hope in God, knowing that your questions may not be answered. Each day make a point to look beyond your situation to the all-knowing God of truth, who will not leave you nor fail you. Learn about His attributes and cling to them in hope. The path of life that you travel is different from what you expected, but He will guide you.

"I will lead the blind by ways they have not known, along unfamiliar paths I will guide them; I will turn the darkness into light before them and make the rough places smooth. These are the things I will do; I will not forsake them" (Isaiah 42:16).

Lord, I am truly in the dark, and it scares me. In my fear, I lash out wildly. Shine Your light in my heart. Lead me along this new path. Amen.

Spiritual Doubts

The death of a loved one can leave you feeling spiritually off balance. Question God, but allow Him to work mightily in you.

Shelly's teenage son appeared to be doing well when, unexpectedly, he committed suicide. She says, "I did go through one period where I was so upset that I probably had my faith shaken to the deepest that it has ever been shaken. I said, 'Lord, it is not supposed to happen like this.' We prayed for the prodigal return. We prayed for the change around. We prayed, and it was happening. And everything was going the way it should have. Hope was restored in our hearts, and then to have this happen.

"I can remember being upset to the point of saying, 'Well, Lord, have we been believing all this in vain? Are You there, or is this just another myth like so many in our history have tried to create because they couldn't understand why things happened the way they did?' When I look over that period of questioning, I think that is probably what has caused me to grow and be so much greater a Christian."

Your greatest spiritual growth comes through your questions and trials. You may not like a situation, but often you must accept it and seek growth, not stagnation.

Is God a myth? You will find the answer to this question is an unequivocal *no*. Allow Him to show you His glorious power and might.

"God of all grace, who called you to his eternal glory in Christ, after you have suffered a little while, will himself restore you and make you strong, firm and steadfast" (1 Peter 5:10).

Almighty God of the universe, forgive me when I limit You, doubt You, and expect You to fail me. I am so small compared to You, yet You love me more than I can comprehend. Amen.

Limited Answers

Here is the challenge: Do not use your suffering as a time to discover if you believe in God, but focus instead on discovering what you believe about Him. In times of suffering, God does not change, but what you believe about Him, what you understand about Him, may.

You will likely have questions to which you will never receive answers. It is human nature to want all the pieces to fit, to want to make sense of things. But there are times when that will not happen.

"I was real angry because I couldn't get answers," says Dora of her daughter's death. "I now realize that there really is no logical reason why my daughter suffered. It is what it is, and to say that she suffered and died for my betterment or for our growth does not make sense. So I've come to realize that I'll never get an answer to that question."

As a human living on this side of death, you will not receive answers that truly satisfy you. The only satisfaction will come when you accept Jesus as Lord of your life and live each day seeking to walk in His Spirit.

"Now we see but a poor reflection as in a mirror; then we shall see face to face. Now I know in part; then I shall know fully, even as I am fully known" (1 Corinthians 13:12).

God, instead of focusing on the questions, I want to start focusing on the Answer—You. Help me to better understand Your attributes and Your plan for my life. Amen.

Walk by Faith, Trusting God

"For we walk by faith, not by sight" (2 Corinthians 5:7 NASB).

You are called to walk by faith, especially when there are unanswered questions in your heart. You are to trust God, even when you do not have the explanations you feel you need.

Dr. Joseph Stowell says, "If you look at your problem and then look at God, you always end up throwing stones at God for the problem. If you look at God first and look at your problems through Him, through His sovereignty—that He is in control of everything, that He has permitted this in your life for a reason, that He is a just God, that He will settle the score for you—you will see that He is an all-powerful God who can turn this situation to that which is good and right.

"So the way to avoid the vulnerability of these nagging questions that distance you from God and make you liable for Satan's attack in the midst of your despair is to really focus on what you know to be true about God and to live in the exclamation point of that truth, not in the question marks of what you don't know about your problem."

Faithful God, I must look at You first. Teach me about Your goodness and sovereignty. Teach me to see the big picture and not just the pebbles of my unanswered questions. Lord, I'm willing to try. Amen.

Move Beyond the Why

At some point in time, if you are to continue toward healing, you must let go of the questions. Your questions may be answered later or they may not, but it is in the process of moving toward healing that you are most likely to get the answers you want.

Margi, who lost her husband, says, "I eventually came to a point in my life where I just said to the Lord, 'I'm going to stop asking You why, and I will begin asking You how. How can I use this in my life so that it will glorify You? I want to be able to use this to witness to others and encourage them through whatever it is You are trying to teach me.'"

Change your whys to hows, and seek to grow toward healing by helping other people.

> Therefore encourage one another and build each other up, just as in fact you are doing. . . . Live in peace with each other . . . warn those who are idle, encourage the timid, help the weak, be patient with everyone. Make sure that nobody pays back wrong for wrong, but always try to be kind to each other and to everyone else. Be joyful always; pray continually; give thanks in all circumstances, for this is God's will for you in Christ Jesus. Do not put out the Spirit's fire; do not treat prophecies with contempt. Test everything. Hold on to the good. Avoid every kind of evil.
>
> May God himself, the God of peace, sanctify you through and through. May your whole spirit, soul and body be kept blameless at the coming of our Lord Jesus Christ. The one who calls you is faithful and he will do it." (1 Thessalonians 5:11, 13–24)

God, it seems so hard, too hard. Help me to understand that I cannot do anything without Your enabling. You only expect me to love You and learn about You, and Your Spirit will do the rest within me and through me. Amen.

Understanding God's Ways

"Understanding the ways of God with my little finite mind would be like a little corpuscle in my big toe trying to figure what I'm thinking in my mind," said Dr. Bill Bright. "I can trust Him; I don't have to understand."

Why do humans feel the need to understand and to be in control of everything that happens in their lives? This reaction may be human nature, but that does not make it right.

At the beginning of time, man was created in the image of God (Genesis 1:26–27). But man was tempted by Satan to sin and failed the test. Since that time, humans have continued to be tempted and to fall. This is our sinful nature. All people are born sinners; we are born to want to take control and have the upper hand in our lives, but we are doomed to failure.

This is why Christ came as the God/man to earth. He came to live, die, and rise again as payment for the sins of all people for all time. Only a sovereign God could possibly do such a thing and be successful! If you believe this about Christ and surrender your life to Him, you will receive the benefits of His work of salvation. You do not need to fully understand Him, just believe in Him and trust Him in all things.

"But God demonstrates his own love for us in this: While we were still sinners, Christ died for us" (Romans 5:8).

"Christ died for our sins. . . . he was buried, . . . he was raised on the third day. . . . He appeared to more than five hundred [witnesses]" (1 Corinthians 15:3–6).

"I will put my trust in him" (Hebrews 2:13).

God, You are good, and I trust You in all things. Amen.

Moving Forward in Faith

In the Psalms you read of men crying out to God with endless questions.

> I cried out to God for help; I cried out to God to hear me. When I was in distress, I sought the Lord; at night I stretched out untiring hands and my soul refused to be comforted.
>
> "Will the Lord reject forever? Will he never show his favor again? Has his unfailing love vanished forever? Has his promise failed for all time? Has God forgotten to be merciful? Has he in anger withheld his compassion?" (Psalm 77:1–4, 7–9)

These questions move from cries of despair to cries of praise to God for His faithfulness. The psalmists knew God's faithfulness. They knew that God would not only hear their plea for help, but that He would also be faithful to answer them.

"Then I thought, 'To this I will appeal: the years of the right hand of the Most High.' I will remember the deeds of the LORD; yes, I will remember your miracles of long ago. I will meditate on all your works and consider all your mighty deeds. Your ways, O God, are holy. What god is so great as our God? You are the God who performs miracles; you display your power among the peoples" (Psalm 77:10–14).

Dr. Norman Peart encourages you to come to God with your questions and your heart cries and to discover what God would have you do for Him. Pray these words of Dr. Peart's:

> "Lord, I don't understand. I'm asking You and being very honest with You. Please answer according to Your will, but also, can You show me how I am to deal with this? What would You have me to learn? How would You have me to operate from this point on? Amen."

Remember the Larger Picture

Sometimes when you ask why, He answers by reminding you of the eternal picture. Learn to live your life in light of eternity. Live each day from the perspective of one whose life lasts forever.

Dr. Joseph Stowell says, "I can't underscore enough how important it is to prepare for grief and sorrow ahead of time. One of the ways to do that is to get a grip on eternity, on the world to come. Learn to live here in the light of there so that you are seeing all of your daily affairs and daily routines in light of the world to come. You need to see all of your interactions and reactions and value systems in light of the value systems of the world to come. Then when grief or sudden loss or wrenching sorrow and deep disappointment shatter your world, you are already schooled in all the realities that give you strength in that moment."

There is much more to this life than just doing your best day by day until you die. The big picture is that a glorious eternity is in store for those who know the saving grace of Jesus Christ.

"Surely there is a future, and your hope will not be cut off" (Proverbs 23:18 NASB).

"And this is what he promised us—even eternal life" (1 John 2:25).

Eternal Savior, thank you that You have given me abundant life through a relationship with You. Every time I get bogged down with life on this earth, remind me of the reality of a glorious, eternal future in heaven. Amen.

Future Understanding

One answer God gives Christians to the question why is the assurance that one day you will be able to see things from His perspective.

"He is going to wipe away those tears by giving you knowledge," states Dr. Erwin Lutzer. "Finally, you shall look at everything from His viewpoint. Finally, you shall rejoice in the justice of God. Finally, you shall see the mercy and the lovingkindness of God set against His holiness and His greatness. And when you see that, you will be content."

God is just and good, and His plan is wholly good.

"He will wipe every tear from their eyes. There will be no more death or mourning or crying or pain, for the old order of things has passed away" (Revelation 21:4).

God, forgive my impatience; I would rather see Your perspective now. Grant me the wisdom and the patience to wait on You and to trust in Your perfect plan. Amen.

He Gives Himself

Because God sees your real need, He wants to give you an answer far better than the answers you seek. You may demand reasons and explanations, but what you need is something more—you need the Lord.

"For in him we live and move and have our being" (Acts 17:28).

Think about the astounding reality of this Bible verse. God is all-sufficient for you. Your very being is in Him. You need Him for survival; you do not need answers.

Joni Eareckson Tada says, "Because God is at the center of the universe holding it all together, and because everything in Him moves and breathes and has its being, He can do no more than give Himself. To do anything less is to be less than Himself. Why seek pat, dry, formulized answers when you can actually receive the flesh-and-blood reality of the love of God?"

God would not be God if He were not sufficient for everyone.

God of life, I need You. My loved ones need You. Help me to place You first and ask questions only after I have done so. Amen.

A Sharpened Focus

"When you know that this life is not all there is," says Anne Graham Lotz, "and you know that one day you are going to be standing before God giving an account of your life, and you know that there is a great big eternity out there when we are going to worship the Lamb and forever glorify Him, it gives you a seriousness about life now. It sharpens your focus and motivates you to live every moment of your life fully to the glory of God."

Train yourself to focus on eternity. Focus on the big picture, not on your own limited life on earth.

In some ways you probably feel more unfocused than you have ever felt in your life, as if you are walking around in a constant fog of grief. In other ways you may feel more alert than ever because you are observing life from a completely different perspective. Many things—from the simple to the complex—take on a different meaning or level of importance to you. Sharpen your focus on the God of eternity by reading His Word daily. Stop trying to handle your tumultuous life alone.

"If the axe is dull and he does not sharpen its edge, then he must exert more strength. Wisdom has the advantage of giving success" (Ecclesiastes 10:10 NASB).

> *Eternal God, grant me the wisdom and the focus to recommit my days to You. Help me to understand the seriousness of following Your eternal plan as written in the Bible. Amen.*

He Sympathizes with Your Sorrows

The Lord Jesus Christ knows what you are going through. No one else can make this claim.

"For we do not have a high priest who is unable to sympathize with our weaknesses, but we have one who has been tempted in every way, just as we are—yet was without sin" (Hebrews 4:15).

Jesus Christ came to this earth and experienced life from a human perspective. The Bible says He was tempted in every way; therefore, He can sympathize with all of your weaknesses. He knows your pain.

Anne Graham Lotz says, "It's a wonderful comfort to know that our Lord Jesus Christ is not indifferent to our pain. He's not oblivious to it. It's not that He doesn't care. He's up there at the right hand of the Father, ever living to pray for us in the midst of our suffering and difficulty. He's someone who suffered, and He's someone who has had problems, and He knows how to pray for us."

Lord Jesus, pray for me. Surround me with Your constant prayers. Amen.

Trust His Character

How do you perceive God? Who is He to you?

"Get solidly in your mind who God is," said Dr. E. V. Hill. "He is not a smart man somewhere who finished from Yale or Harvard who is trying to figure out day-to-day problems for people. . . . He is the eternal I AM. He is the eternal last word. And He is love.

"So when He does something or permits something to happen, you are the one who has to wade through all of this human thinking of what God should have done. God is the Answer. It has been my experience that if you continue to have faith and continue to stay at your post, God somehow will explain it to you. He doesn't have to, but I've seen it over and over. I've seen people come up to me and say, 'Pastor, it's been a long time, but I'm beginning to see now. I'm beginning to see.'"

God is the answer to every question and every need.

"God said to Moses, 'I AM WHO I AM'; and He said, 'Thus you shall say to the sons of Israel, I AM has sent me to you'" (Exodus 3:14 NASB).

The *New American Standard Study Bible* (Zondervan 1999) explains that "I AM WHO I AM" in Exodus 3:14 is the name that expresses God's character as the dependable and faithful God who desires the full trust of His people.

God, I want to know You and trust You as the eternal I AM. May I find security and rest in this all-encompassing aspect of Your character. Amen.

The Sovereignty of God

One who is *sovereign* has supreme power, authority, and excellence over all. Name a person on this earth who could possibly fit the above description.

God alone is sovereign. Root yourself in this truth.

"The most singular important truth I've ever learned is what my God is like, and that is what holds me," says Kay Arthur, whose husband took his life. "My God is sovereign. He rules over all. When God gets ready to move, no one can stop Him from moving. And no one can say unto Him, 'What doest thou?' because what He does is perfect. It doesn't look perfect, but He's over all and there are no accidents. So when my husband died, the truth that held me together was the sovereignty of God."

In Daniel 4, God casts King Nebuchadnezzar out of a position of wealth and authority because the king attributed the greatness of his kingdom to his own power. When the king finally realized and acknowledged that God alone is sovereign, God restored him to the throne, and Nebuchadnezzar's life became even better than it was before.

> At the end of that time, I, Nebuchadnezzar, raised my eyes toward heaven, and my sanity was restored. Then I praised the Most High; I honored and glorified him who lives forever. His dominion is an eternal dominion; his kingdom endures from generation to generation. All the peoples of the earth are regarded as nothing. He does as he pleases with the powers of heaven and the peoples of the earth. No one can hold back his hand or say to him: "What have you done?" . . . Everything he does is right and all his ways are just. (Daniel 4:34–35, 37)

God, Your ways are just and right. I do not understand it, but I must believe it. Amen.

The Goodness of God

Can you truly say that God is good?

"One of the worst things you can do as a Christian is to go around with this plasticized mask on saying, 'I love God, and He's so good,' when your heart is breaking inside," says Dr. Joseph Stowell.

"Sometimes you may say, 'God is good,' with tears running down your cheeks, but He is good, and He will see you through, and He never wastes your sorrows. He didn't waste the sorrows of His Son on the cross. He won't waste your sorrows. He, by His magnificent power, will transform them into that which is good—that which brings gain to the kingdom and glory to His name."

Everything God does is good. Believe this with your heart, and hold on to this truth for unfailing strength in times of sorrow.

"'Why do you call me good?' Jesus answered. 'No one is good—except God alone'" (Luke 18:19).

Lord God, I cannot pretend that everything is fine, that everything is good because it's not. But I want to be completely truthful when I say that You, God, are good. Amen.

He Is Faithful

The Lord is faithful to you. He will not desert you.

"God, are you really here or what?" asked Shelly after the death of her son.

She says, "I'm so glad that I came out of that. There was just a faith that surged up and said, 'Yes, You are; You've always been there; You always will be. God, You're doing something here. And I know I'm not ready to see all of it right now, so help me walk in the healing that I have today.'"

So many things are overwhelming right now. Just remember to take one step at a time, one day at a time.

Join the psalmist David in this prayer to the Lord:

> "O Lord, do not forsake me; be not far from me, O my God. Come quickly to help me, O Lord, my Savior" (Psalm 38:21–22). Amen.

Only God Knows

You may have an extra heaviness of heart because you are concerned that your lost loved one did not know Christ and that you will not see him or her in heaven. Remember, no one on earth can know another person's heart or eternal destiny. Only God knows that.

Keep a proper perspective as you work through this.

Dr. Joseph Stowell says, "The most important thing to remember is that God is fair and just and wise and loving. Whatever He does with your loved one will be fair and wise and just and loving. God cannot deny Himself. You do not know what your loved one did in that last flickering moment of life in the quietness of his or her soul. Just give your worries to God and say, 'God, You are a fair, loving, wise, just God, and my loved one is Yours, and whatever You do with him or her, I know that someday I will praise You for the wisdom of that decision.'"

It is through the grace of God that people can receive eternal life. We, as fallen humans, cannot fully understand grace. Grace is an undeserved gift of life from God to man. How fortunate we are to have such a loving God.

"Just as sin reigned in death, so also grace might reign through righteousness to bring eternal life through Jesus Christ our Lord" (Romans 5:21).

Loving God, I cannot know the eternal destiny of my loved one for sure, but I do praise You and thank you for Your gift of grace. You have compassion on me, no matter how undeserving I may be. Thank you for this reassurance. Amen.

Conclusion in God's Hands

You must trust in the mercy and justice of God. If you leave a matter in His hands, you can trust Him to do what is right.

God really does give you important answers, but often not the answers you were expecting. If you trust in Him, He will give you the answers you need.

"I have to trust in Him because I don't understand why things have happened, but I know that He holds the future," says Heidi, whose husband was killed.

God gives you answers and the greatest answer He ever gave is in His Son Jesus. It is when you have Jesus in your life that you are best equipped to find answers and to find the healing that you need.

"I call on the LORD in my distress, and he answers me" (Psalm 120:1).

Lord, I will continually call on You, and I will trust You to answer my cries. Amen.

If God Is Good, Why . . . ?

Grief often brings with it theological questions. Why did God allow this or cause this to happen? Why now? Why to this person? Moral issues often arise out of the cauldron of emotions in grief. A sense of outrage is embedded in the grieving process, especially when children and good people die, sometimes creating an inner demand for justice.

Dr. Ray Pritchard says, "There are questions for which answers are hidden in the mind and heart of a loving God. All we can say is this: God has so designed the moral universe that, as the Bible says, the rain falls on the just and the unjust.

"We live in a fallen world, a world that's distorted by sin, and ever since sin entered the human race in the Garden of Eden there has been sin, sickness, pain, suffering, and death. So I don't think anyone will be able to know why one child gets cancer, why one marriage breaks up, why one person loses his job and another one is promoted. Sometimes we'll come up with superficial answers, but truly I've discovered that the deeper and more heartrending the question, the harder it is to come up with an answer on a human level."

While God does not always give answers to your questions, He always gives Himself. You can focus your attention instead on the faithfulness of God, His comfort, and His promise to work all things together for good (Romans 8:28). You can trust Him when you do not have all the answers.

"He causes his sun to rise on the evil and the good, and sends rain on the righteous and the unrighteous" (Matthew 5:45).

Lord God, even though I do not understand why, I know I don't need these answers in order to move on. Your ways and Your thoughts are truly higher than mine. Amen.

your greatest resource

Is God Interested?

God is a supreme being who is interested in and concerned about you, and He wants to be involved in the process of your healing. This is amazing.

"Think of who God is," said Dr. Bill Bright. "Astronomers tell us there are over a hundred billion galaxies separated by trillions of light years, and this God, who created it all, became a man: the God/man Jesus of Nazareth. He died on the cross for us, and it is all a gift. It is awesome, that this great, holy, Creator, God of the universe should care."

It is so difficult for our limited human minds to embrace the greatness of God and His ultimate plan. It is difficult to move out of a self-centered existence.

"When I consider your heavens, the work of your fingers, the moon and the stars, which you have set in place, what is man that you are mindful of him, the son of man that you care for him? You made him a little lower than the heavenly beings and crowned him with glory and honor" (Psalm 8:3–5).

Amazing God, turn my inward-looking eyes outward to You. You are interested in all that goes on in my life—my emotions, fears, disappointments, and confusions—and You want to heal me through Christ. Thank you. Amen.

Your Spiritual Life

Perhaps you have not explored your spiritual life in too much detail. You may feel uncomfortable doing so, or maybe you don't know where to start.

Begin with the prayer "God, is there something more for me?"

"Then listen for His answer in His Word," suggests Joni Eareckson Tada. "Begin reading the Psalms, which are written by men inspired by the Lord of the universe, full of emotional heartache, turmoil, doubt, anxiety, and fear. Let God speak to you through those Psalms. Then go to the Gospels: Matthew, Mark, Luke, and John. I would suggest starting with the book of John. Read about this God in flesh, this Jesus who walked the earth. Read about the way He reached out to the widow, the hurting child, the mother with a fever, and the single woman scorned at the well. Read about His love for these individuals, and you will know and feel His love the same."

Discover the wonders of a relationship with the Lord Jesus. Become actively involved in reading His Word, and listen with your heart.

"And he said to me, 'Son of man, listen carefully and take to heart all the words I speak to you'" (Ezekiel 3:10).

Lord, I want to be tuned in to You, but my mind is so easily filled with clutter. Speak to me in Your Word, and teach me to listen. Amen.

Source of True Healing

"Without a relationship with Christ, healing in every case will be superficial," says Dr. Larry Crabb. "I just can't face the depth of my pain without knowing Christ. Knowing Christ there's always hope. And the deeper the pain, the clearer the hope actually can become.

"Without Christ, I can't face it. I can only face what a pill can solve. I can only face what an affair can solve. I can only face what drinking too much or eating too much or spending too much or crying a lot or watching TV or reading or watching soap operas can solve, which isn't the real me."

Think of the actions or activities that you have been pursuing in an effort to alleviate the pain. Christ's healing love will always go deeper than anything you could find on this earth. With Christ, there is forgiveness and hope, no matter how hard the struggle, no matter how deep the pain, no matter how unforgivable you may feel.

Read this miraculous promise that is available for all who call on the name of Jesus:

"By faith in the name of Jesus, this man whom you see and know was made strong. It is Jesus' name and the faith that comes through him that has given this complete healing to him, as you can all see" (Acts 3:16).

God, I try to escape the pain through a myriad of activities from busyness to tears. But the reality of my healing is found in You. Amen.

A Relationship with God

The Lord wants so much more than to just visit you during a difficult time in your life. He wants to be involved in your life forever. This is the purpose for which you were born.

"Salvation is a gift. You need to ask Jesus for it. He has died and paid the price. But unless you ask Him to be your Savior and Lord, you do not have a relationship with Him," says Dee Brestin.

In order to be saved from this bleak existence, you must first believe and then ask. Salvation is not something you earn; it is a free gift of God.

"Until now you have asked for nothing in My name; ask, and you will receive, that your joy may be made full" (John 16:24 NASB).

Savior God, my life has a specific purpose in You. Help me to live out that purpose. Amen.

Accepting His Love

Most people find it easy to believe that God loves other people, but the Bible says the heavenly Father loves each person the same. You can be confident of His love for you.

Bruce Marchiano says, "If you can take the way you feel about your own kids and multiply it a billion times, you might begin to come close to the way He feels about you."

Accept His love right now. Close your eyes in prayer and ask His Spirit to fill you with His love. There is no greater joy than to know His love.

"See how great a love the Father has bestowed on us, that we would be called children of God; and such we are" (1 John 3:1 NASB).

Heavenly Father, Your love for me is amazing. What a wondrous love this is! I am Your blessed child! Amen.

His Love

When you surrender your life to Christ Jesus, you become wholly aware of His great love for you. Your past sins are wiped away, and you can be assured that He will never leave you.

"The steadfast love of the LORD never ceases, his mercies never come to an end; they are new every morning; great is thy faithfulness. 'The LORD is my portion,' says my soul, 'therefore I will hope in him'" (Lamentations 3:22–24 RSV).

God loves you so much that there is nothing you can do to cause Him to turn away from you. He is always there for you; He is your hope; and He is all you need.

Dr. Larry Crabb says, "Christ is looking at you and saying, 'Take the worst discouragement that you ever felt, the deepest pain you ever felt, the worst sin you ever committed. Combine them all and they are not enough to make Me move away from you.'"

Father God, I'm so glad that You will never leave me. You love me so much; I can barely comprehend it. Yes, Lord, my hope is in You. Amen.

Contemplate the Cross

"The clearest demonstration of the love of God is the cross," says Dr. Larry Crabb. "Without an understanding of the cross, you're never going to get God's love clear in your mind.

Do you feel unlovable? Have people turned away from you in your grief? Has anyone glibly offered to pray for you or shared Scripture with you without really taking time to listen to you? Have you heard the story of what Jesus did on the cross, but do not feel it personally? Instead of focusing on how inadequate other people are at expressing their love for you, direct your attention to the cross of Christ. Take time to listen to its message of love.

Crabb continues, "This hanging on the cross is the richest, clearest, most convincing demonstration of God's love. Without contemplating the cross and looking at it, Christians, you draw the wrong conclusions sometimes."

Direct your attention to the cross at Calvary. Here is where you are reconciled to God, where you receive the fullness of Christ through His shed blood. If you continued to direct your focus to the cross through-out this day, the next day, and the days after that, you would know—without a doubt—His love for you. You would begin to live your life on a higher plane.

"For God was pleased to have all his fullness dwell in him [Jesus Christ], and through him to reconcile to himself all things, whether things on earth or things in heaven, by making peace through his blood, shed on the cross" (Colossians 1:19–20).

Loving God, the Bible says that it was Your pleasure to reconcile me to You through this amazing sacrifice on the cross. Help me to focus on the cross and to understand the intense personal signifi-cance that I will find there. Amen.

Seeking to Know God

In today's culture, people are typically unaware of the daily urgency of living for God. It is imperative to choose to live for Christ today because you do not know if you will be given another chance to decide. You do not know what the future holds. The only certainty is that those who surrender their lives to Christ will be given the gift and the hope of a glorious eternal life with Him.

Jesus said, "I tell you the truth, whoever hears my word and believes him who sent me has eternal life and will not be condemned; he has crossed over from death to life" (John 5:24).

If you have already made the decision to commit your life to Christ, where are you in that commitment? Do not be content with a shallow faith and basic biblical knowledge. Delve into the Bible, search the Scriptures, pray powerfully, and listen carefully to what God is longing to teach you.

> Wisdom calls aloud in the street, she raises her voice in the public squares; at the head of the noisy streets she cries out, in the gateways of the city she makes her speech: "How long will you simple ones love your simple ways? How long will mockers delight in mockery and fools hate knowledge? If you had responded to my rebuke, I would have poured out my heart to you and made my thoughts known to you. (Proverbs 1:20–23)

Mighty God, I am not content to continue in my own simple ways. I want to know You as I have never known You before. Amen.

Learning to Worship

You were created to *worship* God. *Worship* means "to honor or reverence; to regard with great or extravagant respect or devotion" (Merriam-Webster). Do these words describe your response to God?

Dr. Ray Pritchard says, "I would define worship in the broadest sense as the soul's response to God. It is anything that I do in my soul where I am truly aware of my heavenly Father, and I am turning to Him in the time of need. It might be with joy. It might be with praise. But very often it's with a broken heart.

"I think that in those moments when you have lost someone very precious to you, God is honored when deep inside you turn to Him and cry out, 'Oh God, oh Lord, You are awesome. Your ways are beyond finding out. Lord, I do not understand, but I bow before You because You are an awesome God.' That to me is worship."

Hezekiah was a king who trusted God with wholehearted devotion both in good times and in bad. The Bible records that "there was no one like him among all the kings of Judah, either before him or after him" (2 Kings 18:5). Even in the midst of bitter tears, Hezekiah approached God with a reverent, worshipful heart, and God heard his prayer:

"'Remember, O LORD, how I have walked before you faithfully and with wholehearted devotion and have done what is good in your eyes.' And Hezekiah wept bitterly" (2 Kings 20:3).

O Lord God, my heart cries out to You. I worship You with reverence. You are Lord of all. Amen.

Yielding to His Lordship

God is not a therapist; He is not just someone you approach to make it through a difficult time. He is Lord and Savior. Your greatest joy will come when you yield your whole life to Him.

"Know that you have to leave it up to Him, and you have no control over life or death—that's what sustained me through it all," says Gretchen, whose husband died.

When you honor Him as God, you are better able to accept the circumstances of life.

"Woe is me for my hurt! My wound is grievous: but I said, Truly this is a grief, and I must bear it" (Jeremiah 10:19 KJV).

Father, yielding to Your Lordship is difficult for me, but I want to give my every thought and effort to You, not just to get me through the rough times, but as an act of worship to You. Amen.

Security

When you believe in Jesus and receive Him, you are ushered into the most secure position in the universe. It does not mean things will be easy, but it does mean He will always be with you and sustain you.

> The boat was already a considerable distance from land, buffeted by the waves because the wind was against it. During the fourth watch of the night Jesus went out to them, walking on the lake. When the disciples saw him walking on the lake, they were terrified. "It's a ghost," they said, and cried out in fear. But Jesus immediately said to them: "Take courage! It is I. Don't be afraid."
>
> "Lord, if it's you," Peter replied, "tell me to come to you on the water."
>
> "Come," he said. Then Peter got down out of the boat, walked on the water and came toward Jesus. But when he saw the wind, he was afraid and, beginning to sink, cried out, "Lord, save me!" Immediately Jesus reached out his hand and caught him.
>
> "You of little faith," he said, "why did you doubt?" And when they climbed into the boat, the wind died down. Then those who were in the boat worshiped him, saying, "Truly you are the Son of God." (Matthew 14:24–33)

Your security is in Christ. You are safe and empowered when you remain in Him.

"The more you focus on the problem, on the bad thing that is happening to you, your life just goes down, down, down," says Anne Graham Lotz. "It's like Peter when he was walking on the waves. When he started looking at the waves and all of his circumstances, he started to sink. He started to go down, and he needed to keep his eyes on Christ."

Lord, I lift my eyes to You. Keep me from focusing on the negative, and teach me to embrace the good, which is only in You. Amen.

What Is at the Center of Your Life?

In the solar system, planets have a predictable orbit because the sun is a stable gravitational "center." Imagine what would happen to those planets if the sun suddenly disappeared.

You, too, need a stable center for your life, or your life could go spinning off into orbit. Perhaps you feel as if you are floating crazily and aimlessly right now.

Take care not to place another person at the center of your life; your life cannot revolve around a person because no matter how much that individual loves you, he or she is fallible and can unintentionally fail you.

Dee Brestin says, "Put your trust in God. It sounds simplistic. I think that often particularly women have a tendency toward depending on people instead of God. They cling too tightly. They don't think they will ever be alone. They almost tend to make that person like God, and they're shocked when that person either lets them down or dies. How important it is to know that you have a Friend who is closer than a brother, who will never let you down and will never die."

In the end, only one thing is permanent. Your relationship with God, if you have one, cannot be taken away. Because this relationship is so critical to your stability, it's important to know for sure that you have the kind of relationship with Him that will ensure He is permanently in the center of your life.

"Those who know your name will trust in you, for you, LORD, have never forsaken those who seek you" (Psalm 9:10).

Lord God, You will never leave me or let me down. Forgive me for placing other people and things at the center of my life. I want You as my secure foundation. Amen.

A Heart of Peace

The phenomenal result of worshiping God and submitting to His Lordship is that you experience peace in your heart, a peace that goes deeper than the circumstances around you.

Phyllis, whose sister died, says, "Daily the Lord was providing me with spiritual bread. I still was looking for that pouring out of His grace and peace, and I just expected any time I was going to have this overwhelming feeling of peace in my life, but it was not like that. It was just a day-by-day supplying of the bread that I needed for that day."

After her husband's death, Jodie says, "I also experienced a lot of peace from the Lord after I started throwing these things at His feet, because I knew I couldn't handle them. His peace that passes all understanding was very real to me."

The Bible describes God's peace as a peace that "transcends all understanding," or "surpasses all comprehension" (Philippians 4:7). This is the only kind of peace that can flow deeper than pain and sorrow.

"Peace I leave with you; My peace I give to you; not as the world gives do I give to you. Do not let your heart be troubled, nor let it be fearful" (John 14:27 NASB).

Giving Father, I pray for Your peace in my life. Amen.

Inviting Christ into Your Life

Surrendering your life to Christ is a step of faith and an act of will. God is most interested in the sincerity of your heart, not the words you pray. He recognizes a genuine desire to surrender to Him.

"I know that in your heart if you say, 'Jesus, I believe in You. I know that You're my Savior,' He hears it. He hears your heart," says Cindy Morgan. "I think He pays a lot more attention to your heart than your words."

Invite Christ into your life today. He gave His life for you.

You see, at just the right time, when we were still powerless, Christ died for the ungodly. Very rarely will anyone die for a righteous man, though for a good man someone might possibly dare to die. But God demonstrates his own love for us in this: While we were still sinners, Christ died for us. Since we have now been justified by his blood, how much more shall we be saved from God's wrath through him! For if, when we were God's enemies, we were reconciled to him through the death of his Son, how much more, having been reconciled, shall we be saved through his life! (Romans 5:6–10)

Lord Jesus, thank You for saving me from this old life and giving me a new life in You. Amen.

How Your Perception of God Affects You

Points to think about:

- Your identity, security, and confidence are all deeply woven into your perception of God.

- You may have a false perception of God because of the human tendency to project on to Him the unloving characteristics of people you have looked up to.

- You may believe that God is going to treat you as others do.

- Your perception of God must come from the Scriptures and not from your past relationships, some of which may have been very harmful.

Robert McGee in *Search for Significance* says, "There have been many times in my life when I felt that God was going to punish me by causing me to lose all that I had, either because I'd done something I shouldn't have, or because I failed to do something I should have. This erroneous perception of God had driven me away from Him on many occasions when I've needed Him most, and is completely contrary to the One whom Paul describes as the 'Father of mercies and God of all comfort [2 Corinthians 1:3]'" (Word Publishing, 1998).

Father God, my relationship with You is not about my effort to obey or to be a good Christian; it is about who You are and who I can be through You. Amen.

stuck in grief or moving on?

Good Grief

Good grief is accepting the fact that your loved one has died, accepting the sorrow and pain, and knowing there is more to come. Good grief is getting through the days, the months, and, eventually, through the years.

Dr. Erwin Lutzer says, "There was a young woman who saw me for counsel. She was madly in love with her husband, and he died unexpectedly. She was contemplating suicide. She said, 'I simply cannot live. I want to die, and I want to be with him. That's all that I care about.' So I explained to her that what she needed to do was to get through the first year. I promised her that the sun would shine again.

"She saw me several months later, and she said, 'You know, the sun is beginning to shine. I have now discovered I can make it without him.' And she's on her way. Grief takes time but you will find it gets better, and you must recognize that it is a period of transition to a brand-new kind of life for you."

Your life will never be the same again, but you will get through the grief. The grieving process is a transition into your new life.

"He will renew your life and sustain you in your old age" (Ruth 4:15).

> *Lord, I did not want a new life. I liked my old one just fine, but I understand that going back is not an option. Therefore, Lord, I will move forward. Teach me to seek You and embrace You and grow in this new life. Amen.*

Bad Grief

Grief is a process. A *process* is a series of actions and gradual changes that one progresses through. The grieving process involves forward movement—going from one emotion, one level, one day to the next.

Good grief involves identifying the loss, recognizing the grieving process, accepting that life will never be the same, and continuing forward on the journey. There is also bad grief: continually thinking about the person who died and refusing to let him or her go.

"Let me give you an example of bad grief," says Dr. Erwin Lutzer. "Here's a woman whose husband has been dead for fifteen years, and she will not touch his study, but leaves it exactly as he left it, fearing that if she were to touch it or sell the books, it would be a sign of dishonor and disrespect.

"Let me give you another example of bad grief. A woman convinced her husband to go to a concert that he didn't want to go to. So they go to this concert, and he's killed in a car accident. For fourteen years she goes to his grave every single morning, bemoaning the fact that she convinced him to go to something that he didn't want to go to. That grief is not of God. That is bad grief."

Grief that is not of God will not bring healing and peace. Humble yourself before God, and seek His forgiveness if you have a preoccupation with your lost loved one and have refused to let him or her go.

"Humble yourselves, therefore, under God's mighty hand, that he may lift you up in due time. Cast all your anxiety on him because he cares for you" (1 Peter 5:6–7).

Holy God, it is hard to let go. Forgive me for holding on so tightly. Help me to release my feelings and fears to You each day. Amen.

Frozen in Grief

Grief freezes you in place; it freezes your emotions, and it can become so bad that you are trapped in a prison of your own making.

In the North when the first frost of the season comes, the lakes begin to ice over. At this point the ice can still be broken or thawed. But as the winter season progresses, layers of ice build up until the lake is so solid that even a truck can drive across it.

Dr. John Trent uses this image to help us understand how, over time, you can become frozen in layer after layer of grief if you do not deal with your emotions and your negative mental images as they come. He says, "You get all those images and pictures built up, and the ice can be thick. So whether you're frozen or whether you're stuck, the key to thawing things out is like how the spring comes. It comes when we turn the warmth of the sun, in this case God's Son, on those negative pictures."

For each negative emotion, each image that plays and replays itself in your mind, you must express it and let God's Son melt it with His love.

"He sends his word and melts them; he stirs up his breezes, and the waters flow" (Psalm 147:18).

Heavenly God, shine Your Sonlight on my thoughts and emotions today. Thaw this block of ice that imprisons me, and free me to move again. Amen.

Write Your Memories

Writing down your memories is a way to become unstuck if you are stuck in grief. Set aside a regular time to write out all the positive experiences you can remember that include your loved one. One memory will lead to another, and you will have much to write. This exercise shines light on the positive memories, which will help you keep the negative memories in perspective.

"When you lose someone," says Dr. H. Norman Wright, "what you have left basically are the memories. At first they're so sharp that they hurt. In time those memories begin to dull. They diminish. That in itself is another loss that you have to go through. In writing about it, you don't lose those memories. They're always there in black and white."

Writing down memories is a special process that takes time and courage.

"For I wrote you out of great distress and anguish of heart and with many tears, not to grieve you but to let you know the depth of my love for you" (2 Corinthians 2:4).

Lord, give me the discipline and the courage to sit down and write out special memories about my loved one. Thank you, Jesus, Amen.

Address Unresolved Issues

Having unresolved issues with the person who died will cause you to be stuck in grief. These issues may be petty disagreements over work or family life, or they could be deep-rooted conflicts that were never settled. You can still settle those issues in your own heart.

"You can't get unstuck from grief until you deal with the issues that stuck and gummed things up in the first place," says Dr. Ray Pritchard.

To complete the grieving process, you must go back and deal with unresolved issues. These matters can be resolved. A pastor, counselor, or support group may help you with this.

You could also write a letter to the loved one with whom you had the disagreement or misunderstanding. Give details and ask for forgiveness. Because the person you lost cannot read the letter or respond to you, this exercise is totally for your benefit. Finally, tear up the letter. The matter is settled and finished. You can do no more.

Tell God about these conflicts. Tell Him what the disagreement was, how you felt then, and how you feel now.

"Review the past for me, let us argue the matter together" (Isaiah 43:26).

Lord God, I keep thinking, If only. *But I cannot go back, so I must go forward with Your help. Lead me to a Christian counselor or support group that can help me settle the issues causing such turmoil in my heart. But first, Lord, let me tell You all about it . . .*

Acknowledge Hidden Grief

Hidden losses—miscarriages, abortions, stillbirths—bring deep grief that can be difficult to move forward from. You may feel that those around you are reacting far too lightly to this loss. You may even try to hide your grief, unsure of it.

Your grief is real and justified. Despite what others are thinking or saying to you, you must give yourself permission to grieve. The Bible holds all human life to be equally valuable—from the womb to the final seconds of life and beyond.

For you created my inmost being; you knit me together in my mother's womb. I praise you because I am fearfully and wonderfully made; your works are wonderful, I know that full well. My frame was not hidden from you when I was made in the secret place. When I was woven together in the depths of the earth, your eyes saw my unformed body. All the days ordained for me were written in your book before one of them came to be. (Psalm 139:13–16)

Creator God, my pain is deep, and I hide it from others. But, Lord, I acknowledge this grief to You, and I pray for healing on my journey. Amen.

Release Your Emotions

Barbara Johnson shares practical advice that she had once given to a woman who could not stop crying because of grief. Her plan involves accelerating your emotions by releasing them for a set time each day. She says, "This woman worked at a department store, and she was selling clothes. And she was crying all over the clothes. She said, 'I just can't stop crying. I'm just crying all the time.'

"I said, 'Well, go into your room and be sure you're home alone. Turn on some sad music. Lock the door. And then just pound the pillow and cry and grieve and let the emotions out. Set a timer for thirty minutes. Then every day lessen the timer one minute. By the end of thirty days you will have exhausted yourself with all this crying.'

"She called me after about a week and she said, 'Barbara, that really worked. I mean, I've only done it a week, and I can work all day at the store and I don't even cry on the clothes anymore.'

"So, it does help when you can ventilate and drain some of that abscess and pain out. See, tears are a good escape. I think God sent us tears as an escape measure. We need to cry."

Release your tears for a time, but learn to compose yourself for other times.

"This is what the LORD, the God of your father David, says: I have heard your prayer and seen your tears; I will heal you" (2 Kings 20:5).

Sometimes, Lord, I just have to cry.

Look for the Exceptions

Think of something good that has happened to you lately. If you do not feel you can label anything as good, think instead of the "exceptions" to your sorrow. Think of any times this past week when you were not focused on your sorrow. What were you doing during those times?

"The mind can't occupy itself with two thoughts at a time," says Jim Grassi. "If you focus on those things that are good and pure and right and fun and new and exciting and challenging, it's going to be harder for those other thoughts to seep into your head."

Your healing journey will contain positives, or exceptions to the negative, as you continue forward. Teach yourself to recognize these forward steps.

"A simple man believes anything, but a prudent man gives thought to his steps" (Proverbs 14:15).

Lord, I know I cannot walk aimlessly through grief; it is too tangled and torturous. Show me the positive steps I have made so far so I can be encouraged by them. Amen.

Decide to Move Forward

The most important thing to understand if you are stuck in grief is that only you can make the decision to get unstuck. Only you can make the decision to move on.

Dr. Tim Clinton observes, "You close yourself off from interactions in life that normally would be healthy for you. You're so sorrowed that you close your world in. You start disengaging from life to control your world. But the more you disengage, the more you've cut off that life supply."

Choose to move forward in your grief—rebuild relationships, serve others in your community, express your emotions, share your story, begin a new sport, hobby, or activity. Your effort to control your life and cut off relational ties will not help anyone, least of all you.

When Ruth lost her husband, she did not disengage from life. Boaz commented on this, saying to Ruth, "I've been told all about what you have done for your mother-in-law since the death of your husband— how you left your father and mother and your homeland and came to live with a people you did not know before. May the LORD repay you for what you have done. May you be richly rewarded by the LORD, the God of Israel, under whose wings you have come to take refuge" (Ruth 2:11–12). Ruth became the great-grandmother of King David through whose physical lineage came Jesus.

Jesus, I know that I must move on. I am making the decision right now to get myself unstuck from this place in my grief. I need You to replenish my life supply. Amen.

Making Progress

You probably know what it is like to be stuck in a traffic jam. At such times you wonder, *What is the problem? Why aren't things moving on?* Yet there is a reason, even when you cannot see what it is. If you have found yourself stuck in grief, making no progress day after day or month after month, there's a reason for the gridlock.

Think back to the healing suggestions that have been discussed the previous few days. Have you acted on any of these suggestions? These ideas will help you make forward progress:

1. Write out your memories.

2. Address unresolved issues.

3. Acknowledge hidden grief.

4. Release your emotions.

5. Look for the exceptions to your sorrow.

6. Make a conscious decision each day to move forward.

On your journey through grief you will experience some delays and detours, but it is important that you do not get stuck at any partial level of healing.

"I have considered my ways and have turned my steps to your statutes. I will hasten and not delay to obey your commands" (Psalm 119:59–60).

God, through my pain, I turn to You, and I will move forward. Amen.

The Time Must Come

A person in the grieving process should never be rushed by others. You need to fully process your feelings and emotions, and you should not feel guilty about taking the time to do that. However, in order to proceed with healing, there will come a time when you have to say, "Enough. It is time to move on."

Your sinful nature will resist this movement because it always wants the path of least resistance. It is easier to give in to self-pity or other negative emotions than to get involved in activities where you have to deal with other people. But moving back into life is God's plan for you, and His Spirit will help you do this.

"For the sinful nature desires what is contrary to the Spirit, and the Spirit what is contrary to the sinful nature. They are in conflict with each other, so that you do not do what you want" (Galatians 5:17).

Holy Spirit, I've had enough. It is time to move on. Lead me forward in strength so that I will not give in to my weakened emotional state. Amen.

Resuming Life

When a loved one dies, the week of the funeral is usually very busy. It is filled with details and obligations and visits from friends. But in the weeks and months that follow, if you are honest, you may be surprised to see those around you resuming their normal, everyday lives. You may feel, "How could they?"

Yet you know this is natural. Life does go on, but you may wonder how you will ever be part of that life again. You cannot merely "turn off" your grief; you will carry a part of that grief with you always. But as you walk through your grief journey, you must take conscious steps forward each day.

Jodie, whose husband died, says, "I got tired of getting up the next morning with puffy eyes and all of that, and I thought, *You know, there's got to be an end to this.* But all I could do was just keep asking the Lord, 'Lord, please just help me get over this. Please just get me to a point where I can handle it.'

"Slowly I got better. But every once in a while the feelings will come, and I just know that the Lord collects those tears, and they're special to Him. Just cry out to the Lord because He's the healer."

Let the Scriptures motivate you to press on forward.

"I press on toward the goal to win the prize for which God has called me heavenward in Christ Jesus. All of us who are mature should take such a view of things. And if on some point you think differently, that too God will make clear to you. Only let us live up to what we have already attained" (Philippians 3:14–16).

Lord Jesus, guide me in Your Word and show me what You want me to do today. Empower me with Your Spirit to live. Amen.

Experiencing Closure

For some people, closure occurs over a long period of time. For others, it occurs at specific moments. Closure can come through the words or comfort of another person, an important memory, a letter, a graveside visit, a Scripture, a new understanding, financial help, or a service to another. God will provide a healing closure for you, and He will bless you in that closure. Pray for closure and look for it.

God blessed this widow with financial provision and by enabling her to keep her sons at home when she feared she could not.

> "My husband is dead, and you know that he revered the LORD. But now his creditor is coming to take my two boys as his slaves." Elisha replied to her, "How can I help you? Tell me, what do you have in your house?" "Your servant has nothing there at all," she said, "except a little oil." Elisha said, "Go around and ask all your neighbors for empty jars. Don't ask for just a few. Then go inside and shut the door behind you and your sons. Pour oil into all the jars, and as each is filled, put it to one side."
>
> She left him and afterward shut the door behind her and her sons. They brought the jars to her and she kept pouring. When all the jars were full, she said to her son, "Bring me another one." But he replied, "There is not a jar left." Then the oil stopped flowing. (2 Kings 4:1–6)

This financial provision was enough to pay off all her debts and to bring an end to the economic crisis her husband's death introduced.

God will help you to find closure for the many struggles you face in grief. Remember, though, that God provides for each person in different ways. He will meet your needs in His time and by His perfect plan.

Holy Spirit, bring me to the point of closure and peace so that I can think of my loved one with a smile on my face and reassurance in my heart. Amen.

Steps Toward Closure

Closure is crucial to your grief journey, and at some point you must take action to help bring it about. Start by identifying the person, memories, objects, and emotions you have been hanging on to too tightly. Here are suggestions to help you come to a place where you can release these. One idea is to make a scrapbook of memories. Another idea is to do volunteer work in memory of your loved one. You could also give some of your loved one's possessions to a needy family.

Virgil found a way to release his feelings after his wife died: "She died in April, and on Mother's Day the kids wanted to take flowers and go to her grave and just express how they felt. So we sat around the grave site and shared our feelings."

Releasing is not forgetting; it is the act of setting free. Your loved one was such a blessing to you. Cherish the memories, but pass the blessing on to someone else now.

"Freely you have received, freely give" (Matthew 10:8).

Lord, I am ready to experience this freedom. All that I have been hanging on to, I release in Your name. Show me where to go from here. Amen.

Letting Go

To move on means (1) you have to acknowledge that things will never be the same again, and (2) you have to desire God's plan for your life now. Letting go of a lost loved one is tough, especially when the love is deep, and he or she has filled a need in you that was never filled until you met that person.

"To really admit to yourself, 'This person is gone, and life's got to go on, and I've got to buck up and turn the corner and get going,' is probably one of the toughest transitions in the grief process," says Dr. Joseph Stowell.

Your plan for life was suddenly changed. But God has a purpose for you, and you were created to fulfill that purpose. That is why you are here on earth right now. Find God's plan for your life and seek fulfillment from Him.

"The LORD will fulfill his purpose for me; your love, O LORD, endures forever—do not abandon the works of your hands" (Psalm 138:8).

"But I have raised you up for this very purpose, that I might show you my power and that my name might be proclaimed in all the earth" (Exodus 9:16).

> *Lord God, things will never be the same again, and I will never be able to go back to the way things were. I admit this, Lord, and I will move forward with a purpose, seeking to fulfill Your plan for my life. What do You have for me to do? Amen.*

Look Beyond the Past

It would be dangerous to drive down the street if your attention were focused solely on the rearview mirror, looking at what is behind. Grief tends to make you look to the past, to what you lost. The pain of that loss, it's true, will be with you forever, but to move on, you must focus on the future as well as on the past.

"You can either stay in that grief, or you can move on. But you will move on with the grief," says Linda, whose baby was stillborn. "You always have that, and you can't expect that one day you won't ever feel sorry that you lost a loved one. That will always be part of you."

Use your past to build on your future. Seek the God of the past, the present, and the future for a hope that will sustain you.

"I am the Alpha and the Omega, the First and the Last, the Beginning and the End" (Revelation 22:13).

Lord God, You are my only hope. I do not want to forget the past, but I cannot live there either. Amen.

Keep the Past in Perspective

Be careful not to let your past control your future.

"My first wife is a memory," says Virgil. "She'll always be a memory. She'll always be there. But I can't let her control my life."

Your loved one will always hold a special place in your heart, but daily decisions cannot be made based on emotions tied up in this person's death. Decisions today should be relative to the present and to the future. Your hope lies before you and not behind you.

"There is surely a future hope for you, and your hope will not be cut off" (Proverbs 23:18). This hope is available for those who have placed their trust in Jesus Christ.

Dear Jesus, my past is so precious to me, but I know that I must live in the present and look forward to the future. Amen.

Live Responsibly

"I've seen individuals who are still living in a state of memorial, a state of going back and rehearsing and feeling bad about what has happened and really verging on cursing God and walking away from Him," says Dr. Norman Peart.

"Come to God honestly and accept the fact that this has happened. It is a big step when one can say, 'This is now life, and I must live it responsibly. I must begin to take steps in life and establish counselors, activities, and responsibilities that push me back into the world.'"

In what areas of your life are you not living responsibly?

Think of a specific step you can take today that will enable you to become more active in life. Depending on where you are in your grief, it may be a phone call to a family member or friend. It may involve signing up for a class, sports team, or club. Perhaps volunteer work is for you. Get out and see people. Build relationships.

"The wise look ahead to see what is coming, but fools deceive themselves" (Proverbs 14:8 NLT).

Holy God, I cannot change what has happened, but it is my responsibility to make wise choices in the situation I am in now and to move forward in love. Amen.

Receive God's Help

Even though you may not understand why you feel stuck in grief, the Lord understands everything about you. He still works miracles. Tell Him what your needs are. Confess your failures, and receive help from Him.

"Because God created you in His image, you are of great worth to Him," said Dr. Bill Bright. "He can lift your load instantly if you let Him. Cast all your cares on the Lord. He is not only a God of power and wisdom, He's a God of love. His love matches His creative power, so you can trust Him with everything."

God will help you. He knows you better than anyone; He knows what goes on inside your heart and mind. Trust in Him to help you break free from the chains that bind you.

"Cast your cares on the LORD and he will sustain you; he will never let the righteous fall" (Psalm 55:22).

Lord, I cannot understand why You care so much for me, but today I give you my emotions, actions, reactions, and attitudes. I take these burdens off my own back and place them in Your arms. Transform my life, Jesus. Amen.

Honesty with God

Yes, God already knows your every thought, emotion, and struggle, but He wants you to come to Him and admit your struggles and give Him your burdens. Let this be a daily action.

God is greater than everything you currently face and anything you will ever go through.

"You need to be honest," says Dr. Norman Peart. "You need to come and let the Lord know what's already there. You may often try to be 'religious' or 'Christian'—and come with a facade. In reality you're doing yourself a great disservice because He wants to reach that deepest point in your life, and it only comes when you open your life and show Him what He already knows. Just let it come, let it flow. He can deal with it."

God desires your sincere heart. What a comfort to know that you do not have to pretend with God.

"In Christ we speak before God with sincerity, like men sent from God" (2 Corinthians 2:17).

Lord of all, I want to be honest with You—no more pretending, no more holding it all in. Amen.

Two Healthy Responses

Pastor Buck Buchanan describes two healthy responses that people can have during the grieving process. The first is to be honest about the depth of the pain, but to choose not to be resentful. He says, "My mom was that way after my dad died. She said, 'I'm not going to feel sorry for myself.'"

Another healthy response is to use the pain to help others. Pastor Buchanan continues, "Take the hurt, embrace the pain, and then realize that it is probably the tool and the gift God has given you to use now. Then begin to minister to other people and share their experiences."

Notice that both responses involve admitting and accepting your pain and choosing to move forward.

"Draw near to God and He will draw near to you. Cleanse your hands, you sinners; and purify your hearts, you double-minded" (James 4:8 NASB).

Lord God, I choose to move forward. I will draw near to You in the midst of my pain. Show me how to respond to the pain in a way that is healthy and that honors You. Amen.

Confess Self-Preoccupation

We need to be straightforward at this point. Some of you are stuck in grief because you have allowed your loss to become the central focus of your life, dominating your existence. Your loss has become larger than all other relationships, larger than your purpose for existence, larger than God.

But how does one get unstuck? What does one do with the loneliness and suffering?

Elisabeth Elliot says, "He gets down on his knees, lifts up his hands in the presence of the Lord, and says, 'Lord here is this self-pity. I confess it as a sin. This self-isolation, I confess it as a sin.' And the blood of Jesus Christ cleanses you from all sin, and He can deliver you. He wants to deliver you from all self-preoccupation."

You must recognize that your self-preoccupation is a sin and you need to be freed from it. When you admit this to God and seek His forgiveness and help, He will clean your heart and free you from this entrapment.

"How much more, then, will the blood of Christ, who through the eternal Spirit offered himself unblemished to God, cleanse our consciences from acts that lead to death, so that we may serve the living God!" (Hebrews 9:14).

Living God, I want to serve You, not myself. I am only making things worse by focusing on my loss, which, in reality, is focusing on myself. I confess my self-preoccupation, and I ask that You forgive me and deliver me from my sinful habits. Amen.

Responses That Cause People to Be Stuck in Grief

Are you struggling with any of the following responses?

- acting as if the loss is not affecting you
- pretending you are still in control
- giving in to despair as your normal attitude
- allowing bitterness or self-pity to control you
- refusing to let the departed go
- holding on to your anger against God
- not talking about the aspects of your loss
- "medicating" your pain with drugs, alcohol, busyness, etc.

Any of the above responses can cause you to be stuck in grief. Tackle each area one by one. For instance, if you are outwardly acting as if your loss is not affecting you, make a point today to let someone know just how much you are affected deep down. Sharing honestly is one sure step to moving on in grief.

Alone, it would be impossible to work through the above issues and succeed. With God, all things are possible. This next Bible verse says that God is able to do far more than what you can even imagine!

"Now to him who is able to do immeasurably more than all we ask or imagine, according to his power that is at work within us, to him be glory in the church and in Christ Jesus throughout all generations, for ever and ever! Amen" (Ephesians 3:20–21).

Glory to You, Lord. You answer my seemingly impossible prayers.
Help me as I face the struggles that are pulling me down. Amen.

Seek Help

"Listen to counsel and accept discipline, that you may be wise the rest of your days" (Proverbs 19:20 NASB).

What can you do if you are still stuck in grief?

Dr. H. Norman Wright says, "Tell somebody about it. Tell somebody who knows what to do, 'I'm feeling stuck. I don't know where to go.' Because somebody else can give you the resources or direct you to appropriate help."

Seek the advice of a mature Christian friend, a pastor, or a counselor to find resources that will be helpful for you.

Wise Father, lead me to a person who can help me find my way forward along this grief journey. Give me wisdom as to whom I should speak and the strength to follow through. Amen.

Do Not Try to Do It Alone

One of the benefits of being a part of a church is that you do not have to move through this process alone. There are friends and companions to go on the journey with you.

Gretchen says, after her husband's death, "When I got in a Bible study, that just really opened up my whole life. That is what has really made me a different person. I met new friends there, and one of them is my praying friend. We just call up each other and cry on each other's shoulders and pray for each other and open our hearts to each other. Things like that are really what keep me going."

Get involved with a local Bible study or church group. You do not need to be alone.

"Every day they [the believers] continued to meet together in the temple courts. They broke bread in their homes and ate together with glad and sincere hearts" (Acts 2:46).

Father, with You I am never alone, but I need the companionship of friends who will carry a portion of my grief as they listen to, laugh with, and cry with me. Amen.

Help Others Stuck in Grief

You may feel so weak and needy that it seems impossible you would have anything to give. But there are people around you who need your help. Don't withhold that word of encouragement, that phone call, that friendly note. There is a place for your ministry too.

"Everyone is wounded," says Rev. Noel Castellanos, "and one of the incredible things about the Christian life is that God can take wounded people and turn them into givers and ministers in spite of the woundedness.

"I think one of the tragedies I've seen is when people focus so much on their own hurt that they can never look outside of themselves to see how they can use their hurt to minister to somebody else."

Think of someone today who could use an encouraging word. Call or send a card to that person.

"He will be an instrument for noble purposes, made holy, useful to the Master and prepared to do any good work" (2 Timothy 2:21).

Great God, may I think of others first and stop focusing on myself. Amen.

Self-Pity

"A Christian needs to take himself by the scruff of the neck and begin thinking as God thinks and cut out the self-pity," says Elisabeth Elliot.

Self-pity is a dangerous emotion that can slither in and block all your forward progression toward healing.

"That is a dead-end street that you are choosing for yourself," continues Elliot. "If you decide that the whole world needs to feel sorry for you, and you need to be surrounded and hovered over and propped up, that is certainly what you would call self-isolation.

"It doesn't have to be. If you offer yourself to Jesus Christ as an instrument of peace, He is very likely to make you an instrument of peace to someone else."

How can you use your hurt to minister to somebody else?

"Do nothing from selfishness or empty conceit, but with humility of mind regard one another as more important than yourselves; do not merely look out for your own personal interests, but also for the interests of others" (Philippians 2:3–4 NASB).

Lord, I've been self-absorbed, and I want to change. May I see others in a new light today, looking for ways I can meet their needs or share in their concerns. Amen.

Helping Others Helps You

Nancy, whose husband died, says, "It's a slow process of actually getting back into the swing. It will never be the same as it was before, and you have got to accept that.

"But there are so many things that the Lord opens up to the person who is open to receive it that the sadness will go into the background a little bit. When you help others, you forget about yourself."

What can you do to help another person today? Brainstorm some ideas on a piece of paper. Here are some suggestions: baking, watching children, doing minor home repairs, visiting a local rest home, helping at an animal shelter, preparing a meal for a sick or busy mother, or helping teachers and students at a local school. Who could use your helping hand?

God has blessed you with a particular gift. It may not be any of those listed above, but be assured that you do have a gift that is meant to be used to help others.

"Each one should use whatever gift he has received to serve others, faithfully administering God's grace in its various forms" (1 Peter 4:10).

Holy God, make it clear to me what my special gift is. Show me how I can use this gift to help another person. Amen.

The Benefits of Moving On

Although moving on involves making some hard decisions, there are great rewards to the person who dares to make those decisions.

"I never thought I would ever be normal again. But the pain eased eventually, and I got back into my life," says Nancy, who lost her husband.

Dare to move on.

"Therefore, since we are surrounded by such a great cloud of witnesses, let us throw off everything that hinders and the sin that so easily entangles, and let us run with perseverance the race marked out for us" (Hebrews 12:1).

Righteous God, I will run this race with Your help. Amen.

What It Means to Move On

Moving on *does not* mean . . .

- you forget the person.
- you never feel the pain of your loss.
- you believe that life is fair.

Moving on *does* mean . . .

- you experience a lessening of the pain.
- you can treasure your best memories of the person who has died.
- you can realistically accept the different aspects of your loss.
- you can form new relationships, try new things.

Moving on also means . . .

- you grow in grace and in your walk with God.
- you accept your loss and forgive others.
- you understand that both joy and loss are a part of life.
- you believe that God is good, even when life isn't.

"I have told you this so that my joy may be in you and that your joy may be complete" (John 15:11).

Holy God, sometimes moving on seems impossible. Continue to remind me that I cannot move on through my own strength, but only through an extension of Yours. Amen.

Feeling Guilty About Being Happy

Guilt is subtle and insidious.

Guilt whispers that you should continually grieve and that it would be wrong for you to enjoy life even just a little. It will perch on your shoulder and chant, "You should feel good about feeling bad. This is your life. This is your lot." The reality, however, is that you should enjoy life more fully because you have grieved.

"Finally the day does come when you do begin to feel better," says Dr. Ray Pritchard. "That is the grace of God. Then you begin to feel guilty. That is normal too. Don't give in to that feeling of guilt."

Thank God for His saving grace. Then immerse yourself in God's Word and use it to strike down guilt when it starts whispering in your ear.

"For the word of God is living and active. Sharper than any double-edged sword, it penetrates even to dividing soul and spirit, joints and marrow; it judges the thoughts and attitudes of the heart" (Hebrews 4:12).

Lord Jesus, sometimes I feel like I'm betraying my loved one because I'm starting to feel better. Help me to truly understand how wrong these thoughts are, and help me to stand firm in the power of Your Word. Amen.

Giving Thanks

"In everything give thanks; for this is God's will for you in Christ Jesus" (1 Thessalonians 5:18 NASB).

This Bible verse is sometimes misconstrued. It doesn't say to give thanks *for* all situations, but *in* all situations—big difference.

When you seek God in prayer and through His Word, you learn about His attributes, and you come to know His complete love and faithfulness and rise above the situation as you see it. Here is where you are truly thankful.

According to Dr. Bill Bright, "His ways are so far beyond your ways, you can't even comprehend; therefore, when problems arise you can say, 'God loves me. Nothing happens to me that is not filtered through His love; therefore, by faith on the authority of God's Word and what I know about God, I can say all things that happen to me are for my good and for God's glory.' God makes no mistakes. God honors your expression of faith when you say 'thank you' through your tears with broken hearts. When you trust Him, He turns tragedy to triumph. That is where you learn."

Lord, thank you for Your faithfulness to me and Your patience with me. Thank you that You are in control. Amen.

He Gives Himself

Healing is not about doing better or being stronger or going to church more. It is about experiencing a love that will never let you go.

Joni Eareckson Tada says, "Your deepest need when you are hurting is to have God, like a daddy, reach down and pick you up and hold you and reassure you that everything is going to be okay. He lets you know that your life is not in nightmarish chaos, your world is not splitting apart at the seams. Somehow and somewhere there is order and stability to it all. And that's why God never gives advice; He gives Himself."

Let go of the shreds of your life you have been hanging on to and embrace God.

"A father to the fatherless, a defender of widows, is God in his holy dwelling" (Psalm 68:5).

"You hear, O LORD, the desire of the afflicted; you encourage them, and you listen to their cry, defending the fatherless and the oppressed, in order that man, who is of the earth, may terrify no more" (Psalm 10:17–18).

Heavenly Father, hold me in Your arms and comfort me. Reassure me that everything is going to be okay. Amen.

Surrender to the Suffering

"Sometimes when you're hurting and you're suffering, all you think about is getting out of it," says Anne Graham Lotz. "Your prayers are all geared to 'Lord, deliver me. Get me out of this.'"

Stop fighting the suffering, and submit to God's will for it. God has a purpose for you right now, based on all that you have experienced up to this moment. Wait patiently on God, and continually seek His will for you.

"For I consider that the sufferings of this present time are not worthy to be compared with the glory that is to be revealed to us" (Romans 8:18 NASB).

Lord, I surrender to the suffering. What do You want me to do? I give the glory to You. Amen.

Self-Sufficiency

When life is comfortable, you lose that awe, that fear of God, putting Him in a compartment that is convenient for you. When things are going well, you might put God on the back burner because you don't exactly need Him at that time.

"Self-sufficiency is a terrible place to be," says Dr. Joseph Stowell, "because it is the worst deceit you can bring on yourself. You need God. You need God every minute of your life. I believe God knows that, and He desires fellowship and dependency from you, radical dependency in terms of your relationship with Him."

Each person needs to be taken to a place where God alone is sufficient. Suffering takes you to that place. And suffering does not happen to some people and not to others; it is a crucial part of every person's life.

"Consider what God has done: Who can straighten what he has made crooked? When times are good, be happy; but when times are bad, consider: God has made the one as well as the other" (Ecclesiastes 7:13–14).

God, I need You. Please heal me. Amen.

Adversity Unlocks the Doors

A Christian's troubles advance God's purposes, purposes only He can fully understand. As a human, you try so hard to understand. But if God could be fully understood, where's the power and sovereignty in that? What would make Him any different than just another smart human? He is above all; His ways are so perfect that a mere human could not possibly understand on this side of heaven. This is why you can place your absolute trust and your life in Him, despite the pain and the heartache.

Because He is the God above all, when you get to heaven and see the world from His point of view, you will be astounded by the perfection of His loving plan.

Dr. Richard Bewes says, "The world outside doesn't understand that. The world outside tends to see adversity as a dead end. We don't, not in the Christian church. Christians see it as a gateway to progress, to advancement with the knowledge of God, to the very kingdom of God itself."

Reach through the pain to grasp hold of the knowledge of God.

"So that no one would be disturbed by these afflictions; for you yourselves know that we have been destined for this" (1 Thessalonians 3:3 NASB).

"Through many tribulations we must enter the kingdom of God" (Acts 14:22 NASB).

God, I reach past the oppression of this world and cling to You. You are the almighty sovereign Lord. Amen.

growing through grief

Greater Compassion for Others

It is amazing how grief enables people to relate to one another at a deeper level than before. Until you've experienced grief, you cannot empathize with someone else who is going through it. During your healing process, you may find yourself becoming more sensitive to the hurts and needs of others.

"Sometimes I can't even recognize the person I was before," says Dora, who lost a child. "I think that my ability to empathize or have compassion has been strengthened. I'm not so quick to place judgment on a situation or on a person. What may appear on the outside to be one way, may be a completely different story on the inside."

You know what grief feels like. You know what it's like to disguise your feelings as you go about your daily tasks, keeping a stoic face as you relate to people at work, in the community, or at church.

Use your experience and knowledge of grief to help others. You are the one who realizes that everyone has deep fears and griefs of their own. What act of kindness or compassion will best help those you come in contact with today?

God asks you to follow Jesus' example of kindness, compassion, and forgiveness. Follow His example daily.

"Be kind and compassionate to one another, forgiving each other, just as in Christ God forgave you" (Ephesians 4:32).

Lord God, let me not make assumptions about the people I meet today; instead, guide me to pass along Your kindness, compassion, and forgiveness. Amen.

What Really Matters?

Grief has a way of shaping you and turning your attention away from the busyness of life to what really matters. People in today's fast-paced culture do not stop long enough to contemplate the significant questions of life.

What is important in life?

Look at the big picture. Your life on earth encompasses a short time frame when compared to eternal life. You are an eternal being. You are made to live forever. Keep this in perspective.

So the question best asked is: *What is important in this life that will extend into eternity?*

Dr. Joseph Stowell emphasizes the importance of living today in light of the world to come: "When you really embrace the world to come and bring it back into the world of your own life, everything is radically rearranged. One of the things that is rearranged is your values. For instance, this world tends to value self, tends to value things, and tends to value accomplishment and personal success.

"When you're really committed to the world to come and understand the depth and importance of it, you begin to value other things— like people. People are the only things going on to eternity. So I tend to value my children differently; I tend to value my neighbors differently; I tend to see the people I work with differently. I see them in light of their own eternal destiny."

Do not be uninformed about life's significance.

"It is better to go to a house of mourning than to go to a house of feasting, for death is the destiny of every man; the living should take this to heart" (Ecclesiastes 7:2).

Living God, teach me to open my heart and embrace the knowledge that life after death is an important reality that must be acknowledged in my daily life. Help me to live my life in light of eternity. Amen.

God Uses Low Places

There are some lessons in life that you only learn through times of grief or suffering. This is why it is important that you do not waste your sorrows. Times of suffering show you your limitations and how needy you really are.

Dr. Larry Crabb shares his initial reaction to the news of his brother's death: "I came outside and I remember my wife was waiting for me out in the car, and as I came out, I just stood there and said, 'Bill's dead.' It was a very, very strong moment. But as I recall that moment, I think my first internal deep reaction was not despair. I think my first reaction at that moment was *I must find God as I have never found Him before or I'm not going to make it.*"

People are needy. The world wants you to be tough, strong, and independent. God wants you to lean on Him. God's way is right and wise. Depend on Him as you have never done before, and you will find true peace and power that can never be achieved on your own.

"'Do not be afraid, O man highly esteemed,' he said. 'Peace! Be strong now; be strong.' When he spoke to me, I was strengthened and said, 'Speak, my lord, since you have given me strength'" (Daniel 10:19).

"Then he continued, 'Do not be afraid, Daniel. Since the first day that you set your mind to gain understanding and to humble yourself before your God, your words were heard, and I have come in response to them'" (Daniel 10:12).

> *Holy God, I come humbly before You. I seek strength, understanding, and true knowledge of You. Show Yourself to me, O Lord. Amen.*

Open to Change

Grief places you in a vulnerable position where change is daily and inevitable. Change can be threatening, and it is your nature to resist it. But your greatest opportunity for change can happen during times that are emotionally intense, and the death of a friend or loved one can open you up to new depths of spiritual experience.

Heidi, a widow, says, "People would say to me, 'Heidi, I just wish I had some of your strength.' And one of the things that I would say to them was, 'If you would have gone through the situations in your life like I have, then you would have the strength that I have.' I've experienced a lot of things in my walk with God that have strengthened me. I think because I know who God is and I know His faithfulness in my life, I was able to say that this is not going to knock me down. This is a hard thing, but I have to trust in God."

You have the opportunity to experience unparalleled spiritual growth.

"You will seek Me and find Me when you search for Me with all your heart" (Jeremiah 29:13 NASB).

Lord, I want to be a willing student of You and Your Word. Show me how. Amen.

Set Apart Through Grief

Many people become wiser, more humane, more compassionate, more fully human after experiencing grief. In this way, grief sets you apart. People who have gone through it are different.

"It will change you," says Sylvia, whose parents died. "You will do a 180-degree turn. When you go to a funeral, you will know what those people are going through; you'll know what you can do to help them.

"Before that, I would go to the line, shake hands and say, 'I'm sorry.' And I didn't understand. But after you've lost a loved one, you have a totally different concept of what they're going through. I think you can be a better minister, and I think God gives you some of these things to use in your own personal ministry. So it will change you."

Change is difficult, and all people experience change throughout their lives. God, though, remains the same—a solid refuge and fortress.

"I the LORD do not change" (Malachi 3:6).

"Jesus Christ is the same yesterday and today and forever" (Hebrews 13:8).

Sovereign God, You never change. I can put my anchor in You and know I will remain secure. Lord, I want You to be the foundation of my life so that I will make it through life's difficult times. Amen.

Certain of Eternity

You have heard the cliché "Life is short," but the words do not impact you until you experience the death of a loved one.

"My mom was fifty-six years old when she was diagnosed with colon cancer," says Dr. Robert Jeffress. "The doctor said, 'You have four months to live.' Because she was a noted personality in Dallas, Texas, several TV stations came out to interview her before her death. They said to her, 'Mrs. Jeffress, how does it feel to know that your case is terminal, that you are going to die?'

"This is what my mom said on that interview: 'We're all terminal. The only difference is some of us realize it and some of us don't.'"

You understand the hard truth of that so-called cliché. What will you do with this knowledge? Yes, life on earth is short, but life beyond the grave lasts forever. Be certain of your own eternal destination.

"He who believes in the Son [Jesus] has eternal life; but he who does not obey the Son will not see life, but the wrath of God abides on him" (John 3:36 NASB).

Lord Jesus, You are my Lord and Savior. Forgive me for my sins and failures. I yield control of my life to You. Teach me how to live for You. Amen.

Make Life Count

Grief reminds you that you only have one life to live, and you need to make it count.

"There are some things in life that we put too much emphasis on that really aren't important at all. Family is so important, and too often we take everybody for granted," says Heidi, whose husband passed away.

"With the Lord we too often put Him down a bit on our priority list because 'I have to be these things . . . I have to accumulate this . . . I have to get this . . . I have to work through this problem.' So often we leave Him out."

What does it mean to truly live? According to the Bible: "To live is Christ and to die is gain" (Philippians 1:21).

Embrace this truth in order to live a life that really counts.

Pray this prayer of Heidi's:

"God, I can't leave You out because You're the main source of my life, and without You I am nothing. Amen."

Continue Learning

"I learned lessons that I keep learning over and over," says Janet Paschal, whose grandfather passed away.

Some of life's lessons need to be learned several times, not just once. But each time, you will learn them in a deeper way.

Dr. David Olford states, "That's God's purpose of allowing a lot of things to come into your life—to shape you and to mold you and to purify you. At the same time, there's not only a purpose of God; there's His power to enable you to go through and to shield you and to guard you and to keep you."

Take a moment to consider what lessons you have learned as a result of your grief experience. These are lessons for your good, not lessons about what you should not have done. What good have you learned?

"I applied my heart to what I observed and learned a lesson from what I saw" (Proverbs 24:32).

Holy God, I pray that something good can come out of this situation in my life. Help me to see this, and please take down any barriers that block my view. Amen.

Life's Lessons

One important part of healthy grieving is to learn life's lessons through your loss. Webster's Dictionary defines *learn* as "to get knowledge of or skill in by study, experience, etc."

You have certainly had an experience; now step back and study it for a moment.

What have you come to understand about yourself and others? What knowledge have you gained? Some examples might be compassion, kindness, sympathy, or mercy. Practical applications might include knowing how to provide assistance to others in grief or knowing what to say and what not to say to them.

Dr. Robert Abarno says, "It puts you in a qualified position to relate to the person who is suffering. It's not as though you are telling someone something that you've not experienced. It's a great opportunity."

Now that you have the qualifications, you can effectively help others. Remember, this step is part of your grieving process.

"Grace and peace to you from God our Father and the Lord Jesus Christ. Praise be to the God and Father of our Lord Jesus Christ, the Father of compassion and the God of all comfort, who comforts us in all our troubles, so that we can comfort those in any trouble with the comfort we ourselves have received from God" (2 Corinthians 1:2–4).

Lord Jesus, reveal to me what I have learned through this experience and give me an opportunity to use it. Amen.

Principles for Living

The Bible says there are powerful principles for living that can be learned through grief and loss.

"I know what it is to be in need, and I know what it is to have plenty. I have learned the secret of being content in any and every situation . . ." (Philippians 4:12).

Unfailing strength is found in a relationship with Jesus Christ.

> That is why we never give up. Though our bodies are dying, our spirits are being renewed every day. For our present troubles are quite small and won't last very long. Yet they produce for us an immeasurably great glory that will last forever! So we don't look at the troubles we can see right now; rather, we look forward to what we have not yet seen. For the troubles we see will soon be over, but the joys to come will last forever. (2 Corinthians 4:16–18 NLT)

Sharpen your focus on the things in life that have lasting value, and contemplate your eternal life, being certain about where you will spend it.

Saving Jesus, my strength, my hope, and my joy are rooted in You. I want to live with You forever in heaven. Amen.

Catalyst for Personal Growth

"When you are down in the valley, that is where you are going to grow because that is where the fertilizer is," says Barbara Johnson. "That's where you have to seek out God's help."

In what ways have you grown as a result of your experience? Perhaps your compassion has been strengthened. Maybe you are slower to place judgment on other people who are going through trials. You might be more willing to approach people who seem down or troubled. Decide how you can be a better person today as a result of your time "in the valley."

"He will be like a tree planted by the water that sends out its roots by the stream. It does not fear when heat comes; its leaves are always green. It has no worries in a year of drought and never fails to bear fruit" (Jeremiah 17:8).

Holy God, I will plant myself near You and trust You to bring out the good in me. Amen.

Hearts of Compassion

Jeffrey and Wendy's infant son died. They share how this tragic experience has given them hearts of compassion for other people in grief:

Wendy says, "I can have much more compassion for others because I know how hard it was. I know that sick feeling in the pit of your heart that you think is never going to go away. I had that same feeling for so long."

Jeffrey shares, "It's made me have a lot more compassion for others because now I can look at them and the emotions come back. I know that some people want to be left alone in grief and some people want to talk in grief, and the Lord has just given me a heart to be able to distinguish between the two."

You may be in a situation in which you feel you have not received any compassion for yourself and almost begrudge the thought of trying to help others. God has compassion for you, and He never withholds it. He loves you deeply.

"Yet the LORD longs to be gracious to you; he rises to show you compassion. For the LORD is a God of justice. Blessed are all who wait for him!" (Isaiah 30:18).

"'Though the mountains be shaken and the hills be removed, yet my unfailing love for you will not be shaken nor my covenant of peace be removed,' says the LORD, who has compassion on you" (Isaiah 54:10).

Lord God, Your unfailing love and compassion for me are amazing. Even when I rail against You, You love me just as much. Show me how to have Your compassion for others. Amen.

Family Becomes More Important

Sometimes your newly awakened compassion finds expression in your own family. Often it takes a death to bring a family closer together and to remind each one how important family relationships are.

"It's an awareness that I've got to make the most of my time; it might be my last moment. I have a sense of appreciation for that, a kind of cutting-edge understanding of the preciousness of the moment," says Bruce Marchiano.

Perhaps your family has splits and contentions. Now is the time to take the needed steps to settle differences and mend hearts. With the enabling power of the Holy Spirit behind you, your family's healing can start with you. Pray about this.

"Jesus . . . said, 'Go home to your family and tell them how much the Lord has done for you, and how he has had mercy on you'" (Mark 5:19).

Healing Father, my family is precious and unique. Any rifts between us can be healed, but only by Your power. Give me the words to say to bring my family close together. Amen.

Growing Spiritually

"The death of my parents was a wake-up call of my own spiritual life," admits Dr. Robert Jeffress. "I had wandered away from the Lord and nobody knew it; I was a pastor, a staff member of the church. But in my heart I had wandered away from the Lord. God used that experience as a wake-up call for me.

"I think the process of losing loved ones can be a healthy experience if you allow God to use you and mold that experience in your life to strengthen your relationship with Him."

One of the most vital changes that grieving can produce in you is spiritual growth. It is possible to grow more in a year of grieving than in several years of life with few difficulties or problems.

One extremely effective way to pray is to use words from the Bible. Make Colossians 1:9–12 a personal prayer by replacing the pronouns with "I" and "me" as you pray:

> *"[I] have not stopped praying . . . and asking God to fill [me] with the knowledge of His will through all spiritual wisdom and understanding. And [I] pray this in order that [I] may live a life worthy of the Lord and may please Him in every way: bearing fruit in every good work, growing in the knowledge of God, being strengthened with all power according to His glorious might so that [I] may have great endurance and patience, and joyfully giving thanks to the Father, who has qualified [me] to share in the inheritance of the saints in the kingdom of light. Amen."*

Rejoice in Suffering?

In the Bible the apostle Paul says that you should rejoice in your suffering. This advice sounds incredible, especially when you are in the midst of pain.

"Not only so, but we also rejoice in our sufferings, because we know that suffering produces perseverance; perseverance, character; and character, hope. And hope does not disappoint us, because God has poured out his love into our hearts by the Holy Spirit, whom he has given us" (Romans 5:3–5).

After looking closer at Paul's words, you will realize that he is not saying to be glad about what happened, not at all! He tells you that you are to use your suffering as a time of personal growth in which you ultimately experience an outpouring of God's love into your heart.

Dr. Ray Pritchard says, "Christians who most deeply experience the love of God are those who have not fought against God at the point of their suffering, but they've said, 'Lord, I don't understand. God, this doesn't make any sense. I wish this would go away, but, Lord, I'm going to cooperate with You. I'm going to walk with You through this.'

"Through that, God gives them perseverance; He develops character; character becomes hope, and in the end, their hearts are soft, and then they experience the love of God."

Lord, I'm not happy with this, but I will make the best of it. Pour out Your Spirit on me, and give me perseverance, character, and hope. Lord, I sure need hope. Amen.

The God of Hope

One of the consistent testimonies in Scripture is that faith can grow strong during the darkest times of adversity. It is during those darkest moments that you come to know personally that your Lord is the God of hope.

"One thing about being in grief is that your sorrow is certain, and your loss is so real you literally taste it to the depth of your being," says Dr. Joseph Stowell. "You have to have a certainty that is bigger than the certainty of your sorrow.

"That is why you must train yourself in biblical hope where you are absolutely convinced that God is and that He has a world to come for you and that on the other side everything will be okay. That certainty has to be bigger than the certainty of your sorrows."

Ideally, this biblical training should come *before* times of adversity, so you can be at least somewhat prepared to face it. But if you are not absolutely sure that God is everything He says He is, then tell Him your doubts and confusion. Study the Bible to learn more about Him. We suggest that you begin reading the book of John or Mark.

If you are sure that Christ Jesus is your only secure hope for life, and life after death, then praise His name, and seek to know Him more fully.

"Praise be to the God and Father of our Lord Jesus Christ! In his great mercy he has given us new birth into a living hope through the resurrection of Jesus Christ from the dead, and into an inheritance that can never perish, spoil or fade—kept in heaven for you" (1 Peter 1:3–4).

Jesus, I am certain to the depth of my being that You are the living God and that everything will be okay through You. Amen.

Your Home Is Not Here

Faith not only empowers you to get through your difficulties, but it also assures you of a coming day when tears and sorrows are no more. Faith recognizes that this world is not your ultimate home.

"There's a longing in my soul that requires me to look up, requires me to say, 'This isn't all there is,' because it isn't enough," says Dr. Larry Crabb. "When I am hurting, others come up with the formulas and the procedures to do this and this and this and then I will be fine. My answer is this: I'll never be fine until I'm home."

What does the word *home* typically mean to you? Know that you were created for a different home, a better home, an eternal home with God. This life here is not all there is.

"Now we know that if the earthly tent we live in is destroyed, we have a building from God, an eternal house in heaven, not built by human hands" (2 Corinthians 5:1).

Heavenly Father, may I fix my eyes on You and not get dragged down by the struggles within me and around me. Please give me a taste of what is to come so I can make it through. Amen.

Eternal Perspective

When you begin to see heaven as your true home, you can develop an eternal perspective that sees all sorrows as passing.

"It is possible to trust God in all things," says Dr. Joseph Stowell. "You may have a hard time getting there, but you won't get there unless you believe in the world to come. If this is all you have, if it's just this world, then bitterness is your only option.

"But if you believe that there is a God who is higher than you are and wiser than you are, and He has a world prepared for you where all Christians will be together again and be with Him in absolute joy and bliss, then that brings strength to your sorrow."

Place your trust in God and in His preparations and plans for you.

"Do not let your hearts be troubled. Trust in God; trust also in me. In my Father's house are many rooms; if it were not so, I would have told you. I am going there to prepare a place for you. And if I go and prepare a place for you, I will come back and take you to be with me that you also may be where I am" (John 14:1–3).

Lord and Savior, I trust that You will someday bring me home to live in heaven with You. For now, I need to try and look at my sorrows in light of eternity. The things of this world are much clearer when I have a higher perspective. Amen.

Grow Closer to God

In moments of grief you always have the choice of how you are going to respond. Dr. Ray Pritchard describes Job's response to his intense losses and tragedies: "The Bible says that when he had lost everything, he bowed his face before the Lord, and he worshiped.

"When you face those moments when the entire world has turned against you, you have a choice. You can either turn away from the Lord and walk away from the only hope that you have, or you can fall on your face before the Lord and say, 'Oh God, have mercy. Oh God, I do not understand, but I do believe that You are the eternal God, and I commit my soul to You.'

"If you let your grief lead you back to God, in the end your soul will be purified, and you will come into an experience of God greater, deeper, and closer than you have ever known before."

Job chose to worship God and in the end was blessed abundantly.

"Then Job arose and tore his robe and shaved his head, and he fell to the ground and worshiped. He said, 'Naked I came from my mother's womb, and naked I shall return there. The LORD gave and the LORD has taken away. Blessed be the name of the LORD.' Through all this Job did not sin nor did he blame God" (Job 1:20–22 NASB).

> *God, You are powerful and living and real. Have mercy on me; I do not understand why I am going through this. Bless me, Lord, I want to experience You deeper and closer than ever before. Amen.*

The Road to Heaven

Do you know how to get to heaven?

The Bible clearly states there is only one way to get to heaven: "Jesus answered, 'I am the way and the truth and the life. No one comes to the Father except through me'" (John 14:6).

A person cannot enter heaven through good deeds and moral behavior. You cannot enter heaven by attending church or by having Christian parents: "This [is] not from yourselves, it is the gift of God—not by works, so that no one can boast" (Ephesians 2:8–9).

Eternal life is a free gift from God, but it is only given to those people who believe in and surrender control of their lives to Jesus.

"He who believes in the Son [Jesus] has eternal life" (John 3:36 NASB).

Lord, I want to make sure that I'm going to heaven. And I want to live each day with the knowledge of my eternal destination. Thank you, God. Amen.

Entering Heaven:
The Four Rs

Dr. Richard Bewes uses four Rs to explain how to get to heaven:

1. Recognize who is knocking on the door of your heart. That person is Christ!

2. Repent and acknowledge that you have been wrong. Do a mental U-turn.

3. Reflect on who [Jesus!] is coming into your life. He has died for the forgiveness of your sins. He will be Lord of your life, and this will demand changes.

4. Receive Him, as His Spirit enters your life. It's as simple as saying, "Come in, Lord Jesus."

Come to the Lord with a sincere heart. "The LORD does not look at the things man looks at . . . the LORD looks at the heart" (1 Samuel 16:7).

Lord Jesus, I know that You stand at the door of every person's heart. Come in, please. Forgive me for the wrongs I have done. I want You to be Lord of my life. Amen.

What Next?

"The most exciting thing that ever happened to me—the greatest decision I've made in my life—was to turn over my life to Jesus Christ and have a new life and be told that God has a plan for my life," says Chandra.

If you have surrendered your life to Christ, you are a new creation. You have entered into a new relationship with God through His Son, Jesus Christ. This is the first step on an exciting spiritual journey.

"Therefore, if anyone is in Christ, he is a new creation; the old has gone, the new has come!" (2 Corinthians 5:17).

When your old habits and patterns of thinking try to come back— and they will try—immediately turn them over to God and choose instead to do something pleasing to Him. It is helpful to have a plan in place. Find a Christian friend whom you can call at any hour of the day for encouragement and prayer. Be involved in a regular Bible study and keep up with the study. Help others in the church and community through volunteer work.

Jesus, I am a new creation! The decision to follow You is life changing, and that's what I want and need. Lead me to new activities and relationships that honor You. Amen.

Embracing the Change in Your Life

Grief will either make you a better person or it will cause you to harden your heart as you resist its lessons. You have the opportunity for unparalleled spiritual growth. This will not happen quickly, but you can grow deeply. By learning that life is a precious gift, you can do more than just exist; you can live on a higher plane.

It was when Isaiah's friend died that he had a deeper experience of God.

> In the year that King Uzziah died, I saw the Lord seated on a throne, high and exalted, and the train of his robe filled the temple. Above him were seraphs, each with six wings: With two wings they covered their faces, with two they covered their feet, and with two they were flying. And they were calling to one another: "Holy, holy, holy is the LORD Almighty; the whole earth is full of his glory." (Isaiah 6:1–3)

Lord, I want to live above all the garbage that goes on in my mind. I want to grow spiritually and discover You like never before. Amen.

Learning Through Grief

"Adults generally change through a significant emotional event. What more significant emotional event is there than the loss of a loved one?" says Dr. John Trent.

When logic doesn't seem to apply and being in control is not an option, you are left feeling vulnerable. This is the point at which you are ready to learn. Recognize the need to learn more about God in order to live.

"He learned obedience from what he suffered" (Hebrews 5:8).

Father God, I am ready to listen and learn from You. Help me to be still before You in worshipful silence. Amen.

Learning Helps Bring Healing

"Take every counsel, every word that has come to your heart in the deep place where you are, because it is in that place that you surrender," says Shelly, who lost a son. "It is that place where your will is broken. It is that place where the veil is lifted, and all of a sudden you see what you need to see, and the instruction will come into your heart.

"So embrace it and hold on to it until you can see the image that God wants you to change into while you are in that deep place. Then look forward to the mountaintop again. There was a time when I couldn't have said that, but I can say that now."

Jesus instructs you to learn from Him and follow His teachings: "Take my yoke upon you and learn from me, for I am gentle and humble in heart, and you will find rest for your souls" (Matthew 11:29).

It is through a life dedicated to Jesus Christ that you will find healing for your grieving soul. At the deepest place of despair, God is there. He wants you to look to Him and learn more about Him through Bible study, prayer, church, and through a mature Christian mentor.

Lord Jesus, open my heart to Your instruction. Give me the strength and the will to get deeper into Your Bible and to be committed to a Bible study group. Amen.

grief recovery tool kit

Grief Recovery Tool Kit

During a crisis, it is important to have the proper tools and equipment at your disposal. For the next few weeks, you will be introduced to several "tools" that will help you make it through grief and reconstruct your life. Pick the resources that best suit you.

In the Bible, David made the decision to seek God and rebuild his life after his son died (2 Samuel 12). Dr. Norman Peart comments on David's decision: "David could not waste the rest of his life focusing upon the wrong, the hurt that was there. He instead had to build upon that life because at some point he was going to see the God he was aiming for."

The time has come to rebuild your life.

"They will rebuild the ruined cities and live in them. They will plant vineyards and drink their wine; they will make gardens and eat their fruit" (Amos 9:14).

Lord, what am I aiming for? I think aimless would best describe me sometimes. But I am willing to try these grief tools and rebuild my life one day at a time as I focus on You. Amen.

Keep a Journal

A journal is not written for anyone but you, so you do not need to worry about the grammar, how it looks, or what you write. A journal allows you to express your deepest feelings and, over a period of time, to see the progress of your healing.

"The journal is so useful for me because I can look back and say, I really made it through this," says Dora, whose daughter died.

"I wrote down random thoughts as I was sitting by her bedside: 'She's so weak; it seems she will never progress off the ventilator. I miss her. I really miss her. I miss my girls, my husband, my life. The anger is so great. I woke up this morning at three with a pain in my body, in my heart, a pain I could not turn off, an angry pain, a shouting pain, a pain that would not keep quiet. Lord, help me, please. Help my daughter. Help her to live. I want her to live a normal, happy life. I'm tired. Please, dear God, help my little girl.'"

More than two years after her daughter's death, Dora continued her journal:

> My daughter taught me to love. It's a simple word that has a vast meaning. Love can mean compassion, uncensored and true, living in the moment. Love can be unconditional and unprotected and vulnerable, which is a scary place to be, a place most of us choose not to be. My daughter taught me it is this place of love that holds the meaning of life for us. The reason we're put here is to receive those precious gifts of love from the Lord and to surpass our own boundaries and give love.

"Give ear to my words, O LORD, Consider my groaning" (Psalm 5:1 NASB).

> *Lord, I need to do this. Each day I need to write down whatever comes to my mind, whatever I am thinking about or feeling. I release these thoughts to You. Help me to grow and to love. Amen.*

Share with a Friend

Pray for God to bring you a friend you can talk with about your loss. Let your friend know what you need from him or her. You might prefer writing your friend a letter that expresses your feelings, your needs, and your thankfulness for the friendship.

Sylvia, who lost her parents, had a close friend who helped her through her grief: "He was just a friend I could go to and talk to and know that he understood; that was the main thing, just having somebody to listen to me."

Never underestimate the comforting power of friendship.

"You have comforted me by speaking so kindly to me" (Ruth 2:13 NLT).

Provider God, I pray that I keep up my friendships with those who are true to me, even when I don't feel like making the effort. Amen.

Grief Support Group

We encourage you to join a biblically based grief recovery support group to aid in your healing. It does not matter how long ago your loss occurred; grief support groups are for people at all stages of the grieving process. (Information about *GriefShare*® support groups can be found at the end of this book.)

"It's in the sharing and the group's caring for each other that the healing is accomplished," says Dr. Jim Conway.

Healing is a mending together for the purpose of making something whole again. Your heart, mind, and body can become whole and in excellent working condition again through Jesus. But healing does not mean there will be no scars. It means that you were once broken, but through time and effort you are being made whole again.

"He heals the brokenhearted and binds up their wounds" (Psalm 147:3).

Jesus, it's hard to imagine I will ever be healed. Help me to remember that healing is not forgetting, but it is remembering with love and tenderness and joy. Amen.

Maintain Humor

Barbara Johnson says it is good to keep your sense of humor during this time of grief; in fact, keeping a sense of humor is one of the healthiest things you can do: "Oh, I think that's very important. You see, one laugh equals three spoons of oat bran. And one laugh will burn six calories. And one laugh is like jogging on the inside. I think God intended for us to laugh.

"Job 8:21 says, 'He will fill your mouth with laughter and your lips with shouts of joy.' So laughter is very important. Many people don't have a sense of humor, and they suffer longer and harder than those who can let a little laugh bubble out."

> *Lord of all, bring something humorous in my path today. Teach me to relax inside and let "a little laugh bubble out." Amen.*

Enjoy God's Creation

Open your eyes today to the gift of God's creation. Make a point to look up and notice and savor what you see.

"The heavens declare the glory of God; the skies proclaim the work of his hands. Day after day they pour forth speech; night after night they display knowledge. There is no speech or language where their voice is not heard. Their voice goes out into all the earth, their words to the ends of the world" (Psalm 19:1–4).

The beauty of creation is crying out daily for you to see and to worship the Creator in response. Live life on a different level today—a higher level.

Elisabeth Elliot says, "It's our human nature to fret and stew and try everything in the world to satisfy ourselves, but that is never going to be the answer. I myself have found tremendous comfort and joy in observing God's creation."

Creator God, what treasures and beauties do You have in store for me today? What new wonder is just waiting to be seen? Amen.

Directing Your Thoughts

Memories can be a blessing, but they can also have the opposite effect. When you remember your loved one, what dominates your thoughts—good, wholesome, loving memories? Or things you would rather not remember at all?

"Scripture tells you to direct your focus and attention to those things that are pure, right, and true," says Jim Grassi. "It doesn't say focus your attention, all your anxiety, and all your worry on all the things that are bad."

With God's help, turn your thoughts around. This may be a daily, moment-by-moment battle if negative thinking has been a pattern for you.

"We demolish arguments and every pretension that sets itself up against the knowledge of God, and we take captive every thought to make it obedient to Christ" (2 Corinthians 10:5).

Lord, I am prepared to take my negative thoughts captive and make them obedient to Christ—beginning now! Amen.

Get a Pet

Statistics show that people who have a pet to care for live longer and have fewer health problems. Get a pet. It will become a new area of emotional investment.

"I came home with two schnauzers," says Bruce, whose wife died, "and they have been really good. They've been a lot of work, but I hope that they're learning as much as I am. We're good friends now, and they've helped through the loneliness. They give me something other than pictures and things to talk to. I tell them about my wife."

If you haven't visited a pet store lately, you might be surprised at the variety of animals you can have as pets. Perhaps you aren't a dog or cat person; consider having a rabbit, a lizard, a hamster, or a fish. A pet provides companionship and someone to talk to. (Pets are excellent listeners.) Pick a pet that fits your lifestyle because pets are a responsibility, but are usually worth the effort!

You might also consider visiting your local animal shelter or dog pound. They are always looking for loving homes for their animals.

Pets are not specifically mentioned in the Bible, but it does say, "A righteous man cares for the needs of his animal" (Proverbs 12:10).

You may already have a pet. If not, would you pray the following prayer?

Lord, please help me find an animal to take care of. Amen.

Powerful Prayer

Prayer is powerful. Never underestimate what prayer can accomplish. James 5:16 says that the "prayer of a righteous man is powerful and effective." Come confidently before God with your prayers, knowing that He can answer above and beyond what you ask (Ephesians 3:20–21).

Melissa shares one of the many times God answered her prayers after her husband died: "One evening I came home, and I didn't have any food. I had a little pack of soup in my pantry. That was it. I just prayed to the Lord and I said, 'Well, Lord, You know I'm glad to have this.' But being pregnant, I needed to eat more nutritionally. Also, I had only two maternity dresses, and I had started working and wanted to look nice. I just cried out to Him. He knew exactly what I needed. I was just sitting there praying, and as I was praying, a UPS truck drove up to my house and brought me a package. And in this package were ten brand-new maternity outfits, fifteen pairs of stockings, and cash so I could go to the grocery store."

As a Christian, you are doing yourself a great disservice by not tapping into the power available to you through God's Holy Spirit within you.

"And pray in the Spirit on all occasions with all kinds of prayers and requests. With this in mind, be alert and always keep on praying for all the saints" (Ephesians 6:18).

So many times I don't trust in You, Lord. So many times I "logically" conclude that I might as well despair because my prayer could not possibly be answered. Forgive me. Your Spirit is life to those who believe. Amen.

Prayer Is Vital

The moment you surrender your life to Christ, the Holy Spirit comes upon you and lives in you to guide you and intercede for you. When you do not know what to say to God, when words completely fail you, the Holy Spirit is always there speaking for you.

Dr. Norman Peart says, "It's somewhat like in a wartime scene where there are those who are right on the edge of the battle with the walkie-talkies, communing back with the base and saying exactly what was needed on the front. In that period of time, I believe the Holy Spirit is doing more than most people give Him credit for or realize."

Through the power of the Holy Spirit you can do more than just exist from day to day. You can live life at a higher level than the world has to offer. Listen to His Spirit today. Believe that His awesome presence is filling you. Trust that He knows what you need better than you do.

"In the same way the Spirit also helps our weakness; for we do not know how to pray as we should, but the Spirit Himself intercedes for us with groanings too deep for words; and He who searches the hearts knows what the mind of the Spirit is, because He intercedes for the saints according to the will of God" (Romans 8:26–27 NASB).

Holy Spirit, I do not know the words to pray. Intercede on my behalf because You know exactly what I need. I bow down before You now with a listening heart. I want to experience the fullness of Your Spirit within me. I want to live Your way. Amen.

The Bible: God's Inerrant Word

"All the thousands of books in my library and the libraries of the world combined cannot even begin to compare with this holy, inspired, inerrant Word of God," said Dr. Bill Bright.

God's Word is holy and perfect, relevant and true. If you only believe parts of the Bible, you are limiting your view of God. God is revealed throughout the Old Testament and the New Testament. We encourage you to take a step of faith to receive the whole Bible as true. You may still have many questions about it, but God will answer those as you go along.

God's words in the Bible are a reflection of His nature. To show His matchless power, God used many different men to write the Bible while at the same time making sure that every word written was exactly what He wanted. So although many men were involved with the writing of the Bible, the Bible shows a wonderful unity of God's plans and purposes for life.

"But know this first of all, that no prophecy of Scripture is a matter of one's own interpretation, for no prophecy was ever made by an act of human will, but men moved by the Holy Spirit spoke from God" (2 Peter 1:20–21 NASB).

> *Sovereign Lord, You are immeasurable. I will never fully grasp and understand Your great love for me, but I earnestly seek to learn more about You in Your Word. Amen.*

The Bible: Useful in All Situations

"All Scripture is God-breathed and is useful for teaching, rebuking, correcting and training in righteousness, so that the man of God may be thoroughly equipped for every good work" (2 Timothy 3:16–17).

All Scripture is helpful and relevant to your life. But the Bible is more than a good self-help book; it is a treasure trove of godly principles and truths that can radically change your life for the better.

"I know there are a lot of books, and people gave me a lot of books, but I think the best book is God's Word," says Bruce, a widower.

Heavenly God, when I open Your Word, open my heart to understand what You are saying to me. Show me the value of a biblical lifestyle, a life rooted in You. Amen.

The Bible: Read It

No matter how difficult it is for you to concentrate, no matter how busy your schedule, no matter what emotion you are feeling—discipline yourself to read the Bible daily.

Kay Arthur says, "Many times it's very hard for people who are grieving to read the Word because the pain is so great, because they cannot concentrate, because their thoughts keep running back to their pain or to the situation or to the wound, and it's hard to focus."

God's Word brings healing, growth, and life. By reading His Word daily, you will be prepared to face anything the day may bring. You will be victorious in all areas—physical, emotional, mental, and spiritual—through Christ.

"He sent His word and healed them, and delivered them from their destructions" (Psalm 107:20 NASB).

I need You, Lord Jesus. I need Your Word. Deliver me from myself. Amen.

The Bible: Meditate on It

What does it mean to *meditate* on Scripture?

"The word *meditation* in Scripture is literally the word for a cow chewing its cud. That's actually a pretty good metaphor. Read the Scripture passage a first time. Then read it a second time. Read it a third time. Like many people during grief, you are being bombarded by so many different emotions, thoughts, relatives coming, and things to do that your attention span gets shriveled. Take the time to meditate on Scripture," says Dr. John Trent.

Reflect on God's Word. Examine it. Question it. Remember it. Always pray.

"Do not let this Book of the Law depart from your mouth; meditate on it day and night, so that you may be careful to do everything written in it. Then you will be prosperous and successful" (Joshua 1:8).

"But his delight is in the law of the LORD, and on his law he meditates day and night" (Psalm 1:2).

Lord God, may Your Word be my delight as I "chew" on it daily. Amen.

The Bible: Understand It

"The unfolding of your words gives light; it gives understanding to the simple" (Psalm 119:130).

When you approach God's Word with a grieving, desperate spirit, you are more open to listen to what God is saying to you through the Bible. It is an amazing experience when you come to the point where you feel you can't survive another moment without God's Word, when God's Word becomes your lifeline and your necessary focus. Then you will understand the power of God's Word, and you will understand the strength of surrendering.

Dr. Norman Peart says, "During a time of grief and difficulty, spending time in God's Word is really more significant; it's at a higher level because you are more open to what He is saying and what you may not have heard before. You are in a situation where every word means something; every word could be life or death in just how you feel."

Lord, Your Word has penetrated my darkness. I want a better vision of who You are. I have been blind for so long. Draw me to the light of understanding. Amen.

Discipline Yourself

You may have to force yourself to concentrate on God's words and instructions.

"He's the physician. This is the medicine. You take it," says Kay Arthur.

Disciplining yourself to read the Bible daily is not easy when your emotions are interfering with your thoughts. The Bible addresses this struggle:

> My son, if you accept my words and store up my commands within you, turning your ear to wisdom and applying your heart to understanding, and if you call out for insight and cry aloud for understanding, and if you look for it as for silver and search for it as for hidden treasure, then you will understand the fear of the LORD and find the knowledge of God. For the LORD gives wisdom, and from his mouth come knowledge and understanding. He holds victory in store for the upright, he is a shield to those whose walk is blameless, for he guards the course of the just and protects the way of his faithful ones. Then you will understand what is right and just and fair— every good path. For wisdom will enter your heart, and knowledge will be pleasant to your soul. (Proverbs 2:1–10)

"My son, pay attention to what I say; listen closely to my words. Do not let them out of your sight, keep them within your heart; for they are life to those who find them and health to a man's whole body. Above all else, guard your heart, for it is the wellspring of life" (Proverbs 4:20–23).

Grant me discipline, Lord God. Amen.

Healing Through the Psalms

The book of Psalms provides great comfort for those who are suffering and in pain.

"Certainly when someone has lost a husband, a wife, a very dear friend, or perhaps a child, there is an awesome gaping hole of loneliness," says Dr. Ray Pritchard. "One of the best things I know to do is to open to the book of Psalms and to read those great psalms where David, with those same feelings, is crying out to God."

Let words of Scripture be your prayers to God. Choose a psalm to pray each day. Here are a few to get you started: Psalm 5, 23, 31, 40, 57, 61, 69, 86.

"I waited patiently for the LORD; he turned to me and heard my cry. He lifted me out of the slimy pit, out of the mud and mire; he set my feet on a rock and gave me a firm place to stand. He put a new song in my mouth, a hymn of praise to our God. Many will see and fear and put their trust in the LORD" (Psalm 40:1–3).

O God, I trust in You. You are my refuge, my rock, and my daily help. Amen.

Joy Comes in the Morning

"Weeping may endure for a night, but joy comes in the morning" (Psalm 30:5 NKJV).

God's promises in the Bible are for you. Choose to embrace them and live them out in faith. Beth, who lost both her husband and her mother within a year, read God's promise in Psalm 30:5 (above). Not only did she find comfort in this verse, but she also acted on it in faith.

She says, "I had a difficult time in the mornings waking up, facing the day; it's sort of that 'what do you have to live for?' feeling. So, particularly special to me was that verse about joy coming in the morning. Every morning I'd say, 'Lord, what day is my joy coming? What day is my joy coming?'

"Finally I woke up one morning, and my joy had returned. That doesn't mean that I was fine from then on. It doesn't mean I didn't cry and break down and so forth. But there was that peace and that joy that had been missing for those months. It was just wonderful to have that back again."

Lord, I believe Your promises. May my actions be a reflection of my beliefs. Amen.

Where Does Your Help Come From?

"The Scripture that the Lord gave to me was Psalm 121: 'I looked to the hills from whence cometh my strength.' And that was my encouragement, and it was just a day-by-day matter of looking to the Lord and asking Him for what I needed," says Phyllis of her sister's death.

Phyllis actively lived out this psalm. She did not read it and walk away from it—she made it a part of her daily life. Choose a psalm that is special to you and live it!

Psalm 121 is a wonderful psalm to memorize and act on. This psalm expresses assurance in God's unfailing presence, protection, and help:

> *I will lift up my eyes to the hills—from whence comes my help? My help comes from the LORD, who made heaven and earth.*
>
> *He will not allow your foot to be moved; He who keeps you will not slumber.*
>
> *Behold, He who keeps Israel shall neither slumber nor sleep.*
>
> *The LORD is your keeper; the LORD is your shade at your right hand. The sun shall not strike you by day, nor the moon by night.*
>
> *The LORD shall preserve you from all evil; He shall preserve your soul. The LORD shall preserve your going out and your coming in from this time forth, and even forevermore.* (NKJV)

> *Amen.*

A Sacrifice of Praise

Praise is a tremendous resource that brings healing. The Bible says again and again to praise God. That means to worship, honor, and thank Him. Even when you do not feel like praising God, do it because you believe in the power of praise.

"You offer God praise when it hurts," says Joni Eareckson Tada, "and it costs you something. It costs your logic; it costs your pride. God then is so much more highly honored because He knows that you deem Him so, having offered such a sacrifice."

Hebrews 13:15 tells you to offer the "sacrifice of praise" to God with lips that thankfully acknowledge, confess, and proclaim the glory of His name. Your healing is intertwined in this daily praise.

"Therefore by Him let us continually offer the sacrifice of praise to God, that is, the fruit of our lips, giving thanks to His name" (Hebrews 13:15 NKJV).

Holy God, You are worthy of my praise. I honor and lift up Your name, and I thank you for Your daily goodness. Amen.

Praise Breaks the Bonds

According to Dr. Bill Bright, "Praise is a way of being liberated from the bondage of grief. God inhabits the praise of His people. Surround yourself with praise music. Invite your friends to come and praise God with you, and praise Him even with your tears, even if your heart is not in tune with what your lips are saying at first. It will not be long until your heart will catch up with praise.

"Many, many times during heartache and sorrow, I have praised God with tears streaming down my cheeks because I know that God is a God of love."

The Bible says that God dwells in the praises of His people. He lives among praises and is continually surrounded by them. What an incredible way to abide with the Holy God.

"But thou art holy, O thou that inhabitest the praises of Israel" (Psalm 22:3 KJV).

Holy, holy God, I praise Your name. You are worthy to be revered above all things. I praise Your name. Amen.

Making Music unto God

Every person walks to the rhythm of different tunes. The music of your life can be a source of praise to God.

"It is good to praise the LORD and make music to your name, O Most High" (Psalm 92:1).

You may be a singer, a hummer, an instrumentalist, a dancer, or an avid listener. God made you musically unique.

"Let them praise his name with dancing and make music to him with tambourine and harp" (Psalm 149:3).

"Sing joyfully to the LORD, you righteous; it is fitting for the upright to praise him" (Psalm 33:1).

Put on some praise music or take an early-morning walk and sing with the birds! Do this again and again and experience healing through music.

"Worship the LORD with gladness; come before him with joyful songs" (Psalm 100:2).

Lord, I sing my own song to You today. I will sing to You when I rise up in the morning, as I go about my day, and when I retire at night. Jesus, keep this song in my heart and change my life. Amen.

Choose a Productive Activity

"You don't really care about anything," says Sue, who lost her husband. "Nothing has any meaning to you. But I would suggest that you get involved in something to help other people, a soup kitchen, or something you can do without a lot of thought."

Replace your indifferent, negative outlook with something good and productive. The Bible verse below explains that you are not only to cease your wrong behavior, but you are to replace it with an activity that helps other people.

"He who has been stealing must steal no longer, but must work, doing something useful with his own hands, that he may have something to share with those in need" (Ephesians 4:28).

Loving Father, it's time for me to step away from my thoughts and problems and do something for someone else. Guide me today to take an active step toward this. Amen.

Exercise Brings Healing

"Dear friend, I pray that you may enjoy good health and that all may go well with you, even as your soul is getting along well" (3 John 1:2).

You have probably not paid too much attention to your exercise habits (or lack thereof!). Regular exercise is an important part of your healing. Exercise contributes not only to your physical wellness, but also to your mental and spiritual health.

Choose an exercise that you are likely to stick with. Keep in mind that it is good for you to get out of the house. You might enjoy walking, swimming, dancing, or basketball. Find out what sports activities are available in your community.

"I've gone into an exercise program," says Kay, whose brother died, "and I feel much better. I walk every day, three miles a day. I walk early in the morning, right at daylight. It gives me time to think and time to pray."

God has entrusted you with your body to care for it.

"Do you not know that your body is a temple of the Holy Spirit, who is in you, whom you have received from God? You are not your own" (1 Corinthians 6:19).

Holy Spirit, exercising regularly seems like an impossible feat sometimes. Help me to start an exercise plan and remain faithful to it. Amen.

Your Diet

What you eat affects your day more than you may realize. A balanced diet increases your energy, strength, concentration, and your ability to ward off illnesses. It also makes you feel better about yourself, because your diet affects your thoughts and your emotions.

"You need to think through your diet," suggests Dr. Jim Conway, whose wife died. "Typically, people going through grief eat very poorly. During the early days of my grieving, I would open up a can and eat out of it, while standing at the kitchen counter!"

A balanced diet is not only an important tool in healing from grief, but it is also a way to glorify God. It honors God when you take care of your body, His creation.

"So whether you eat or drink or whatever you do, do it all for the glory of God" (1 Corinthians 10:31).

Glorious God, eating healthy is hard enough to do when I'm not grieving. Maybe now is a good time to change my ways. Please help me in this. Amen.

Helping Others

Helping other people eases your pain and gives you the chance to turn your grief into something good.

"I was asked to come in and counsel this mother and daughter. The daughter was dying of a tumor, just as my daughter had died," says Dora. "At first, they were hesitant to approach me. They weren't sure if I could handle facing the pain and the grief again.

"When I was asked, I jumped at the opportunity because I thought, *This is a good chance for me to turn my daughter's death into something really good and something that I could help other people with.* That proved to be very, very helpful for me in my recovery process."

Everyone in this world needs some kind of help, and someone needs you today.

"Each helps the other and says to his brother, 'Be strong!'" (Isaiah 41:6).

God, when I don't feel strong, help me to remember that my strength is in You. Show me someone in need today. Amen.

Remembering Good Memories

Flashbacks and reruns of disturbing memories can be exhausting. For those in grief, the memories can hit you unexpectedly. Time will fade the bad memories, but be sure to make a conscious effort to remember the good.

"I would see him in my mind when he was really sick," says Sue following her husband's death, "but that fades. People told me that would fade. Now I see him praying in church, which is good. At first I had a lot of the negative flashbacks, but over time I saw the good things."

Reminisce good memories about your loved one with someone else. You may want to write down those memories. Above all, enjoy the good memories and gain strength from them.

"You were wearied by all your ways, but you would not say, 'It is hopeless.' You found renewal of your strength, and so you did not faint" (Isaiah 57:10).

Lord, renew my strength and refresh my mind with peaceful, happy memories. Amen.

Making New Memories

As you move forward on your journey, you create new memories each day. Enjoy the good memories of the past, but be aware of the new memories that occur daily.

What special activity or event do you have planned for today or this weekend? Whom will you invite to join you? Make a new, happy memory.

Job suffered great tragedy in his life, but as time went on, the Lord gave Job new opportunities to form happy memories. The Bible says, "The LORD blessed the latter part of Job's life more than the first. He had fourteen thousand sheep, six thousand camels, a thousand yoke of oxen and a thousand donkeys. And he also had seven sons and three daughters" (Job 42:12–13).

Lord, renew my mind as I walk with You today. Amen.

Branch Out

If your life has been monopolized up until this point with grief and other grieving people, it is time to branch out. Get involved in a group that includes a variety of people with a similar interest (people who are not grieving).

"I had no neighbors to visit me except a young girl across the street," says Gretchen, "and she kept saying, 'You need to belong to the garden club. You just stay in all the time.' She'd wait about six months, and she'd catch me at the mailbox, and she'd say, 'You still don't want to join the garden club?' I'd say, 'No, I can't.' She said, 'Well, I'm just going to put your name on the list anyway.' And I said, 'If it ever comes up, I probably won't be able to go on account of my husband's illness.' She said, 'We'll see about that.'

"Well, my husband died the sixteenth of August, and my name came up in September to join the neighborhood garden club. That was just the hand of the Lord. It was a way for me to get out and start meeting my neighbors."

In whatever group you choose to be involved in, you will be an asset. If you think your presence does not benefit the group in any way, you are wrong. God made each person to be an important part of the whole.

"The eye cannot say to the hand, 'I don't need you!' And the head cannot say to the feet, 'I don't need you!' On the contrary, those parts of the body that seem to be weaker are indispensable" (1 Corinthians 12:21–22).

Lord, where do You need me? Amen.

Adding Variety to Your Life

Don't just use one resource for recovery—use several. We have mentioned a number of tools to aid in your grief recovery: a journal, sharing, humor, pets, diet, exercise, the Bible. These tools require work and effort, and they will all help you in some respect. Incorporating a variety of resources will keep you from getting in a rut that would otherwise inhibit your progress toward healing.

Dr. Jim Conway explains it this way. "The process of adjusting to grief is the process of working through these things by talking to people. You also need the music dimension. You need to be spending time in the Scriptures, especially the Psalms and the Proverbs, letting God reach in there and massage your heart.

"You need to spend time praying and reading your Bible. It's important to have that quiet reflection with God. You also need to think through your diet. Don't just eat junk food; force yourself to eat a balanced diet. Additionally, physical exercise drops off, so work at the whole physical component. Also, think about getting into other kinds of groups. If you're only in grief groups, you're only hanging out with grieving people. Join a standard Bible study group with people who are not grieving, but don't get into singles groups; you're not ready for that yet."

Think about what has worked well for you on your healing journey. What new tools can you try out?

"Let the word of Christ dwell in you richly as you teach and admonish one another with all wisdom, and as you sing psalms, hymns and spiritual songs with gratitude in your hearts to God. And whatever you do, whether in word or deed, do it all in the name of the Lord Jesus, giving thanks to God the Father through him" (Colossians 3:16–17).

One thing is clear, Lord: I've got to do something!

It's Your Move

It's hard to take responsibility when so many areas of your life seem out of control. But if you can't manage your life, how can you be answerable for it? It is true that you cannot control what emotions you will feel or how certain events come to pass, but you need to be responsible for how you handle your own circumstances.

As Dr. Norman Peart says, "God is in control. He has not left the scene. He has not left the control panels, and He is going to work it all out for His glory. At the same time, that means that there are some responsibilities we have."

Part of moving on is to figure out where your responsibilities lie. The biblical answer to this question is to start right where you are. What were your areas of service and responsibility before you lost your loved one? You don't need to jump into them all at once, but they will be your beginning point.

"Brothers, each man, as responsible to God, should remain in the situation God called him to" (1 Corinthians 7:24).

Lord, show me where you have called me to serve. Help me to begin so I can take responsibility and move on. Amen.

god's spiritual hospital

God's Spiritual Hospital

"I view the church as a hospital," says Dr. H. Norman Wright. "Invite the people in who are struggling, who are hurting."

The church is not just a place for whole and healthy people to attend. When you are hurting and in need, the church is the community where you can find help. Whether you need immediate treatment or long-term care, God has designed the church to minister to your needs.

Dr. Larry Crabb says, "In the field of the soul, there are no professional surgeons; there are only caring Christians. I think that's a critical thing for us to realize."

People in the church will enable you, through their love, to move forward on your journey. They may not know the exact words to say, and their timing will not always be right, but be assured that they love you because they love the Lord.

"Dear friend, you are faithful in what you are doing for the brothers, even though they are strangers to you. They have told the church about your love. You will do well to send them on their way in a manner worthy of God" (3 John 1:5–6).

Lord God, it is time for me to visit your hospital—the church. Guide me to a church that will welcome me with open arms, and give me the courage to speak up and not hide in the back. Amen.

Emotional Intensive Care

You may feel that emotionally you need critical care. Seek help from a Christian church. The church is a place that welcomes hurting people. Remember, no church congregation is perfect. You may have been let down by the church recently or in the past. Yes, the church is filled with imperfect people, but the church is also filled with people who are trying to love more deeply and trying to live the kind of life that God has called them to.

"It's just like your emotions are going into intensive care. What can you do?" says Sylvia of the loss of her parents.

Let yourself be loved.

"The entire law is summed up in a single command: 'Love your neighbor as yourself'" (Galatians 5:14).

Lord, I want to be loved. I need to be loved. Amen.

Help Is Through the Church

Open your mind to the idea that help can be given through people in a church.

"If you're not a Christian, give it a try," suggests Jan Northington. "Come to church. Find out who this God is and what Jesus can be for you. I think it's a place where you'll find warmth, understanding, and encouragement, even if you are a little undecided as to whether you want to make this kind of commitment. Church is a place to start, and it's a place to find love and acceptance and help. That's what you need right now."

The church has valuable spiritual and emotional resources, beyond what you might realize. Give your local body of believers a chance to help you.

"After all, no one ever hated his own body, but he feeds and cares for it, just as Christ does the church" (Ephesians 5:29).

Christ Jesus, You are the head of the church, and by Your example the people in the church love and care for those in their community. I would like to get to know these people. Amen.

The Door Is Open

The church is very important to God. It is His representative upon the earth. What people think about God is often influenced by what they think about the church. The doors of the church are always open to hurting people.

"You have all that support," says Luevenia, whose husband died. "Church people are ready and willing to rally around you. That's part of being a Christian in a church. I think it's just worth everything. People aren't flawless, but you can rest in the assurance that they are good people in every sense of the word."

Have you walked through those open doors?

"Is any one of you in trouble? He should pray. Is anyone happy? Let him sing songs of praise. Is any one of you sick? He should call the elders of the church to pray over him and anoint him with oil in the name of the Lord" (James 5:13–14).

Father God, give me the courage to seek help in the church. Also, I pray that my own doors are open for anyone who needs my help. Amen.

A New Family

When you become a part of a church, you become part of a family, God's family. Believers of Jesus Christ will rally together in love and support for those in need.

"I don't think we would have made it through without family support, without the church family," says Betty, whose daughter-in-law died. "Here it is fifteen months later, and our church family is still supporting us. The Sunday school class brought in meals for three months. The women came in and helped me with the children.

"I literally quit my job and moved in with my son to look after the children. Those two o'clock feedings for a grandma are not easy. The women would come in from nine to three to help me so that I could catch up with my sleep and keep up. The meals kept coming in."

If you did not receive this kind of support from your church, let your pastor or a church leader know your needs. The church body cannot help if they are not aware of your needs. This is not the time to say you have everything under control, because you don't.

Let yourself be ministered to by your church family, and you, in turn, can provide help for someone else at a different time.

"Therefore, as we have opportunity, let us do good to all people, especially to those who belong to the family of believers" (Galatians 6:10).

Savior God, my church family is such a blessing to me. Free me to accept their help with sincere appreciation. Amen.

You Need Others

How many people are praying for you regularly? You need other people, and you especially need their prayers.

Barbara Johnson says, "Right when you're down in the middle of the pain and you're going through this, that's when you have to say, 'Hey, I'm a Christian, but I'm really hurting. I need you to pray for me, and I need you to love me because right now I'm not effective as a Christian. I just can't be bubbling out about how joyful I am. I will in time, but right now I need you to comfort me and I need God's love to comfort me.'"

When you first lost your loved one, you likely had several people praying for you and your family. But what about now? What about now when the grief is still deep and everyone seems to expect you to have bounced back into life?

Call a friend who will quietly listen and who will pray. Be sure to ask people for their prayers. They might not think to offer if the topic is not brought up!

"I always thank my God as I remember you in my prayers" (Philemon 1:4).

Comfort me with Your love, O Lord. Hear the prayers that are being said for me. Amen.

Lend Me Your Faith

"Faith is what carries you through," says Dr. H. Norman Wright. "It is vital. But the problem is, during an intense loss or trauma or crisis, sometimes you wonder, *Where is my faith? Where is my hope?* And that's when you need somebody else to walk alongside you and say, 'Let me lend you my faith and my hope until your own comes back again.'"

A strong Christian friend will be invaluable on your grief journey. This friend will listen, be available, and uphold you in prayer. He or she will spur you on to a deeper relationship with Christ.

"I long to see you so that I may impart to you some spiritual gift to make you strong—that is, that you and I may be mutually encouraged by each other's faith" (Romans 1:11–12).

Your friend, in turn, will grow and be blessed by the almighty God who greatly rewards those who follow His commands.

Lord, show me who this strong Christian friend is. You have provided people to walk alongside me and to lift me up when I stumble. I do not want to miss out on this blessing. Thank you, Great Provider. Amen.

Be Involved in Others' Lives

Involvement requires investment. Getting involved in other people's lives is not easy. You have to choose to take the time and show love to others. It will not always come naturally.

"You need to find the courage to get deeply involved in other people's lives and experience the mess and frustration, the sense of impotence, the sense of not knowing what to do," says Dr. Larry Crabb.

You may be thinking, *I have my own problems. I don't have the time. I don't have the energy. I don't have anything to offer.*

Excuses!

Step out of your comfort zone and do something great for God. People need you, and it's up to you to find out who they are and what you can do to help.

"If you really keep the royal law found in Scripture, 'Love your neighbor as yourself,' you are doing right" (James 2:8).

Holy God, I want to do right. Even when my energy and courage are failing, push me forward to help and love another person who needs me. Amen.

Stay Involved in Others' Lives

"When you listen to somebody and he or she shares what's really happening, the pat answers don't work, and you don't know what to say," says Dr. Larry Crabb. "But it's at that point when you don't know what to say that if you back away, you lose the opportunity to touch. In your inadequacy can you stay involved?"

Don't back away because you are afraid of getting involved in another person's sorrows and problems. No one is wholly adequate, but everyone has a choice: (1) stay involved and truly show love and help or (2) back away, afraid of making things worse.

Take the risk, and God will provide the strength.

"Serve one another in love" (Galatians 5:13).

Great Lord, yes, with You I really can be strong. Amen.

Take the First Step

"Religion that God our Father accepts as pure and faultless is this: to look after orphans and widows in their distress and to keep oneself from being polluted by the world" (James 1:27).

Others will want to show their love for you during grief, but will often not know how to do that.

Wendy and Jeffrey lost their infant son. Wendy says, "We both felt like everybody in the entire world was trying to avoid us. They didn't want to ask us how we were doing because they were scared that we might actually tell them! They wouldn't know what to say, or they just didn't want to talk to us at all because they knew we were probably very sad people. So that might rub off on them.

"I wish I had counted the number of cards we received, because that's a very easy thing to do. But as far as phone calls? We have very good friends, and it wasn't that they didn't care; it was just that they didn't know what to say. So they didn't call."

If you are in need of a phone call or a listening ear, you may need to take the first step. Or, if you need to offer someone else a listening ear, pick up the phone and call. The Bible instructs people to look after one another and to stay true to His Word.

Father, I'm on both ends of this. I need people to help and encourage me, and, at the same time, I want to be there for those who need my support. Amen.

Give a Hug

Sometimes a hug is all that is needed.

Jeffrey, who lost his son, says, "The first Sunday we went back to church after this happened, one of the ladies walked in, and we did not know her at all. She walked over, and she saw our name tags. She just grabbed both of us and hugged us and started crying. And she didn't speak a word.

"That meant more to us just to know that she had a heart, and she had compassion. She didn't know what to say, and she didn't say anything. But she was willing to let her emotion show and embrace us."

Christians are carriers of God's power. A simple, heartfelt hug provides a release of that holy, healing power. Always look for the opportunity to spread God's goodness daily and in a variety of ways.

> One of the teachers of the law came and heard them debating. Noticing that Jesus had given them a good answer, he asked him, "Of all the commandments, which is the most important?"
>
> "The most important one," answered Jesus, "is this: 'Hear, O Israel, the Lord our God, the Lord is one. Love the Lord your God with all your heart and with all your soul and with all your mind and with all your strength.' The second is this: 'Love your neighbor as yourself.' There is no commandment greater than these." (Mark 12:28–31)

Lord God, may Your healing power be released in me as I take the opportunity to love. Amen.

Called to Love

You have the opportunity to demonstrate the kind of love that God calls you to in His Word. As you do this, your healing will be accelerated.

> What good is it, my brothers, if a man claims to have faith but has no deeds? Can such faith save him? Suppose a brother or sister is without clothes and daily food. If one of you says to him, "Go, I wish you well; keep warm and well fed," but does nothing about his physical needs, what good is it?
>
> In the same way, faith by itself, if it is not accompanied by action, is dead. But someone will say, "You have faith; I have deeds." Show me your faith without deeds, and I will show you my faith by what I do. (James 2:14–18)

Act on your beliefs. What specific things can you do to help someone in need? If you do not know of someone in need, ask God to bring a name to your mind. Then be brave and call that person and offer your help. Persist until you have something specific to do. You can also call your pastor or church leader and ask for suggestions of people who might need your help.

Lord, I want to do something. I want to take action and not just think about taking action. Spur me on. Amen.

Develop New Relationships

"We were just so close to so many couples, but once [my husband] died, the invitations weren't there. That really hurt," says Gretchen. "I just prayed to the Lord, 'Well, Lord, I just need new friends.'

"I have been very blessed that He has given me a number of good widow ladies that I have been able to do things with and share with. Some of them are much older than me, and they don't drive in the day-time. Some of them are walkers, and they can't drive. I feel that I can be helpful in doing things for them and carrying them places and having a luncheon and that sort of thing. God has really been good."

For Gretchen, it wasn't about hurt feelings and self-pity. She chose to reach out to new people, and she knew she had love to give because of God's love for her. She spoke to God frankly: "I just need new friends." And God was faithful in answering.

"We love because he first loved us. If anyone says, 'I love God,' yet hates his brother, he is a liar. For anyone who does not love his brother, whom he has seen, cannot love God, whom he has not seen. And he has given us this command: Whoever loves God must also love his brother" (1 John 4:19–21).

Father God, when I don't fit in as I once did, it hurts me. Give me a positive outlook and hear my prayer: "Lord, I just need new friends." Amen.

You Are Not the Same

You are not the same person you were before. Too much has changed within and without. Do not try to fall back into the same patterns, because you will only struggle to fit into a lifestyle that no longer fits. In order to live this new life, you must first identify the areas of your life that you struggle with, and then take steps to learn how to move forward in those areas. For instance, you might find yourself in new situations that you are not comfortable in without your loved one, or you might have new responsibilities that you do not know how to fulfill because your loved one used to take care of them for you.

Here is where you need to grow. God will provide what you need to experience true growth. Pray for wisdom as you develop new patterns of living.

Gretchen says, "My husband could talk to anybody about anything for any length of time, and I just always let him do it. I wasn't a big talker, but the Lord gave me some of that talking ability after he died. And I've been grateful for that because I was very happy in just letting my husband carry the conversation with people. Now, every time I go to something that I really wished I didn't have to go to, I just call on the Lord. The Lord is so faithful. Every single time I get through it and wind up enjoying it."

By God's grace you can be changed. You do not have to try and be the person you were before, because that is not possible. Instead . . .

"Put on the new self, which is being renewed in knowledge in the image of its Creator" (Colossians 3:10).

Lord, even though I don't necessarily want to change, I know that I must. Give me confidence and wisdom in the areas that I struggle with. Amen.

Be Willing to Reach Out

"In everything I did, I showed you that by this kind of hard work we must help the weak, remembering the words the Lord Jesus himself said: 'It is more blessed to give than to receive'" (Acts 20:35).

You have probably been the recipient of much help throughout your time of grief. That is a great blessing. But think about Jesus' words: "It is more blessed to give than to receive." Now it's your turn to be the giver.

"Look around and find someone else who's hurting," says Linda, whose baby died, "and minister to that person, whether it's just a card or a phone call. It seems like when you reach out to someone else, your grief begins to heal and it doesn't seem as overwhelming to you. You can see beyond it."

> *Lord Jesus, it sure is hard to see beyond myself. What can I do to reach out in love to another person today? Amen.*

Share the Blessing

After the deaths of Sylvia's parents, she began to take more notice of people who had lost a loved one.

She says, "I had not paid that much attention to them before. When another woman in our church lost a father, I could feel the pain that she was going through when she sang in the choir on Father's Day. Right after church when she came down, I went up to her and I said, 'I know exactly how you feel.' She said, 'You will never know how much this means to me.' Through noticing and watching people who are undergoing grief, you can be a big help."

Your compassion and empathy can bring healing to another person in grief. Be willing to give and to share.

"Your love has given me great joy and encouragement, because you, brother, have refreshed the hearts of the saints" (Philemon 1:7).

Father, let me be Your instrument of love and healing to others. Amen.

Your Sorrows Can Help Others

God comforts you in your sorrows if you allow Him to. You, in turn, are to comfort others.

"One of the advantages of going through pain," says Dee Brestin, "is that one day you will be able to comfort others who have been where you are. God is stretching you right now, and it's very painful, but I do think that one day you will be able to comfort someone else."

You first have to allow God to comfort you. Be open to receiving His comfort. Then you will be supplied and ready to give that same comfort to another person. You will not have to drum up the energy to do this or feel that it is a chore. You will be so full of God's comfort that passing it on will come naturally, *super*naturally.

"All praise to the God and Father of our Lord Jesus Christ. He is the source of every mercy and the God who comforts us. He comforts us in all our troubles so that we can comfort others. When others are troubled, we will be able to give them the same comfort God has given us" (2 Corinthians 1:3–4 NLT).

Father God, I accept Your comfort. I open my arms to You right now and stand secure in Your loving embrace. May my heart be so full of Your comfort that it pours out on others I meet today. Amen.

Be Available to Help Others

Elisabeth Elliot says, "My advice would certainly be quit thinking about yourself. Don't look around the room and wonder why nobody wants to pay attention to you, thinking to yourself, *Are the people not remembering that I'm a widow?*

"Forget all that and look for someone who looks a little lonely and go and try to encourage that person. Isaiah 58:10 has been a great watchword for me: If you pour yourself out for the hungry, then the Lord is going to satisfy your needs and you will become like a watered garden."

You may think you have nothing to offer right now. But, remember, when people are in the midst of a deep struggle, they need someone who cares, someone who will just be with them.

"If you give yourself to the hungry and satisfy the desire of the afflicted, then your light will rise in darkness and your gloom will become like midday. And the LORD will continually guide you, and satisfy your desire in scorched places, and give strength to your bones; and you will be like a watered garden, and like a spring of water whose waters do not fail" (Isaiah 58:10–11 NASB).

Lord, today I will change my focus from myself to others. I am going to look for someone who needs encouragement or company. Amen.

The Courage to Listen

Dr. Larry Crabb describes this scenario: "You're sitting next to somebody in church or maybe in a small-group setting. It's coffee break time and the person obviously is distressed. Your initial inclination is 'Let me see if I can't go have coffee with somebody else, because if I stay with this person who is hurting, I won't know what to do. Let me go chat with some buddies and some friends where I feel very adequate.'"

He continues, "We tend to underestimate the profound power of listening. We think of that as anemic: *'Well, at least I listened, but what good does that do?'* I think the biggest lesson I've learned as a friend or as a husband or as a counselor is this: It isn't what I know or my competence that makes the difference; it's when I find the courage to be there in the presence of God, that's where the difference is found."

Be courageous; do not stay where you feel comfortable and safe. Take a chance for someone else today and listen. Listen to God urging you forward and listen attentively to someone who is hurting. When a person sees you are truly listening, that person feels valued. This validation brings deep healing.

"He who answers before listening—that is his folly and his shame" (Proverbs 18:13).

God, I feel very inadequate sometimes. Teach me that with You in my life, I am complete, and my presence is needed to help others who are hurting. Amen.

Everyone Has a Ministry

The Bible often compares the church to the human body with many members and many parts. Each part is needed for the body to function properly. In the church there are many members, and each one has something important to give.

"From him [Jesus] the whole body, joined and held together by every supporting ligament, grows and builds itself up in love, as each part does its work" (Ephesians 4:16).

The church is called the body of Christ. There is a definite, life-giving connection between everyone in the church body. Life flows from one person to another and back again.

"Somebody who has experienced the comfort of God knows that he or she has something to pour," says Dr. Larry Crabb. "I love the word *pour*. It's a metaphor that doesn't feel clinical; it feels alive. There's something within the person who has been comforted that can actually pour into the other and bathe his or her soul."

Lord Jesus Christ, I am part of Your body. Help me pour Your comfort into another person who needs it. Amen.

Give Permission to Grieve

An important ministry you have to other people is to validate their individual losses. You will not tend to trivialize their losses by giving quick, easy answers. Rather, you know it is better to stand alongside them and feel what they are going through. By doing this, you give them permission to grieve.

Dr. Robert Jeffress states, "Christians need to be given permission to grieve. They do not need to feel like they've fallen if they are grieving. They need to be reminded that what they are experiencing is normal.

"I believe the Bible, the Word of God is alive; it's active; it's sharper than any two-edged sword. But grieving people do not need to be bombarded with Bible verses. I think sometimes the best thing to do for grieving Christians is just to be there, to be silent, and when the time is right, to share a truth that might help them."

You have suffered and are still suffering. Many people around you are suffering as well. Sometimes it is hard to notice because in today's culture, hiding true feelings is common and often expected. The Bible tells you to share in your sufferings. It also says to share in your comfort.

"Our hope for you is firm, because we know that just as you share in our sufferings, so also you share in our comfort" (2 Corinthians 1:7).

Lord God, someone around me needs to grieve. He or she may be holding it back and suffering even more because of that. I want to help that person understand it is okay and necessary to grieve. Amen.

Words of Comfort

When sharing with someone else who is grieving, words often fail you. Do talk. That person needs to hear from you, but let your words be few and specific.

Emy, who lost her husband, advises, "People shouldn't say, 'How are you?' They should ask about a specific area: 'Is your health better?' or 'Are you getting out more?', something like that rather than making an open-ended question."

Don't just offer empty words of encouragement. Find out what is really going on in another person's life, and keep track of how he or she is progressing through the struggle. Comforting another person with the love of Christ is necessary for your own healing as you begin to better understand the strength and peace found in a life lived for Jesus.

"For just as the sufferings of Christ flow over into our lives, so also through Christ our comfort overflows" (2 Corinthians 1:5).

Holy Jesus, may my words be few, but focused and sincere, as I seek to comfort another grieving person with Your love. Amen.

Helping Another Person in Grief

Not everyone reacts to loss the same. Some may pursue help. Others may avoid it. That can be a sign they are not doing well. You may need to gently and tactfully go after them.

You might be tempted to say, "Oh, someone else will help him. I hardly know him anyway." Or you might think, *She really doesn't want my help.*

In grief, the rules have changed. Step in and help. Worrying about discomfort or embarrassment is not relevant in grief. People need other people to intervene regardless of societal conventions.

"He saw that there was no one, he was appalled that there was no one to intervene" (Isaiah 59:16).

Lord, I need to get over my uncertainty about how to help others or whether to help. Help me to step out in faith and gently bring comfort to another person in grief. Amen.

Having a Grief Night

There is great strength in community, the coming together in Christ and building up of one another to love and good deeds. Dr. Larry Crabb shares how his Sunday school class has responded to this need by implementing a practice called a *grief night:*

1. Plan a time to meet together as a group.

2. To begin the grief night, light a candle to symbolize the one who is not there.

3. Have others ask the grieving person random questions about the loved one who has died. What did he or she do to disappoint you? Which of your loved one's possessions evoke strong fellings or memories? Let the person talk.

4. After about an hour of questions, tears, and sharing, take time to respond to the grieving person. This is not a time for platitudes and advice, but for a pouring out of love.

5. Next is prayer time. Have the grieving person sit in the center of the group, and people who want to can lay their hands on the bereaved person. Then come before God in worship and in pleading and petition for the bereaved.

6. Last is song time. Sing favorites of the one who died or of the one who is grieving.

"Let us not give up meeting together, as some are in the habit of doing, but let us encourage one another—and all the more as you see the Day approaching" (Hebrews 10:25).

> *Loving Father, healing is possible in the community of believers. Lead me to meet together regularly with other people who believe in You. Amen.*

Practical Help

Don't underestimate the value of giving practical help. But be observant. The kind of help needed will vary from one person to another.

Barbara Johnson shares, "I wished people would have just come and told me they loved me and that God loved me, and then helped me feed the dog, take care of the house, dump the garbage, do some things like that. Doing practical things for me would have been good because so many things they said were causing turmoil for me rather than comfort. So I learned that the words should be few and that it is better to do practical things to help the family. Bring some casseroles; feed the children; do the laundry."

If you could use practical help, ask for it. People want to help and usually find it easier to help with a specific task or responsibility.

"So in everything, do to others what you would have them do to you, for this sums up the Law and the Prophets" (Matthew 7:12).

Receive help with open arms and an appreciative outlook. Offer help with the same caring attitude.

Lord God, even when I'm not sure how another person will respond to my overtures, give me the courage to find a practical way to help and to just do it! Amen.

Lessons You Have Learned

Keep your grief in perspective by remembering these truths you have learned:

- Other people have experienced grief.
- Your feelings are as unique as you are.
- You can use the lessons you learn in grief to help others.
- People in grief do not need sermons or lectures.
- In grief, people often must tell their stories over and over.

Your pains and sorrows can become the bridge to reach out and to minister to others, bringing healing to both you and them.

"Comfort, comfort my people, says your God" (Isaiah 40:1).

God of comfort, help me to keep my grief in perspective and to use it to help others. Amen.

Communicating in Grief

Although you have experienced grief, you may be hesitant to approach others who are bereaved. Not knowing what to say, you may tend to avoid them. There is no "right" thing to say. It is your heart of concern and love that you need to express. Be genuine.

These suggestions will help you interact with them:

- Use direct and specific language (naming times, places, and names) to help them reorient from the "blur" of grief events.

- Mention the deceased by name.

- Do not say that you know how they feel. Each loss is unique.

- Do not tell them how good they look to avoid talking about how bad they feel.

- Encourage them to talk about life before their loss.

- Show your humanity.

- Do not be afraid to gently touch them.

- Let them cry and express their emotions.

- Be willing to listen, especially in the evening.

- Don't change the subject to a lighter topic for your own comfort.

- Take your conversation cues from them. Silence is okay.

- Make several short visits.

- Visit when "normal" life returns to everyone but them.

- Minister to the whole family, but do not let them "attach" to you in an unhealthy manner.

"Now that you have purified yourselves by obeying the truth so that you have sincere love for your brothers, love one another deeply, from the heart" (1 Peter 1:22).

Holy God, give me the words to say and help this person know I am sincere. Amen.

Living Eulogy

A *eulogy* is typically a formal, prepared statement of commendation. But *eulogy* can also be defined as "high praise" (Merriam-Webster). You have the opportunity daily to give a living eulogy to those you love.

Rev. John Coulombe explains, "Living eulogies should start at the crib with hands laid on the infants, speaking to them good things about who they are, God's will for them, and God's blessing upon them. Living eulogies should continue through those childhood years, adolescent years, adult years, and death years. It should be a lifestyle. A living eulogy is the greatest gift that you can give. It is telling someone he or she has value and wishing God's best upon his or her life."

Pray the following Scripture for those you love, and let them know that you desire God's blessing on their lives:

> *"The Lord bless you and keep you; the Lord make his face shine upon you and be gracious to you; the Lord turn his face toward you and give you peace" (Numbers 6:24–26). Amen.*

Let this prayer be the start of a living eulogy.

Record a Living Eulogy

You can record a living eulogy on a videotape or audiocassette. Plan a time when your loved ones are all together. Each person could share a favorite song and Bible verse. Go around the room and ask specific questions, or have each person share something nice about the person next to him or her. Reminisce happy memories that include people in the room. Also, share thoughts and memories about loved ones who are no longer with you.

Pastor Buck Buchanan says, "The benefit I've seen is the event itself, just getting the family together. There's a lot of crying; there's a lot of laughing; there's a lot of exchange. You see the family's relationships coming out. It is extremely helpful in healing."

This is the perfect opportunity to let those around you know how much you love and value them for who they are. Sometimes in grief you will cling too tightly to family members who are still living because you fear losing them as well. This does not make them feel loved and valued; that behavior is based on fear.

Bring the family together. Plan a special evening of living memories, laughter, questions, and tears. Let God's love flow through you.

"These days should be remembered and kept throughout every generation, every family, every province, and every city . . . that the memory of them should not perish among their descendants" (Esther 9:28 NKJV).

Father God, You created me to be in a family. Teach me to cherish my loved ones in a way that is healthy and true. Amen.

Listening to God

The rushing and busyness that characterize many lives today can be detrimental to your health, not only your physical health, but also your spiritual and emotional health. Jesus shows you what you need to do in this biblical account of Mary and Martha:

> As Jesus and his disciples were on their way, he came to a village where a woman named Martha opened her home to him. She had a sister called Mary, who sat at the Lord's feet listening to what he said. But Martha was distracted by all the preparations that had to be made. She came to him and asked, "Lord, don't you care that my sister has left me to do the work by myself? Tell her to help me!"
>
> "Martha, Martha," the Lord answered, "you are worried and upset about many things, but only one thing is needed. Mary has chosen what is better, and it will not be taken away from her." (Luke 10:38–43)

When did you last stop and take the time to listen to God?

Holy God, You are worthy of my honor, praise, and undivided attention. Daily You try to speak to me, and many times I rush away from You with barely a nod. Right now, Lord, I will quiet myself before You and meditate on Your holiness and listen. Amen.

longing for heaven

What Happens After Death?

"There's far more here than meets the eye. The things we see now are here today, gone tomorrow. But the things we can't see now will last forever" (2 Corinthians 4:18 MSG).

Whenever you consider God's answer to suffering, loss, and grief, you must also think about heaven. You will only be on earth for a brief time. For those who believe in Jesus, their time in heaven will be forever. In heaven you will see God's final solution for tragedy, disease, death, and injustice.

"Christians understand plenty about death simply because of Jesus Christ our Lord and Savior. He's been there ahead of us," says Dr. Richard Bewes.

Lord Jesus, help me to clarify my beliefs about what happens after death. Show me the truth about eternity. Amen.

Hope for Eternity

"Truly, truly, I say to you, if anyone keeps My word he will never see death" (John 8:51 NASB).

"Jesus said . . . 'I am the resurrection and the life. He who believes in me will live, even though he dies; and whoever lives and believes in me will never die. Do you believe this?'" (John 11:25–26).

God has promised you eternal life through His Son Jesus Christ when you believe in Him and surrender your life over to His will.

"It was a great opportunity to be told that there was a living God and that there is eternal life and that a person doesn't have to be good in order to receive God's gift of salvation," says Chandra. "You don't have to be good in order to live forever. You have to just accept Christ as your Savior and believe in the cross and what Jesus did on the cross for you, the shedding of His blood, and accept Him as your Savior. And at that very moment you start eternal life."

Eternal God, You have promised life to those who believe. I believe, Lord, I believe. Amen.

Exploring Eternal Life

"I pray also that the eyes of your heart may be enlightened in order that you may know the hope to which he has called you, the riches of his glorious inheritance in the saints, and his incomparably great power for us who believe" (Ephesians 1:18–19).

So many people do not take the time or make an effort to discover the truth about Jesus Christ and God's plan for eternity. Our prayer is that you take the time to read God's Word, to pray, and to learn more about Him.

Do not believe all you hear. Find out the truth for yourself. The Bible has much to say about Jesus, eternity, heaven, death, and abundant life.

Dr. Erwin Lutzer says, "Christ is the only one who can forgive you, declare you to be righteous, scoop you up out of the pit of sin, and place you right before the throne of God."

The key to eternal life, Jesus, is You. Help me to learn more and to back up my beliefs with facts. Amen.

God Has Set Eternity in Your Heart

Even if you know that heaven is your eternal destiny, you have probably had days when you've said, "Oh Lord, just take me home now." Do you long for the time when you never have to say good-bye again? When there will be no more sickness, no more suffering, no more growing old?

The Bible says God has set eternity in your heart. To long for a better place is not a vain hope or delusion. You were made for eternity, and because of this, you can never be fully satisfied until you get to heaven.

"Training our minds and hearts, the totality of our being on heaven, is instinctive because our souls are eternal," says Dr. Joseph Stowell. "There's something in us that feels right about believing there is something on the other side of death.

"But instincts don't quite cut it because you have to have some content. When we are born again in Jesus Christ, when we've repented of our sin, embraced the finished work of Christ on the cross, and have been reborn so that the Holy Spirit lives within us, now these instincts for eternity suddenly take on meaning because the Holy Spirit excites and nurtures our desire for home."

Let God's Spirit move inside you and excite you to live life in light of eternity.

"He has made everything beautiful in its time. He has also set eternity in the hearts of men; yet they cannot fathom what God has done from beginning to end" (Ecclesiastes 3:11).

Holy Spirit, I can't wait for heaven. No more tears, no more good-byes, no more sadness, just Jesus Christ and His love. Amen.

Preparing for Eternity

One thing is certain—eternity is in the future for all people. The Bible says that thanks to Jesus, you can spend that eternity with God in heaven. But how can you prepare while still living on this earth?

Dr. Joseph Stowell says, "The Word of God comes along and trains you and talks to you about living life from an eternal perspective. You read through the Gospels, and you become convinced that Jesus Christ is driven by one reality—eternity. His whole perspective is driven by the fact that there is a world to come; this one will soon be done. And what you do here will count for the world that is yet to come.

"Life here really is a dress rehearsal for the world to come. A person who embraces eternity and lives in light of it has his whole world radically re-altered. He looks at people differently. Looks at his money differently. Looks at the things around his life differently. Looks at his own self differently."

Live your life from an eternal perspective, not longing for this one to be over, but driven by a new set of values found in God's Word.

> The law of the LORD is perfect, reviving the soul. The decrees of the LORD are trustworthy, making wise the simple. The commandments of the LORD are right, bringing joy to the heart. The commands of the LORD are clear, giving insight to life. Reverence for the LORD is pure, lasting forever. The laws of the LORD are true; each one is fair. They are more desirable than gold, even the finest gold. They are sweeter than honey, even honey dripping from the comb." (Psalm 19:7–10 NLT)

Lord Jesus, teach me the values of a biblical, eternal lifestyle, and change my world in light of this reality. Amen.

Longing for Home

The Bible says just enough about heaven to make people wonder what it will really be like.

"No eye has seen, no ear has heard, no mind has conceived what God has prepared for those who love him" (1 Corinthians 2:9). Revelation 21 describes the heavenly city—a city so magnificent and vast that you can hardly comprehend it.

> It shone with the glory of God, and its brilliance was like that of a very precious jewel, like a jasper, clear as crystal. It had a great, high wall with twelve gates, and with twelve angels at the gates. . . . The wall was made of jasper, and the city of pure gold, as pure as glass.
>
> The foundations of the city walls were decorated with every kind of precious stone. The first foundation was jasper, the second sapphire, the third chalcedony, the fourth emerald, the fifth sardonyx, the sixth carnelian, the seventh chrysolite, the eighth beryl, the ninth topaz, the tenth chrysoprase, the eleventh jacinth, and the twelfth amethyst.
>
> The twelve gates were twelve pearls, each gate made of a single pearl. The great street of the city was of pure gold, like transparent glass. . . . The city does not need the sun or the moon to shine on it, for the glory of God gives it light, and the Lamb is its lamp. (11–12, 18–21, 23)

The walls will be over 200 feet thick. Each of the four sides of the city will be approximately 1,400 miles long:

"I figured it out one time—396,000 stories high and one half the size of the United States," says Dr. Erwin Lutzer.

Sovereign King, Your kingdom is glorious beyond my imagination. I am prepared to be amazed! Amen.

A Wonderful Reunion

In heaven there will be a wonderful reunion. You will see your family and friends, all of those who have gone on to be with Jesus when they died.

Dr. Luis Palau tells about a man who was grieving his daughter's death: "He would go every Saturday to the grave and stand at the grave and weep in front of his daughter's grave and sob inconsolably. And he would talk to her as though she was there.

"One Friday evening the man attended an evangelistic event and made the decision to surrender his life to Jesus Christ. The next day, he said, 'I was going to go to the grave and suddenly it dawned on me: *Wait. My girl is not here. She's in heaven, and now I'm a believer. I'm going to heaven. I don't have to visit the grave and weep, because my girl is happy in the presence of Jesus Christ!*'"

Jesus changed his life. Now this man lives with the absolute assurance of a happy reunion with his daughter in heaven.

The Bible tells about a future time when believers in Christ (those in heaven and those still on earth) will all join together in the presence of the Lord.

> For the Lord himself will come down from heaven, with a loud command, with the voice of the archangel and with the trumpet call of God, and the dead in Christ will rise first. After that, we who are still alive and are left will be caught up together with them in the clouds to meet the Lord in the air. And so we will be with the Lord forever. There-fore encourage each other with these words. (1 Thessalonians 4:16–18)

> *Lord, I am thrilled to know that good-byes on earth will soon be hellos again. Amen.*

People Will Know Each Other

In some ways life in heaven will be very different from life as it is now. In other ways, it will be much the same. One of the ways it will be the same is that people will know and recognize each other.

"On the Mount of Transfiguration in Matthew 17, Christ's disciples somehow recognized Moses and Elijah even though they had never met them before," says Dr. Thomas Ice. "So I don't know if we're going to have name tags, but, yes, we'll be able to recognize people."

In heaven you will have a new, glorious body, but your soul will be the same one you have now. Your soul is eternal, and other people will surely recognize and know you in heaven.

> After six days Jesus took with him Peter, James and John the brother of James, and led them up a high mountain by themselves. There he was transfigured before them. His face shone like the sun, and his clothes became as white as the light. Just then there appeared before them Moses and Elijah, talking with Jesus. Peter said to Jesus, "Lord, it is good for us to be here. If you wish, I will put up three shelters—one for you, one for Moses and one for Elijah. (Matthew 17:1–4)

Moses and Elijah, first of all, were recognizable. Second, they were seen talking with Jesus. Then Peter suggested putting up additional shelters for them. The Bible does not describe what Moses and Elijah look like, but you can draw logical conclusions from the disciples' observations of the event.

> *Amazing Lord, I am so glad that I will have a transformed body in heaven, and I am even more glad that I will still be me and those I love will know me in an instant. Amen.*

People Will Fellowship Together

Dr. Luis Palau says, "Will we know each other in heaven? Of course we'll know each other. We will not lose our identity. Yes, we'll have an eternal body, but the Bible says many will come from the east and the west and sit down with Abraham and Isaac around the table."

The Bible describes this great feast in Luke 13:28–29: "When you see Abraham, Isaac and Jacob and all the prophets in the kingdom of God . . . people will come from east and west and north and south, and will take their places at the feast in the kingdom of God."

Not only will you know and fellowship with your loved ones, but you will also recognize Christians that you have read about from past times and from all over the world. What a feast that will be!

Holy God, this is amazing beyond my comprehension. Thank you that Your Word gives me a glimpse of the glorious joy to come. I'll be at that feast, Lord! Amen.

Your New Body

"But our citizenship is in heaven. And we eagerly await a Savior from there, the Lord Jesus Christ, who, by the power that enables him to bring everything under his control, will transform our lowly bodies so that they will be like his glorious body" (Philippians 3:20–21).

God promises that your earthly body will be transformed to be like Jesus' glorious body. What does the Bible say about Jesus' body?

"Our glorified body," says Joni Eareckson Tada, "will be a body like the Lord Jesus' body. It was perfectly fit for earth; He could eat a breakfast of fish on the beach with His disciples after His resurrection. His body was also perfectly suited for heaven; He could walk through a wall, or be walking on the road to Emmaus in one moment and appear in the upper room in Jerusalem the next. So we'll have these incredibly marvelous bodies, perfectly suited for both earth and heaven."

Yes, Lord, through all this grief, I am reassured to know that my loved one is enjoying this new, heavenly body. Amen.

Heaven Will Be Beautiful

You have probably seen many beautiful places on the earth. You may have been moved by majestic mountains, immense oceans, or the fine details of a flower. But fasten your spiritual seatbelt, because you haven't seen anything yet.

Dee Brestin shares, "I've been blessed to see some beautiful places on earth—skiing in the Colorado mountains and scuba diving in Hawaii. In Hawaii I saw fish that were striped with yellow and green and that had red polka dots. Just amazing. I got down there, and I thought, *I cannot believe what a beautiful world You have created*. It took God six days to create this, and He has been preparing a place in heaven for us ever since Jesus left earth! Can you imagine how amazing that will be?"

The Bible says that Jesus is preparing a place just for you in heaven. God knows your likes and your dislikes. He knows your favorite colors, preferred temperatures, favorite pastimes. You will be truly at home in heaven.

"In My Father's house are many mansions; if it were not so, I would have told you. I go to prepare a place for you. And if I go and prepare a place for you, I will come again and receive you to Myself; that where I am, there you may be also" (John 14:2–3 NKJV).

"Then the King will say to those on his right, 'Come, you who are blessed by my Father; take your inheritance, the kingdom prepared for you since the creation of the world'" (Matthew 25:34).

How incredible is that, Lord? Heaven will be perfectly beautiful for each person who enters its gates. You are an awesome God. Amen.

Heaven Is Reality

Heaven is real. Real people exist in heaven at this very moment, and you will someday reside there too, if you have a saving relationship with Jesus. You may struggle, though, to visualize a "real" place you cannot get to by car, boat, plane, or space shuttle! The Bible shows that heaven will be both physical and spiritual at the same time.

"The book of Isaiah talks about the new heavens and the new earth, and it speaks of it in very real, solid terms: mountains, trees, lions lying down with lambs, and . . . white horses," says Joni Eareckson Tada.

You will find descriptions of heaven both in the Old and the New Testament of the Bible. The visual language is a powerful tool to help you better grasp this glorious existence.

"'The wolf and the lamb will feed together, and the lion will eat straw like the ox, but dust will be the serpent's food. They will neither harm nor destroy on all my holy mountain,' says the LORD" (Isaiah 65:25).

"The armies of heaven were following him, riding on white horses and dressed in fine linen, white and clean" (Revelation 19:14).

"Then the angel showed me the river of the water of life, as clear as crystal, flowing from the throne of God and of the Lamb down the middle of the great street of the city. On each side of the river stood the tree of life, bearing twelve crops of fruit, yielding its fruit every month" (Revelation 22:1–2).

Holy God, I want to be dressed in fine linen, white and clean, following You all of my days. Amen.

Utter Satisfaction

"Heaven is going to be real," says Dr. Joseph Stowell. "It's not like we end up being clouds of mystical dust wafting through the universe. We're going to be real people, really reacting with a real God and His Son Jesus Christ.

"The heartbeat of heaven is going to be the fullness of unlimited satisfaction and joy in the presence of my Lord forever and ever and ever. Think about the most satisfying experience you've ever had in life, the most joyous, most fulfilling moment you've ever had in life. Heaven will be that moment multiplied by a thousand times forever, no end."

In the Bible, Paul knew that to be in heaven with Christ would be "better by far" than to remain on this earth. Paul longed to be in the joyful presence of God, but he understood that God wanted him to continue His work on earth first. Paul's desire on earth was to spread the good news of Jesus Christ to as many people as he could.

> If I am to go on living in the body, this will mean fruitful labor for me. Yet what shall I choose? I do not know! I am torn between the two: I desire to depart and be with Christ, which is better by far; but it is more necessary for you that I remain in the body. Convinced of this, I know that I will remain, and I will continue with all of you for your progress and joy in the faith, so that through my being with you again your joy in Christ Jesus will overflow on account of me. (Philippians 1:22–26)

Heavenly God, life with You in heaven would be better by far, but for now I will continue Your work here on earth. Amen.

Heaven Is Full of Joy

Another aspect of heaven is the presence of endless joy.

"You have made known to me the path of life; you will fill me with joy in your presence, with eternal pleasures at your right hand" (Psalm 16:11).

Joyful moments on earth are just that—moments. They seem to end so quickly. In heaven joy is eternal.

Joni Eareckson Tada says, "Your best memories are those that are timeless, that seem to live on in your mind and in your heart forever. They seem so crystal clear and so crisp. That's because the joy that surrounds those moments is of the Lord.

"Joy is a fruit of the Spirit, and the Spirit is eternal. So when you experience His joy, it has a sense or a smell of eternity about it. It becomes timeless. Sometimes I think those joy-filled moments down here on earth are like sneak previews to whet your appetite for heavenly glories above. I think that's God's way of yanking your heart every once in a while a little bit closer to heaven out of the mud of earth and onto the solid, real ground of heaven."

Thank you, Lord, that my joy will be full as I live in Your presence. Amen.

Heaven Isn't Boring

One of the things known about heaven from the Bible is that it is not a place of inactivity. In fact, there will not be a single moment in heaven that is boring.

"Our experience in heaven won't be static; it won't be inert," explains Joni Eareckson Tada. "It will be active. It will be dynamic. And it should be, because we as humans are only inspired by the active and the dynamic, never the inert or static."

Dr. Erwin Lutzer says, "In heaven, first of all, we worship God. It is spontaneous worship of God. It is a worship of God that is fulfilling. It is a worship of God that does not weary us. Then, the Bible says His servants shall serve Him. We will be given assignments. I think some of the same vocations here on earth are going to be continued in heaven. I can imagine an artist continuing to do artwork. I can imagine a scientist continuing to study the universe."

Your work in heaven will be completely exciting and satisfying to you. On earth you are fortunate if your work is occasionally exciting or satisfying! Think of the opportunities for hands-on learning and intellectual growth that will be available in heaven from biblical leaders and historical figures who have died before you. Think of meeting the God of the universe!

"To him who loves us and has freed us from our sins by his blood, and has made us to be a kingdom and priests to serve his God and Father—to him be glory and power for ever and ever! Amen" (Revelation 1:5–6).

I worship You, O God, my King. Blessing and honor, forever and ever, belong to You. Amen.

No Sorrow or Pain

In the final chapters of the Bible, heaven is described as a place of wonderful freedom from all pain, sorrow, and suffering.

Darlynn, who lost her grandmother, says, "There won't be any violence there. We won't have to worry about nation against nation or if a bomb is going to be dropped today. We don't have to worry about asbestos killing us, because our bodies are going to be glorified, and we're going to be happy. We're going to smile. We won't have any more tears. So I'm looking forward to being with my family members and my friends. There will be joy."

Believe this promise with all your heart because our God is the great God above all and only speaks what is true:

"He will swallow up death for all time, and the Lord GOD will wipe tears away from all faces, and He will remove the reproach of His people from all the earth; for the LORD has spoken" (Isaiah 25:8 NASB).

Holy Lord, the pain and emptiness of this world do not exist in heaven. I will be set free. Thank you. Amen.

Jesus Is the Treasure

"When it comes to heaven itself," says Dr. Richard Bewes, "all eyes will be on the throne."

All the benefits of heaven that you have read about so far are awesome, but they pale in insignificance to the real treasure in heaven, which is Jesus Christ Himself.

Joni Eareckson Tada says, "So many people think of heaven as a place, but really it's a Person. Jesus, who is at the very center of heaven, is what makes it exciting to me. We have something like a homing detector in our hearts, and it's just not ringing for earth. It's ringing for Him in whom our deepest longings will be answered.

"So heaven is not just a place; it is a Person, that Individual for whom we were made. What makes heaven exciting to me is being with the Lord Jesus where I will be perfectly and utterly at home."

You will marvel at Jesus someday, and His very name will cause you to bow down on your knees in reverence and honor.

"On the day he comes to be glorified in his holy people and to be marveled at among all those who have believed. This includes you, because you believed our testimony to you" (2 Thessalonians 1:10).

"At the name of Jesus every knee should bow, in heaven and on earth and under the earth" (Philippians 2:10).

Teach me to love You, Lord. Show me how to place You at the forefront of my life and my thoughts so that I may experience a touch of heaven. Amen.

Are You Ready?

When the time comes and you die and your eternal destiny is sealed forever, where will you spend that eternity?

"According to God's Word and our Lord Jesus Christ, only those who have received Christ can go to heaven," said Dr. Bill Bright. "That sounds so narrow and bigoted, but the Scripture says there is no name under heaven given among men whereby we must be saved [Acts 4:12]. Jesus put it this way. 'I am the Way, the Truth, the Life, no man cometh unto the Father but by Me' [John 14:6].

"Now that is the most presumptuous, arrogant statement anyone could ever make—unless it's true. *He is God.* Of all the religious leaders of the centuries, there is no one with His credentials. Not only did He live the most holy life ever lived, teach as no man has ever taught, perform miracles such as no one has ever performed, but He died on the cross for our sins in fulfillment of what the prophets of the Old Testament said. Then, miracle of miracles of miracles, on the third day He was raised from the dead and now is available to live within every believer. We invite Him to come into our lives by faith, and when we do, the miracle of new birth takes place."

Are you concerned about your salvation? Consider these questions: Do you believe God sent His Son Jesus Christ to be the Savior of the world? Do you believe Jesus died on a cross, was buried and rose again on the third day? If so, pray this prayer:

Heavenly Father, I need You! I believe You sent Jesus to be the Savior of the world. I receive Him as my Savior and Lord. Come into my life; forgive me of all my sins. Lord Jesus, thank you for dying on the cross for me and for rising on the third day. As you gave Your life for me, I now give my life to You. Thank you for becoming my Lord and Savior and show me how to live for You. Amen.

Your Restoration

Not only does the Lord want to restore you, He wants you to come to know Him in a closer way than you ever knew was possible. When Jesus described His ministry in the fourth chapter of Luke, He quoted a passage from the Old Testament in Isaiah. This will be His ministry to you.

Jesus speaks about His role in your healing:

"The Spirit of the Sovereign LORD is on me, because the LORD has anointed me to preach good news to the poor. He has sent me to bind up the brokenhearted, to proclaim freedom for the captives and release from darkness for the prisoners, to proclaim the year of the LORD's favor and the day of vengeance of our God, to comfort all who mourn" (61:1–2).

His gifts to you: "[to] provide for those who grieve in Zion—to bestow on them a crown of beauty instead of ashes, the oil of gladness instead of mourning, and a garment of praise instead of a spirit of despair" (v. 3).

The results in your life: "They [those who grieve] will be called oaks of righteousness, a planting of the LORD for the display of his splendor. They will rebuild the ancient ruins and restore the places long devastated; they will renew the ruined cities that have been devastated for generations" (vv. 3–4).

Praise God! Look again at those promises that He has given to you: healing, freedom, favor, comfort. A crown of beauty instead of ashes, gladness instead of mourning, praise in place of despair.

Yes, your life will be rebuilt and renewed through Jesus Christ.

Lord, my Healer, Your ministry to me is wonderful and true. I want to know You more and experience Your love more deeply. Amen.

Run to God

Your recovery from grief is likely not complete, but we pray that you are encouraged to grow forward on your journey. We wish God's best for you.

"The greatest and deepest Christians I've ever met are not the ones with the advanced degrees and not the ones who are always happy and cheerful, but they are people who have found God to be faithful in the worst moments of life," says Dr. Ray Pritchard. "Instead of running away from God, they ran toward Him. And they know things about God that the rest of us haven't yet experienced."

Run to God, and praise His name.

"But for you who revere my name, the sun of righteousness will rise with healing in its wings. And you will go out and leap like calves released from the stall" (Malachi 4:2).

Lord, when I have truly surrendered to You, I will be free. Amen.

About the Authors

BILL DUNN graduated from Asbury College and received a master of divinity degree from Princeton Theological Seminary in 1982. During the next fifteen years he served in two pastorates in North Carolina, one in Kill Devil Hills and one in Raleigh. As a pastor he had many opportunities to minister to people in grief and observe its extended influence in the lives of family and close friends. His prayer is that this book will encourage people to move through the process of grief with the help of Jesus.

Bill's wife, Holly, is an emergency physician and has seen the process of grief through that lens. Together they cohost the *GriefShare*® video series used in churches across the United States and beyond.

In 1997 Bill joined the staff of Church Initiative, developing materials to help churches implement effective ministries and outreaches. He is now a pastor in Hanover, New Hampshire, and is working on a Doctor of Ministry degree.

Bill enjoys skiing with his wife at Killington Ski Resort, playing guitar in the worship band at his church, and reading all kinds of books.

Bill and his wife, Holly, reside in Vermont, with their two miniature dachshunds Bella and Uma. They have one daughter, Jessica, who lives and works in North Carolina.

KATHY LEONARD has been writing and editing for over ten years. After graduating with a degree in English from the University of Maryland Asian Division in Okinawa, Japan, Kathy moved with her Air Force husband, Tim, to England. There she wrote feature articles for the Air Force base newspaper and worked as a publicist/graphic designer for the Forty-eighth Services Squadron. After three years in England, Kathy moved to North Carolina where she taught high-school English and was later hired by Church Initiative as a writer and editor.

Kathy was born and raised in Syracuse, New York, where she spent the first eighteen years of her life, active in church, music, dancing, and school. Having been raised by Christian parents, she began her walk with Christ as a preteen. As a result of her time spent at Church Initiative, Kathy has developed a passion to minister to people going through life crises, such as divorce, grief, and addictions, through her writing. She is the author of *Divorce Care: Hope, Help,* and *Healing During and After Your Divorce.*

Kathy and her husband, Tim, live in Palmyra, Virginia, with their two children, Jacob and Alanna.

Acknowledgments

We would like to thank the brave individuals who gave their personal testimonies and allowed us to share their stories of heartache and hope with other people in grief. We would also like to thank the Christian experts quoted in this book who willingly gave their time and teaching to help the grieving. We extend our thanks to the churches and *GriefShare*® leaders around the world who lovingly minister to hurting individuals through the *GriefShare*® program. We pray God's hope and healing for the *GriefShare*® participants and for all those who suffer from the pain of losing a loved one.

Notes

PART 1. When Your Dreams Fall Apart

    1. Barbara Baumgardner, *A Passage Through Grief* (Nashville: Broadman and Holman Publishers, 1997), 95. Used by permission.

PART 2. The Seasons of Grief

    1. To find the *GriefShare*® grief recovery support group nearest you, call 1-800-395-5755 or visit our Web site at www.griefshare.org.

About GriefShare®

GriefShare® is a grief recovery support group program for people grieving the death of a loved one. With groups meeting in locations around the world, this program has ignited hope and healing in the lives of many. *GriefShare®* is a thirteen-week, video and workbook-based resource that combines sound biblical instruction with the dynamic of small group interaction, providing an atmosphere of care and concern with solid, reliable teaching. The groups are designed to be lay led, usually by people who have been through the grieving process themselves.

GriefShare® video sessions and group discussion times are designed to help hurting people travel the journey from mourning to joy. *GriefShare®* brings more than thirty respected Christian authors, counselors, speakers, and pastors into the small group setting via video. The following experts are included:

Kay Arthur

Dr. Bill Bright

Dr. Larry Crabb

Elisabeth Elliot

Dr. Jack Hayford

Dr. E. V. Hill

Barbara Johnson

Anne Graham Lotz

Dr. Erwin Lutzer

Dr. Luis Palau

Joni Eareckson Tada

H. Norman Wright

Visit GriefShare® Online

Whether you are grieving the loss of someone close to you, leading a *GriefShare®* group, or interested in sponsoring a group, you will find helpful information and resources at www.griefshare.org:

- where to find the nearest *GriefShare®* group

- recommended resources dealing with grief recovery and related topics

- free online daily devotions

- additional information about healing from the hurt of a deep loss

- more about the *GriefShare®* ministry

- information about The Church Initiative, Inc., which sponsors *GriefShare®*

- a special leadership forum for *GriefShare®* leaders and facilitators

- advice on how to start a *GriefShare®* group

Find a GriefShare® Group near You

GriefShare® groups are meeting throughout the United States, Canada, and several other countries. Here is how you can find out more about these groups: Search the database at www.griefshare.org and find the location of the nearest *GriefShare®* group by zip code, area code, or city. Or e-mail your zip code to info@griefshare.org to receive a list of the groups nearest you. You can also call 1-800-395-5755 or 919-562-2112.

Order GriefShare® Group Materials

GriefShare is designed to help your church develop a grief recovery seminar/support group. This program equips your church with a Christ-centered, biblical strategy for ministering to people who are grieving the loss of someone close. The *GriefShare®* materials kit includes thirteen video sessions, a leader's guide, a leader-equipping video, workbooks for use by group participants, publicity brochures, and posters.

Order GriefShare® CDs

Listen to *GriefShare®* in your car, at home, or wherever you go. With a set of *GriefShare®* CDs, you can catch up on sessions you missed or find encouragement by listening again to those sessions most meaningful to you. You can also share them with friends and family members to help them understand what you are experiencing as you grieve. You will receive the audio content from each of the thirteen *GriefShare®* sessions on seven CDs.

To place an order or to receive more information,
call 1-800-395-5755
or e-mail *info@churchinitiative.org*.

About The Church Initiative, Inc.

The Church Initiative, Inc., is a nondenominational, nonprofit ministry whose purpose is to create biblically based resources to help churches establish support groups and teaching groups for people dealing with life crises and other life issues. In addition to *GriefShare®*, Church Initiative offers the following ministry resources:

- DivorceCare, divorce recovery support groups (*www.divorcecare.org*)
- Choosing Wisely: Before You Divorce, marriage crisis counseling tool (*www.beforeyoudivorce.org*)
- Facing Forever, evangelism and discipleship tool (*www.facingforever.org*)
- Chance to Change, gambling addiction recovery support groups (*www.chancetochange.org*)
- DivorceCare for Kids, program to help children whose parents are separated or divorced (*www.dc4k.org*)

To place an order or to receive more information,
call 1-800-395-5755
or e-mail *info@churchinitiative.org*.

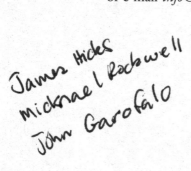